▶ **Modelling in Public Health Research**

DOI: 10.1057/9781137298829.0001

Other Palgrave Pivot titles

William Forbes and Lynn Hodgkinson: Corporate Governance in the United Kingdom: Past, Present and Future

Michela Magliacani: Managing Cultural Heritage: Ecomuseums, Community Governance and Social Accountability

Sara Hsu and Nathan Perry: Lessons in Sustainable Development from Malaysia and Indonesia

Ted Newell: Five Paradigms for Education: Foundational Views and Key Issues

Sophie Body-Gendrot and Catherine Wihtol de Wenden: Policing the Inner City in France, Britain, and the US

William Sims Bainbridge: An Information Technology Surrogate for Religion: The Veneration of Deceased Family in Online Games

Anthony Ridge-Newman: Cameron's Conservatives and the Internet: Change, Culture and Cyber Toryism

Ian Budge and Sarah Birch: National Policy in a Global Economy: How Government Can Improve Living Standards and Balance the Books

Barend Lutz and Pierre du Toit: Defining Democracy in a Digital Age: Political Support on Social Media

Assaf Razin and Efraim Sadka: Migration States and Welfare States: Why Is America Different from Europe?

Conra D. Gist: Preparing Teachers of Color to Teach: Culturally Responsive Teacher Education in Theory and Practice

David Baker: Police, Picket-Lines and Fatalities: Lessons from the Past

Lassi Heininen (editor): Security and Sovereignty in the North Atlantic

Steve Coulter: New Labour Policy, Industrial Relations and the Trade Unions

Ayman A. El-Desouky: The Intellectual and the People in Egyptian Literature and Culture: Amāra and the 2011 Revolution

William Van Lear: The Social Effects of Economic Thinking

Mark E. Schaefer and John G. Poffenbarger: The Formation of the BRICS and Its Implication for the United States: Emerging Together

Donatella Padua: John Maynard Keynes and the Economy of Trust: The Relevance of the Keynesian Social Thought in a Global Society

Davinia Thornley: Cinema, Cross-Cultural Collaboration, and Criticism: Filming

DOI: 10.1057/9781137298829.0001

palgrave▶pivot

Modelling in Public Health Research: How Mathematical Techniques Keep Us Healthy

Erika Mansnerus

Research Fellow, London School of Economics and Political Science, UK

palgrave
macmillan

DOI: 10.1057/9781137298829.0001

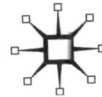

First published 2015 by
PALGRAVE MACMILLAN

Palgrave Macmillan in the UK is an imprint of Macmillan Publishers Limited, registered in England, company number 785998, of Houndmills, Basingstoke, Hampshire RG21 6XS.

Palgrave Macmillan in the US is a division of St Martin's Press LLC, 175 Fifth Avenue, New York, NY 10010.

Palgrave Macmillan is the global academic imprint of the above companies and has companies and representatives throughout the world.

Palgrave® and Macmillan® are registered trademarks in the United States, the United Kingdom, Europe and other countries.

ISBN: 978–1–137–29883–6 EPUB
ISBN: 978–1–137–29882–9 PDF
ISBN: 978–1–137–29881–2 Hardback

A catalogue record for this book is available from the British Library.

A catalog record for this book is available from the Library of Congress.

www.palgrave.com/pivot

DOI: 10.1057/9781137298829

To my father and mother, for Marianna
Omistettu isälleni ja äidilleni, sekä Mariannalle

DOI: 10.1057/9781137298829.0001

Contents

List of Illustrations   viii

Preface   ix

Acknowledgements   xi

1   Introduction: Life-Cycles of Models   1

2   Models and the Stories They Tell Us   8
   2.1   Introduction   9
   2.2   Story of disease transmission   13
   2.3   Telling policy-relevant stories   16
   2.4   Conclusion   25

3   Kinship Relations of Models   29
   3.1   Models and kinship ties   30
   3.2   Kinship: evolving relations and links between models   32
   3.3   Nature of model-based evidence   35
   3.4   Conclusion   41

4   Working Lives of Models   43
   4.1   Introduction   44
   4.2   Revising vaccination policy: from target groups to mass campaign   46
   4.3   Insights into models at work   52
   4.4   Conclusion   57

DOI: 10.1057/9781137298829.0001

5   Encounters with Risks   60
    5.1   Introduction   61
    5.2   Two types of model-based predictions   63
    5.3   Using models in risk assessment: simulating
          pandemic outbreaks   69
    5.4   Conclusion   72

6   When Evidence Is Silent   75
    6.1   Introduction   76
    6.2   What is meant by silent evidence?   78
    6.3   Identifying known unknowns   83
    6.4   Analysing unknown factors   85
    6.5   Conclusion   90

7   Governing by Numbers   93
    7.1   Introduction   94
    7.2   Governing by numbers   95
    7.3   Using models as senior experts   97
    7.4   Quantitative authority of modelling of
          foot-and-mouth disease   101
    7.5   Conclusion   105

8   Lives of Models in the World of Policy   111
    8.1   Understanding models through their lives   112
    8.2   Predicting, preventing and keeping us healthy   114
    8.3   Benefits and limitations of modelling techniques   115
    8.4   Conclusions   116

Glossary   118

References   120

Index   132

DOI: 10.1057/9781137298829.0001

List of Illustrations

Figures

3.1 The family tree of Helsinki models   32
4.1 The RAS-model as a flow diagram of transitions
     between population compartments   55
7.1 Policy Feedback Loop of modelling for policy
     and its stages   100

Infoboxes

2.1 Haemophilus influenzae type b bacteria, Hib   15
2.2 Modelling infectious diseases at the National
     Institute for Health and Welfare in
     Helsinki, Finland   18
4.1 Measles   46
4.2 Rubella   48
4.3 Mumps   51
5.1 Pandemics, especially 2009 A/H1N1 outbreak   68
7.1 Foot-and-mouth disease   103

Tables

3.1 Summary of the analysis of *characteristics* of
     evidential claims   38
3.2 Summary of functional roles of evidential claims   40
7.1 Comparison of the three models developed to
     predict foot-and-mouth disease outbreaks in
     order to highlight main differences between the
     modelling approaches   106

DOI: 10.1057/9781137298829.0002

Preface

The working title of this book the 'Lives of models' summarises my long-term interest in understanding how mathematical models and computer simulations were developed in research groups and were accepted within a policy context. The metaphors of life-cycles or life-histories and stories guided my exploration towards a deeper understanding of what models are, how we work with them and what kind of evidence they provide. My interest in epidemiological models of infectious diseases stems from a PhD study with modellers, epidemiologists and computer scientists in Helsinki. With them I learnt about modelling, became fascinated by the challenges in collaborating with researchers from different disciplinary backgrounds and began to think about how models can be related to each other. What informed my interest in understanding model-based evidence was research on 'travelling facts' – transmission of factual knowledge across research and policy contexts.

By understanding how model-based evidence was disseminated across research and policy context, I became increasingly interested in how models are received in health policy. As the current title suggests, I began to look at how 'modelling for policy' actually happens. How does public health research use mathematical techniques to keep us healthy? These questions led me to explore how modelling became part of the planning and optimisation of vaccination policy in relation to the implementation of the MMR (measles, mumps and rubella) triple vaccine in the UK in the late 1980s. My growing interest in the models-policy

DOI: 10.1057/9781137298829.0003

boundary led me to look into risk research. Modelled encounters with risks show how models can be used effectively to manage and anticipate risks arising from new infections. I also looked at how models are used when predicting outbreaks – both in human epidemiology and most recently in animal health. A case study of the A/H1N1 pandemic outbreak in 2009 led me to consider the limitations of modelling methods, especially when they are used in the early days of an outbreak. Scarcity of data is one of the factors that restricts and affects the reliability of these early predictions. But we also need to cope with the 'known unknowns' in the early days of a pandemic outbreak. These are factors that will be understood when a situation matures. When focussing on the development of modelling as a decision-aid in relation to foot-and-mouth disease outbreak, I also learnt how communication at different stages of the modelling is a way to improve the transparency and reliability of the process.

To help you join this journey in which I will explore various aspects of what models are and how they are best used, I will make some suggestions on how to read the book. Even though it is short and succinct in its expression, it offers a lengthy journey through various areas of modelling. Naturally, the narrative of the book unfolds best for those who read through it fully. The book provides a glossary of key terms at the end to ease the reader with unfamiliar terms, so that those from other disciplinary backgrounds with an interest in modelling are able to follow the case studies. If your background is in the social studies of science and technology, history and philosophy of science or sociology of science, Chapters 2, 3 and 5 will offer insights into what kinds of stories models are able to tell us and how we can understand the nature of model-based evidence and how models help us predict outbreaks. For those of you who come from a policy background Chapters 4, 6 and 7 are rewarding, as they provide case studies of how modelling has been used in public health and animal health policy. Through these chapters, the limitations of modelling methods are also made more explicit. I have applied qualitative research methods with my interdisciplinary interest in conceptual developments in sociology, history and philosophy of science. I have recently written about the methodological approach I use in a joint piece with Susann Wagenknecht (forthcoming, 2014) titled 'Feeling with the organism'. This book can be seen as a closure of my long-term research interest in the development and use of models, yet it is also an opening, an invitation to look more closely at how these fascinating objects of research live their lives.

DOI: 10.1057/9781137298829.0003

Acknowledgements

The journey to write this book based on the fascinating studies of models would not have been possible without generous funding throughout my research career and insightful supervisors and mentors guiding me on my travels. The journey began with funding for my PhD from the Ministry of Education, through the Helsinki Postgraduate School for Science and Technology Studies under the supervision of Professors Matti Sintonen and Reijo Miettinen. After completing my PhD, I had the privilege to work in an ESRC- and Leverhulme Trust-funded research project titled 'Nature of Evidence: How Well Do "Facts" Travel?', led by Prof. Mary Morgan and Dr Peter Howlett in the Department of Economic History, London School of Economics and Political Science (LSE). Questions about evidence led me to think about risk, and an ESRC-funded post with the LSE Centre for Analysis of Risk and Regulation. After I received the British Academy Post-doctoral fellowship (2009–2012), I continued risk studies at the University of Cambridge, Centre for Research in Arts, Social Sciences and Humanities in the Mellon-Sawyer Seminar: Modelling Futures. After that I returned to LSE Health to complete the fellowship. During the BA fellowship, Prof. Tony Barnett was an invaluable mentor with whom I was awarded British Academy Conference Grant, 2012, for dissemination of the key findings of these studies. Prior to continuing my policy-related research with a fellowship from Defra through the Animal Health and Veterinary Laboratories Agency (AHVLA), I was hosted as a visiting fellow in the Department of Social Science,

Health and Medicine, King's College London. My current affiliation with the Department of Social Policy, LSE offers me an intellectual and teaching community.

Learning to think about models, to understand what they are and how they are developed would not have been possible without generous collaboration with modellers and epidemiologists at the Institute for Health and Welfare, Helsinki; Public Health England, Colindale; the European Disease Control Centre, Stockholm, and Animal Health and Veterinary Laboratories Agency, London and Weybridge. I am especially grateful for Dr Kari Auranen and Dr Tuija Leino for our long-term, inspiring collaboration. A special thank you for Francesca Gauntlett and Charlotte Cook at AHVLA, with whom I developed the concept of the Policy Feedback Loop (PFL) and gained insight into model use in animal health, as reported in Chapter 7. I was hosted by the Epidemiology and Risk Policy Advice Team, AHVLA, led by Jane Gibbens, and my fellowship was managed by Ashley Goddard during the winter of 2013–2014.

This journey would not have been possible without generous, inspiring and creative mentoring from Gillie Bolton, who has not only guided me into academic writing but helped me see how it can find its narrative form. I thank the anonymous reviewer for his/her comments and suggestions, which I have taken into account when revising the manuscript. I am grateful for the clear graphics in the figures for Mark Liebenrood, who has done more than I could have imagined by easing my journey of writing. I dedicate this book to my parents and sister.

DOI: 10.1057/9781137298829.0004

1

Introduction:
Life-Cycles of Models

Abstract: *The use of mathematical models has increased and become more common in public health, recently. Along with monitoring activities, public health officials work with modellers in order to organise and analyse surveillance data, for example. In order to learn of the severity and spread of a pandemic outbreak, we can study different predictive scenarios. Mansnerus introduces us to the lives of models in both public health and other fields. She discusses how modelling has gained a dominance in current scientific research and policy-making.*

Mansnerus, Erika. *Modelling in Public Health Research: How Mathematical Techniques Keep Us Healthy.* Basingstoke: Palgrave Macmillan, 2015. DOI: 10.1057/9781137298829.0005.

This book is about us. It tells a story of how our lives are affected by infectious risks and what we can do in order to manage them. However unwanted and unpredictable they are, we are not at their mercy. Mathematical models and simulation techniques have been developed and used to predict, prevent, and study infectious risks. They form invisible machinery behind convincing quantitative evidence needed for decision-making. Their use allows us to anticipate a pandemic outbreak, calculate how to best revise a vaccination programme, and understand how disease transmission happens in a population, for example.

Computer-based modelling and simulation techniques have gained increasing importance in knowledge production and use. They function as measuring instruments, experimental devices, and surrogate systems. They accommodate uncertainties in risk assessment processes and help overcome ethical and financial restrictions of population-wide experiments. Their predictive capacities are valued in climate research and infectious disease studies, for example. Yet, the limitations of model-based evidence have not been fully explored. We remain impressed by their fluency and forget to examine how *the uncertain* becomes *certain* through this computational machinery.

Climate research provides us with one of the most important examples in the development and use of modelling techniques. Already in the 1950s and 1960s, large-scale differential equation models were developed. The very same models form the core of the current climate models that are responsible for the pessimistic estimates of rising temperatures and melting glaciers. However, climate research is, par excellence, a case for the contested nature of model-based evidence. Research has shown that, partly because the facts of the anthropogenic cause of climate change were produced by models and simulations, they became contested, lobbied, ignored and rejected for a good number of years – which, unfortunately, delayed political interventions to reverse the undesirable development (Oreskes, 2011).

Modelling methods can be developed to produce knowledge in basic research, as in physics, but they may well reach into the interdisciplinary fields of environmental policy. This flexibility comes from two sources: from their manipulability, which means that as research tools they provide a way to question and inquire about the world, and from the fact that these techniques are developed in multidisciplinary teams and can accommodate the nuances of the different fields of enquiry. The development of modelling techniques in infectious disease epidemiology

DOI: 10.1057/9781137298829.0005

addresses both these characteristics. Driven by policy-relevant questions, such as 'How do we best protect people against a pandemic outbreak?' or 'What would be the optimal vaccination schedule?', development of modelling techniques is a way to produce new evidence in public health decision-making processes. Elementary for this development is the increase in computational power: from the early mathematical expressions of epidemic outbreaks to current simulation models on infectious diseases, computational capacity represents a key for the usability of modelling techniques and their adaptation as preventive and predictive tools in infectious disease epidemiology. This development is characterised as the *life-cycle* of models and simulation techniques.

Instead of providing a merely internal description of how models are built and how they function in epidemiological research, I will tell a story of their *life-cycle* – a story which combines the production of epidemiological evidence and its use in predicting infectious outbreaks. The metaphor of the 'lives of models' invites us to explore the emergence of modelling techniques in epidemiology, their maturation or 'growing up' through time, the 'working life of models,' and their seniority and potential passing away. These developmental stages in the *life-cycle* of the models form the core structure of the book. The metaphor itself binds together a developmental story that happens through time. It is an epistemic history that evolves from an ethnographer's perspective on models and shows how different modelling methods relate to each other and form 'families of models' within epidemiological research. The metaphor is inspired by recent work that analyses various roles of computer models in environmental policy cycle (van Daalen et al., 2002). Contributions from history and sociology of science in the studies of biographies (Daston, 2002) or the lives of scientific objects (Creager, 2002) have been elemental for developing my understanding of the *life-cycles* of models.

By developing a *life-cycle* of models, I will discuss how mathematical methods, prior to the time when computer-intensive modelling methods entered epidemiological research, and current modelling methods, especially probabilistic transmission models, developed. I will construct a 'family tree' of transmission models built in Helsinki 1995–2001. This family tree not only introduces us to the interconnectedness of modelling approaches, their distribution across different research groups, but also shows how model-based evidence is disseminated across various models. This will lead us to study the 'working life' of models.

DOI: 10.1057/9781137298829.0005

The working life of models means studying their uses in the governance of infectious risks. The predictive capacities of models are a significant way to anticipate risks and examine the applicability and effectiveness of mitigation strategies during a pandemic outbreak. I will identify two types of predictions: explanation-based and scenario-building ones. These predictions serve especially in pandemic risk assessment as tools to quantify, that is, to express through numerical representations how a pandemic potentially progresses. When they function as tools that can fluently express the uncertainties related to an infectious threat, we will see the limitations of models. These limitations, for example, manifest in models' capacity to represent the social aspects of a situation. But the availability of data can also present limitations, as most models we discuss in this book depend on data. These shortcomings, I will suggest, are to be taken into account when models are used as technical aids in the governance of public health risks.

The successful working life of models draws on the development of modelling methods to predict and prevent a measles outbreak in the United Kingdom. Serving along with other sources of evidence, models interpret surveillance data and confirm a potential outbreak that can be prevented by a booster vaccination campaign. Their success may not always last. However useful they are in optimising strategies of antiviral distribution during a pandemic, they at best predict the future by modelling the past. During an outbreak, models encounter silent, absent evidence. Data may not be available, yet as techniques, they try to bridge the gaps in order to alleviate our ignorance. These limitations, although acknowledged by the modellers, may not be communicated to users. Current tendencies to trust in numerical evidence invite us to increase model use and neglect their restrictions.

Following the metaphor according to which models 'live their lives and grow old,' we will look at models as senior experts. With this focus, the seniority of models turns into technical rationality not only to predict public health risks, such as an outbreak of pandemic influenza, but also to plan and optimise preventive actions, such as vaccinations. The 'analytics of governance,' which takes into account a broad set of factors, is addressed as a way to balance the benefits of these techniques without neglecting their limitations. This broader framework, adopted from Michel Foucault, is a way to reverse the development that leads us to be governed by the numbers. I will especially focus on the technical rationality of governance that models represent, and extend the ques-

DOI: 10.1057/9781137298829.0005

tion to power relations between those who govern and those who are governed, which is of special interest when designing preventive interventions, such as vaccination strategies in public health policy-making. This framework of analytics of governance, which takes into account the ways in which knowledge is formed through expertise, and how social identities are shaped in conjunction with technical development, is a way to broaden our perspective beyond the fascination of the technicalities of models and critically assess what lies underneath their authority.

Through the lives of models framework, we will learn how mathematical techniques grow in the service of public health. Their successes and failures or shortcomings can be seen, after all, as aspects of life. But the lives of models are intertwined with our lives. Model-based predictions of outbreaks do not remain as scientific findings in journals; rather, they turn into action and mobilise vaccination programmes. When models enter as experts into the policy domain, they are welcomed as well as criticised. They are welcomed for their capacity to tell stories that inform the next steps in the decision-making process, but criticised for their limitations. In conclusion, this book reflects the tension that remains between the increased use of models as senior experts and the potential shortcomings if their advice is accepted uncritically.

Structure of the book

The structure of this book is as follows. Chapter 2 introduces a narrative framework that shows how models are developed to address policy-motivated questions. Storytelling is a helpful metaphor in order to understand how models are developed historically, what kind of elements are involved in building a model and how these historical accounts can be relevant for our current understanding of models.

Chapter 3 highlights the relatedness of models and how they form 'kinship' relations, as I call the organic development of models that is informed by achievements in collaborating research groups. By establishing the relatedness of models, this chapter will analyse how model-based evidence is disseminated across research groups and to the policy domain. Through this analysis, we will learn about the nature of model-based evidence.

In the fourth chapter, the focus is on the working life of models. The key is to analyse how models operate in the context of public health

DOI: 10.1057/9781137298829.0005

policy. Through the example of revising and implementing the MMR-vaccination strategy in the United Kingdom, this chapter contributes to the debate on the performativity of models.

Models can be built upon available data from previous pandemics, thus, *modelling the past in order to predict the future*. This will be the focus in Chapter 5. As we learned from the 2009 A/H1N1 (swine flu) outbreak, modelling and simulation techniques were widely used during and prior to the pandemic. Pre-pandemic modelling became a way to encounter possible pandemic risks and to assess effective mitigation strategies. This chapter defines two types of model-based predictions: explanation-based and scenario-building. By discussing their reliability, we learn what kind of limitations modelling techniques face.

During the 2009 pandemic outbreak, modelling took place in a reality that was under time pressure. The sense of urgency to make decisions was challenged by the lack of data. Evidence was silent and weak, and modellers did their best to bridge the gaps. In Chapter 6, the main interest is to analyse 'known unknowns', factors of which we have very limited understanding at the beginning of modelling. These factors can be related to the microbiology of the pathogen or to the safety of the pharmaceutical interventions, for example. This chapter looks at how modelling methods alleviate unknowing in the context of pandemic risk assessment.

How do numbers govern the world? How is the authority of computational techniques shaped? Model-based evidence, as shown in previous chapters, is an important part of the whole body of evidence upon which pandemic predictions or vaccination schemes are based. Models, when they function as an evidence base, turn into instruments of governance. Their authority is likely to make us believe in the numerical representations they produce. They act as senior experts guiding and governing health risks, as Chapter 7 will show through a case study on animal health modelling.

When models gain seniority as experts in public health, their lives become intertwined with ours. They not only provide estimates and predictions but also turn them into action. Vaccination policies are renewed, as we learned in the case of measles modelling in the United Kingdom. Yet we know that the modelling process can be described as fluctuation between simplicity and complexity. Chapter 8 discusses these issues. Policy needs are simplified in order to be successfully addressed in models, and model-based evidence faces a heterogeneity in which

DOI: 10.1057/9781137298829.0005

its recommendations may be resisted and disputed. This fluctuation is best captured in the life-cycle of models. This framework accommodates both the critical voices that warn us about overreliance on model-based evidence and the supportive ones that remind us of their beneficial use. After all, we use models to overcome ethical and financial restrictions we face when making sense of infectious risks that affect us all.

DOI: 10.1057/9781137298829.0005

2
Models and the Stories They Tell Us

Abstract: *Models tell stories that can answer vital questions. Models have become essential tools for epidemiological research. How well they address policy-driven questions in public health is explained. In epidemiological research, the mathematical predecessors for current computer-based modelling techniques have a long history. They aimed at policy advice by providing mathematical representations of infectious patterns in populations.*

Mansnerus analyses the early development of probability theory, showing why modelling became beneficial in governing infectious risks. How models are tailored to meet policy needs is revealed through an analysis of interdisciplinary collaboration. Models and mathematical techniques become accessible for us when we see them through the metaphor of storytelling: the transmission of an infection is presented to exemplify this.

Mansnerus, Erika. *Modelling in Public Health Research: How Mathematical Techniques Keep Us Healthy.* Basingstoke: Palgrave Macmillan, 2015. DOI: 10.1057/9781137298829.0006.

DOI: 10.1057/9781137298829.0006

'A *man is always a teller of tales, he lives surrounded by his stories and the stories of others.'*

(Jean-Paul Sartre, 1938, in Bolton 2010)

2.1   Introduction

Time and again we are challenged by new emerging infections and witness their victories amongst us. When the A/H1N1 (Swine flu) outbreak hit the headlines in 2009, we learnt of its rapid spread from country to country, how many people became severely ill, and how many died. Along with these loud narratives, the silent ones whisper worries about common childhood infections.[1] All these stories share something in common: they voice concerns, demand change, and respond to policy calls. They reach beyond the natural habitat of scientific journals, where their findings may be buried and forgotten. After all, these stories are told in order to keep us healthy.

We do not 'live surrounded by stories' passively; we use them to make sense of things.[2] How to improve vaccination uptake? What is a reliable estimate for the spread of a pandemic outbreak? Answers to these questions as told by both historical and current narratives[3] help us understand what models are and how they are used. Their capacity to integrate evidence from various sources, interpret it and express it mathematically explains why modelling techniques became dominant in the field.[4] Even though these techniques developed only when increased computational capacity became accessible to researchers from the 1970s onwards,[5] we can trace their origins to the 'taming of chance' (Hacking, 1990). This signifies the conceptual turn away from deterministic laws governing nature towards the realm of chance dominated by probability theory (Hacking, 1992).

This chapter tells the story of models and their ancestors, showing the inheritance of current sophisticated epidemiological calculations from physics and chemistry. It also explains how a local research programme on modelling infectious diseases was facilitated by interdisciplinary collaboration in the mid-1990s in Helsinki, Finland. The second section introduces how mathematical techniques *emerge* in epidemiology . With a focus on a current research initiative, section three looks at how models tell the stories of transmission. Modelling methods are developed to

DOI: 10.1057/9781137298829.0006

shape current policies, which is discussed in the fourth section. Finally, this chapter voices the question of how useful these narratives are.

> Epidemiology at any given time is something more than the total of its established facts. It includes their *orderly arrangement into chains of inference*, which extends more or less beyond the bounds of direct observation. (Hampton Frost in Maxcy, 1941, emphasis mine)

At the heart of Wade Hampton Frost's (1880–1938) definition of epidemiology lies the assumption that epidemiological facts can be arranged into chains of inference. These chains integrate and incorporate information into meaningful narratives. By building and using epidemiological models, we order factual knowledge, data, assumptions and estimates into 'chains of inference', into processes from which conclusions can be drawn. What are we actually doing?

Statistical analysis of the regularities in populations became the nurturing ground for the growth of modelling techniques. These regularities were analysed with statistical methods as probabilistic thinking developed and created a language to address them (Hacking, 1990).

As 'enduring ways of thinking' or 'styles of reasoning', statistical methods have their own sources and histories.[6] When epidemiological reasoning is seen in this light, we can bridge the past with the present. What does this mean?

Styles of reasoning define or characterise the leading way of thinking which is typical of a field of research or discipline (Hacking, 1992, 2010). Such a style of reasoning incorporates the commonly accepted modes of experimentation, inference and argumentation that define disciplinary identities. Modelling techniques are not the property of a single discipline, and they were not developed in isolation. Therefore it is challenging to develop the notion of styles of reasoning in relation to mathematical modelling in epidemiology. Our interest is in seeing how techniques reach from policy interests to epidemiological research. This means extending the idea of styles of reasoning towards chains of inference that reach from models to policy.

What, then, constitutes a style of reasoning in epidemiology and how does it emerge? The answer will show how mathematical techniques emerge in epidemiological thinking. The long chains of inference that order data and incorporate factual knowledge and estimates also weave into them the applicable, policy-driven goals of epidemiological research. In this sense, the chains of inference, as Hampton Frost suggests, take us

DOI: 10.1057/9781137298829.0006

beyond the 'bounds of direct observation'. This is the pivotal moment when we use models to tell us stories about infections.

Development of early modelling methods

How modelling methods[7] became servants for public health policies is told through stories of transmission. These stories capture the core of epidemiological research: the prediction of infectious outbreaks and the prevention and control of their spread. These interests were embedded in the early modelling methods, although they become more evident in current efforts to optimise vaccination programmes. Back in the 18th century, Daniel Bernoulli (1700–1782) studied probability theory and developed its applications to assess smallpox mortality. His research can be seen as an origin of the efforts to model infectious diseases mathematically.

In 1760, Bernoulli was asked to present the results from his mathematical model of smallpox to the Royal Academy of Sciences in Paris. His model calculated life expectancy at birth assuming that smallpox was completely eliminated.[8] The purpose was to persuade people to support variolation[9] and to find evidence for that practice. Bernoulli's epidemiological model assumed that everybody would participate in the variolation campaign, which indicates that he may not have been aware of *herd immunity*.[10] The model itself was pioneering as it addressed the need for evidence for policy through developing a mathematical method. Bernoulli's motivation to persuade the public to believe in the benefits of variolation is echoed in the increased use of epidemiological modelling as evidence for the benefits of vaccination (Dietz and Heesterbeek, 2002; Gani, 2010).

Vital statistics captured statistical reasoning of how births, deaths and diseases affect populations. William Farr's (1807–1883) pioneering work involved collecting and organising mortality data while serving the General Register Office. His discovery of the *computability* of these statistical records is in line with our attempts to trace the predecessors for current modelling. Farr's legacy can be seen in the systematic collection of population data. When the data are available, they become strength for the models, and when they are missing (or weak), they undermine the model-based evidence, as we will later learn in relation to pandemic modelling. However, behind Farr's work was the slow change from deterministic laws that governed reasoning to statistical laws that reflect the role of chance and uncertainty (Farr, 1885/2000; Langmuir, 1976).

DOI: 10.1057/9781137298829.0006

In the early 20th century, cycles of measles outbreaks caught William Hamer's (1862–1936) interest. The way in which measles epidemics fluctuated between England and France encouraged him to systematise his observations through appropriate mathematical expressions. The pioneering mathematical model of 'measles cycles' defined the rate of transmission from an infective to a susceptible individual. Borrowing the law of heterogeneous mixing from chemistry, both Hamer and later Ross applied it to clarify standard incidence, which is the 'average number of contacts per individual in a constant time unit' (Brauer, 2009). In other words, they assumed that individuals mix with each other like 'gas molecules in a test tube'.

Yet the spread of infections in a population is a more multifaceted process than the simplified version of the heterogeneous mixing of 'gas molecules in a test tube' suggests. When the cause of the infection was identified, a more accurate understanding of the transmission dynamics emerged. Historically, this identification was based on the development of germ theory,[11] which acknowledged microbes as the primary cause of infections. Based on this, the dynamics of transmission had to address the complex interaction between humans and pathogens. Immunity is developed either naturally from an infection or from vaccinations that interrupt the transmission. In every population, there are individuals[12] whose immunity cannot be boosted by vaccinations. They are protected by herd immunity, which means that the whole population is protected when a sufficient number of individuals is vaccinated (Fine, 1993). When developing mathematical techniques to depict transmission dynamics itself, these factors need to be taken into account: the number of contacts a single individual encounters, the probability of transmission in that contact, and pre-existing immunity in that individual. As we will see, only a mathematical model can bring them together into a coherent story.

Studies on malaria control allow us to say that epidemiological modelling is research that is worth a Nobel Prize. Sir Ronald Ross (1857–1932) was awarded this prestigious prize in 1902 for studies that showed how both mosquitoes and humans were involved in the complex mechanism of malaria infection, which was published as the Ross-Macdonald model (McKenzie, 2004). He also formulated the deterministic theory for the spread of epidemics, which was later developed further by William Kermack and Anderson McKendrick (Kermack and McKendrick, 1927). The deterministic theory helped divide the population into

DOI: 10.1057/9781137298829.0006

compartments, or subgroups, and model the transition rates between these different subgroups effectively. This compartmental structure of a population is still useful (and used) in designing models; it shows what the subgroups in a population are (susceptible to the infection, infected, immune or recovered) and allows the calculation of transitions between these groups (Kermack and McKendrick, 1927; Ross, 1911).

Through these brief historical narratives, it becomes clear how mathematical techniques became part of epidemiological reasoning. In these stories, the prediction of outbreaks and the ways to protect public health more and more efficiently are recurrent themes. The range of infections also highlight how widely applicable mathematical methods are. What is common to these early developments of mathematical techniques when they are part of epidemiological reasoning? Each of these techniques or models can be read as a step in the process of making sense of all the factors that affect disease transmission. In the early 1920s, epidemiology also opened up in an experimental direction.[13] One can see these two strands of epidemiological research as synergistic. By bringing together experimental knowledge and model-based evidence, a more comprehensive understanding of infectious diseases evolved. Model building itself brings together various sources of information and allows us to make inferences beyond direct observation, as Hampton Frost's idea of chains of inference suggests. In the following section, the key question is how models tell their stories – stories that help us understand transmission dynamics in a closed population or assess the effect of vaccinations on population immunity, for example.

2.2   Story of disease transmission

'What do we mean by transmission?' a computer scientist asked.[14] He had worked on an interdisciplinary modelling project in Helsinki (see Infobox 2.2) for several years. A lack of understanding was not behind his question. The models answered his question by bringing the intertwined factors of transmission into play in a simulation tool.

How did the models of *Haemophilus influenzae* type b bacteria (Hib) transmission tell their story? In order to understand transmission, we need to identify a bacteria and its strains, and then establish a correlation between the bacteria and the severe disease forms it causes. Immunity slows down or prevents transmission. As we have learned, herd

DOI: 10.1057/9781137298829.0006

immunity can protect the whole population, even when only a part of it has been vaccinated (e.g. Fine, 1993). We could say that in the modelling exercise two aims were intertwined: to translate the understanding of disease transmission into models and to assess preventive measures. Behind this was a goal stated in the research plans of the project: a need to plan and evaluate different vaccination strategies (Arjas and Takala, 1994, 1996). Vaccinations against Hib diseases were a new and effective form of intervention. In order to express all this in a mathematical model, a more fine-grained understanding of the duration of immunity and other factors was required. The Hib models were eventually able to tell the whole story of disease transmission: all these aspects were to be taken into account. A single model was not able to address them all, and therefore a family of models was developed.

The aspiration to tell this story led the Helsinki modelling project (Infobox 2.2) to plan a simulation tool[15] in the early days of the research project (1994–1996). Yet the complexity of disease transmission as an epidemiological phenomenon forced them to study the different aspects of the transmission process through smaller steps. In order to see how these smaller steps developed, I will discuss how models told the story of Hib transmission.

Understanding transmission in a family

The Good-night kiss model shows how transmission happens in a family. By examining the process of model building, we will also get a sense of how it takes place in an interdisciplinary research environment.

Focusing on the case of Hib and the infections it causes (Infobox 2.1), the Helsinki modellers wanted to build a simple transmission model, and therefore defined a population as a family (i.e. a sample of a closed population). When parents kissed their children good-night, Hib was transmitted among family members. This underlying assumption shows that Hib bacteria are transmitted through saliva as the natural niche of the bacteria is in the nose and throat (the human nasopharynx). The assumption also emphasises that small children are more likely to get the Hib infection.[16] Taking these assumptions into account, the Good-night kiss model became a starting point to model transmission dynamics. The researchers needed to identify *ingredients* that helped bring together the information they had about the phenomenon and express it mathematically. Parameter values were estimated from available data, and on

DOI: 10.1057/9781137298829.0006

the basis of the ingredients, the model calculated family and community transmission rates simultaneously.

INFOBOX 2.1 *Haemophilus influenzae type b bacteria, Hib*

Hib is a commonly circulating bacteria among infants and children. It can cause life-threatening conditions, such as meningitis. In milder forms, it causes otitis media, septicaemia and arthritis. Hib was initially identified in the 1930s through the groundbreaking work of Margaret Pittman, who isolated the different strains of Haemophilus bacteria (a-g). Her work helped develop the first polysaccharide vaccines that appeared on the market in the 1980s. In the mid-1990s more effective conjugate vaccines were introduced. These vaccines, despite being more expensive, have been shown not only to protect against the Hib diseases but also to reduce carriage of the bacteria. This is a beneficial effect for the overall population. The Hib bacteria 'lives' in the human nasopharynx. One does not become immune after having a Hib infection. Hib has some similarities with Streptococcus pneumoniae (PnC), and sharing model-based estimates from Hib studies has helped in the modelling of PnC. Hib causes 386,000 deaths worldwide annually. The Global Alliance for Vaccinations and Immunisations (GAVI) campaigns for Hib vaccinations to the poorest countries.

The Good-night kiss model consists of *ingredients* that can be grouped as statistical methods and solutions (including computational techniques), epidemiological mechanisms and data. The ingredients, however, are not as readily available as flour, eggs and sugar for a cake (Boumans, 1999). In the early days of the Helsinki project, the researchers studied how modelling methods had been developed and used in biostatistics. This learning process took place mainly in joint seminars and was supported by a pioneering modeller from Tübingen University who visited Helsinki. This work led the Helsinki modellers to identify the statistical ingredient they needed to develop, so that they could study how Hib carriage and infection happens in a family. This was expressed as a compartmental S-I-S type model.

We consider an S-I-S type epidemic model, where the infection states are *non-carrier* (S) who is susceptible to becoming a carrier of the bacteria,

DOI: 10.1057/9781137298829.0006

and infectious *carrier* (C) able to spread the bacteria. (Auranen, 1999: 2238; Auranen et al., 1999)

This simple pattern of Susceptible-Infected-Susceptible[17] (S-I-S) captures the transitions between different states of carriage in individuals. It was not a new discovery: the deterministic compartmental models of Kermack and MacKendrick (whom we have already met) were the predecessors who identified this pattern. In order to express the S-I-S pattern in mathematical terms, these transitions were seen as likelihoods, and the modellers applied a stochastic process[18] to express the changes in the states. Yet the statistical ingredient needed to be intertwined with the epidemiological mechanisms. These mechanisms were the background assumptions about the behaviour and transmission of Hib.

This S-I-S model formed the core of the Good-night kiss model. It calculated transmission rates based on transitions between the individual as a non-carrier (who does not have the bacteria in her nasopharynx), an asymptomatic carrier (who has the bacteria, but does not have the symptoms of an infection) or one with the rare invasive infection (who suffers from Hib infection).

The Good-night kiss model incorporated two sets of data as its ingredients. The first set was collected as part of a risk-factor analysis of invasive Hib disease in Finland during 1985–1986, just before the Hib vaccination programme was launched; the second was collected in the United Kingdom during 1991–1992. The data were collected from family members and infants aged six, nine and twelve months. Composed of these ingredients, the Good-night kiss model offered an example of individual-based modelling in a small population.

Initiated by the concern for what would be an optimal vaccination strategy against the serious forms of Hib diseases, the Good-night kiss model set the stage and led to understanding of disease transmission in a family. The model showed how the bacteria circulated among family members, which informed epidemiologists on how to optimise a preventive vaccination campaign for children. With the understanding of how a single model is built, we can relate to the stories they tell us. In this way, stories of transmission become policy-relevant.

2.3   Telling policy-relevant stories

Transmission, we could say, has a dual nature. It can be seen as a threat and a potential: the threat of a serious illness to the public, and the

DOI: 10.1057/9781137298829.0006

potential for prevention. When models tell stories of transmission, they emphasise this duality. They may suggest measures to prevent transmission by improving vaccination programmes, for example. Yet, to prevent transmission means to know about the effects of natural immunity in a population. These aspects of transmission need to be integrated into the policy-relevant stories the models tell us. Therefore, the simulation platform[19] told the story of how transmission happens in relation to its effective prevention through vaccinations. This dual nature of transmission gave rise to a vision of a policy instrument that could express it.

The promise of a policy instrument was to estimate and simulate how quickly the Hib infection is likely to spread and how effective vaccination is against it. This promise was initially a vision that guided the building of a visual user interface for a computer-based simulation model. By making easy changes in the basic estimates of the infection, this tool could control the potential spread of the infection in the population and test scenarios for effective and affordable vaccination strategies. The vision turned into a promise that the simulation tool would help overcome financial, ethical and demographic restrictions when researchers experimented with intervention strategies.

What is needed when an unexpected outbreak (in this case, caused by Hib) occurs? In the early days of the Helsinki modelling project, the answer was clear: a simulation model that could be used as a tool to estimate the course of the outbreak *when* it happens. The simulation model,[20] or tool, is an individual-based stochastic simulation model that was built towards the end of the Helsinki project (see Infobox 2.2). Its predecessor was a visual model with a graphic interface that was programmed by an engineering student in the early days of the project. The initial idea was that this interface would provide a simple tool for estimating the risk of infection by manipulating the parameter values. This first attempt did not, however, turn into a functioning simulation tool, and it took many years of research on modelling before the Individual-based Stochastic Simulation Model (IBSSM) came into being, although without a fancy user interface.

Characteristically, the simulation model integrates three smaller models: a demographic model, a transmission model and an immunity model. These models can be seen as small stories that are necessary to know before the whole narrative of the simulation model tells. Through these smaller models, we can learn how modelling both *stores* and *translates* knowledge. This occurs when the simulation model actually evolves from earlier models, such as the Good-night kiss model[21] or, in other

DOI: 10.1057/9781137298829.0006

INFOBOX 2.2   *Modelling infectious diseases at the National Institute for Health and Welfare in Helsinki, Finland*

Modelling collaboration in Helsinki emerged in the early 1990s as a response to a growing need to analyse available epidemiological data on disease transmission, especially in relation to infections caused by *Haemophilus influenzae* type b bacteria, with more fine-grained mathematical tools – computer-based models. Initiated by a senior epidemiologist at the then-National Public Health Institute (KTL), currently the Institute for Health and Welfare, the collaboration owes its success to the serendipity of available expertise and pioneering modelling projects in other countries. The collaboration brought together researchers with training in statistics, mathematics and computer science that complemented the existing epidemiological research at the NPHI.

Researchers from KTL, the Biometry research group at the University of Helsinki, the Rolf Nevanlinna Institute (RNI) (part of the Department of Mathematics and Statistics from 2004), and the Multimedia Laboratory of Helsinki University of Technology (HUT) (currently the Aalto University) all participated in the project INFEMAT that was initiated by KTL and funded by the Academy of Finland. During the project (1994–2004), a total of 15 models were built. These models are probabilistic models on *Haemophilus influenzae* type b bacteria (Hib), related infections, vaccination effects and transmission dynamics.

words, grows out of the fertile soil they have prepared and nourished. The simulation model uses knowledge from the models built earlier. In this process the earlier Good-night kiss model turned out to be a useful starting point to develop a more sophisticated understanding of transmission patterns.

The Finnish population was built into the simulation platform as a demographic model based on data collected by Statistics Finland. It described the size of the contact sites and the corresponding age groups. Contact sites are day-care groups or school classes, and are therefore age related.[22] To have a full understanding of the demographics, the average family size and structure were also added to the demographic model. This component enabled age-specific and contact-specific monitoring of

DOI: 10.1057/9781137298829.0006

the infection in the simulation model. In other words, it told the story of what would happen if a child in a nursery group got an infection and how quickly it would be transmitted to others in the group.

The simulation model followed as accurately as possible the number of estimated carriers in the model. This information was known from the Good-night kiss model and the simulation brought it into play. It monitored all contacts and counted the proportion of carriers among them. A small, constant background intensity of exposure from the whole population was incorporated into the simulation in order to depict circulation of bacteria and viruses that strengthen natural immunity.

To estimate the severity of Hib infection, immunity against harmful Hib diseases was produced in response to Hib and cross-reactive[23] bacteria. The simulation tool also examined the changes in inherited immunity and monitored its waning over time.[24] Hib vaccination reduces the incidence of Hib carriage, and even when not succeeding in this, it is likely to prevent the progression from carriage to actual disease. The Finnish vaccination strategies of the 1980s were integrated into the simulation, which was also sensitive to different types[25] of vaccines.

This compartmental model, which shows the transitions between different groups of people in the Finnish population, captured the transmission dynamics of Hib into the simulation model. This means that the earlier knowledge gained from the Good-night kiss model was integrated into the simulation model. What was known of Hib transmission in a family was now extended to cover the whole of the population.

Thus, the simulation model was composed of three smaller models that were built prior to its modelling. The initial aim of programming a graphical user interface faded, and the final version of the simulation model lost its accessibility and easy manipulation of parameters to estimate different infections. The building of the simulation model revealed the shortcomings of the modelling process. Unevenly allocated resources between epidemiologists and computer scientists became a hindrance to the development of the model. Maintaining multidisciplinary expertise became difficult. When epidemiologists and statisticians were able to carry on collaborative work, a computer scientist had to find extra resources to continue the work after his initial funding period in the project had ended. In this sense the 'material base' of the models, in the sense of institutional support, influenced the success of the project (Mattila, 2006a, 2006c).

DOI: 10.1057/9781137298829.0006

Despite these limitations, the simulation model was able to tell a story that responded to the initial concerns of disease transmission and optimal vaccinations. It was able to show the increased understanding of Hib transmission dynamics, the beneficial effects from the vaccinations and their preferred scheduling, the ways in which natural immunity can be affected and what might be the consequences of that. What was also established was expertise in epidemiological modelling that was gained during the long years of the Helsinki project. This expertise, along with the models, can be seen as a part of the toolkit to produce evidence for policy processes. Characteristic of the expertise is that it evolved through interdisciplinary collaboration. Again, we need to go beyond the trendy term and look at what actually happened in multi-organisational research collaboration.

The modelling project enjoyed from the beginning expertise from different fields of study: mathematics, statistics, epidemiology and computer science. Yet, turning these different fields of expertise into genuine interdisciplinary collaboration was not a straightforward process. Over the years, the researchers developed close forms of collaboration and learned to understand each other's disciplinary requests when reporting and publishing the models. What was seen as a genuinely interdisciplinary collaboration turned out to be a long process evolving from multidisciplinary (i.e. a collaborative phase in which cross-disciplinary language or methods were not yet developed) to interdisciplinary work (i.e. in which there is a significant overlap in research goals, terminology and understanding that goes beyond disciplinary identities). Central to the process was the development and recognition of a joint research goal, the simulation tool, and modelling which enhanced communication beyond discipline-specific practices. Also of critical importance was close collaboration between a mathematician and an epidemiologist, who learned from each other, and as an outcome of this learning process, the models became a *playground*,[26] which allowed testing for different outcomes and scenarios related to the infectious outbreak (cf. Mattila, 2006b).

The way in which modelling shapes policies occurs through the narratives of transmission, immunity and infection that take place in a particular population. These narratives – historical and current – inform both the research community in terms of estimates of the behaviour of the infection and the policy community in terms of recommendations for new vaccination strategies. They are expressed with an interdisciplinary

DOI: 10.1057/9781137298829.0006

voice. Modelled narratives are collages of integrated singular facts that have been studied in a series of models. In this sense, they capture the processes and practices of forming 'chains of inference'. Yet, through these processes the singular facts become enriched and gain applicability perhaps beyond the immediate audience to whom the story is told. But how well do modelled narratives respond to a policy call?

Responding to a policy call

Hib diseases and transmission do not represent a significant problem in the affluent West. Bacterial meningitis, pneumonia, epiglottitis and other harmful diseases caused by Hib have been swept away in mass vaccination campaigns.[27] But worldwide Hib infections cause approximately 3 million cases of serious diseases each year, and approximately 386,000 untimely deaths in children aged 4–18. Societies that struggle with the disease burden are in the developing world. In order to persuade these societies to reallocate their health-care resources for Hib prevention, modelled stories provide useful evidence.

In the introduction to her PhD thesis, Tuija Leino writes,

> 'In the developing world data on the disease burden are limited and although WHO and Global Alliance for Vaccinations and Immunization advocate Hib conjugate vaccination, the major question remains whether universal vaccination will be at all feasible in the poorest economies. *Will it be cost-effective and, moreover, will it be an appropriate use of resources among other possible health interventions?* Schedules optimising the age of vaccination and the number of doses are crucial for the acceptance for the expensive conjugate Hib vaccines. (Leino, 2003: 10, emphasis mine)

Leino (2003) discusses the rationale of studying vaccinations by modelling: to produce evidence that supports the recommendations for vaccination strategies. These recommendations, as she points out, need to address cost-effectiveness in order to influence the decision. But modelling allows more detailed stories to be told. Based on modelling, the optimal schedule and dosage of vaccinations can be examined. She also shows that the effects from mass vaccinations on the population can be predicted based on an understanding of Hib transmission.

The detailed story of vaccinations needs to be told on a global scale. Both the World Health Organization (WHO) and Global Alliance for Vaccines and Immunizations (GAVI) advocate conjugate vaccines, a new group of vaccines against infections caused by *Haemophilus influenza* type

DOI: 10.1057/9781137298829.0006

b bacteria. The challenge is to persuade the poorest economies to implement these vaccines that are more effective, but also more expensive. The main choice is between polysaccharides and conjugate vaccines. While the conjugate vaccines both prevent Hib diseases and reduce carriage, polysaccharides only prevent the more serious disease forms. Despite their cost, the conjugate vaccines can actually reduce the circulation of Hib bacteria in a population, and are therefore more beneficial.

Along with the cost-effectiveness of the vaccinations, we can also read the story of the importance of optimising the vaccination schedule. This means finding the optimal vaccination coverage[28] so that herd immunity (i.e. population-level immunity) will be reached. For this to happen, the dynamics of natural and vaccine-induced immunity need to be understood by addressing the question of how well the population is protected through their natural immunity.[29] Leino's account shows how a bridge between investigative interests and policy interests can be built by modelling. Policy-driven questions are readdressed and translated into smaller and more precise research questions. This is simply because in order to revise a policy, the behaviour of the infection on population level needs to be well known.

The way in which models tell stories can be described schematically, and this is common to modelling practices in different fields. The schematic simplification of model building in economics, for example, emphasises how a model is built to represent the world, or rather an aspect of the world in four steps (Morgan, 2002: 42):

1. building a model to represent the world;
2. asking questions about the model;
3. manipulating the model to answer the questions;
4. relating the answer to real-world phenomena.

Morgan's view leads us to see modelling as a process of representing the world in a model. It is a way of seeing how the object of modelling comes alive in a model. The object of modelling, 'the world' within the model, can then be investigated by using research questions as manipulative tools. When we manipulate a model and experiment with it, we are making the model in order to tell a story (Morgan, 2001: 361; 2002; 2012). Just as a story is told from a particular point of view, a model is built to address a particular question, to represent the world in a limited way.

This schematic account can be extended so that we can see how model building becomes a response to a policy call. Again, this is not an

DOI: 10.1057/9781137298829.0006

exhaustive account of how modelling happens in epidemiology; rather, it offers a simplified view of the stages involved.

i)   Let us assume that WHO or GAVI[30] intends to advocate a vaccination programme in a developing country. In order to give convincing evidence for a new, expensive vaccine, international health organisations use modelling methods to assess the cost-effectiveness of the initiative. The call may also come from a national government[31] that needs to revise pandemic preparedness plans, for example. The UK Health and Social Care Act 2008 summarises the preventive and protective functions of public health: 'The bill provides a comprehensive set of public health measures to help prevent and control the spread of serious diseases caused by infection and contamination'. Within this set of public health measures are mathematical models and simulation techniques and the stories they tell us.

ii) This general policy call asks for further research that is undertaken in national public health institutes[32] that often serve in advisory roles or at the related university departments. In Helsinki, researchers translated the general interests and concerns into more detailed research questions that concretised how modelling was a way to respond to the initial call (Arjas and Takala in research plans 1994 and 1996). This translation meant that the initiative to study the effectiveness of Hib vaccinations was addressed as four research questions:

'1)   Does vaccination alter the age distribution of Hib diseases and its incidence?

2)   Does vaccination alter the spectrum of Hib diseases?

3)   Does natural immunity vanish from the general population, which would indicate the need for revaccination?

4)   How high must the vaccination coverage be in order to prevent Hib diseases in the population?' (Research plans 1994, 1996)

These questions arose from a research initiative that aimed at enhancing the 'understanding of the dynamics of *Haemophilus* infection and assessing its persistence in a population', and 'developing methods for the analysis of Hib infection and the effect of different intervention strategies' by modelling methods (Auranen et al., 1996: 2235). We have learned how these questions have been addressed in both the Good-night kiss model and in the simulation tool, for example. After all, these questions

DOI: 10.1057/9781137298829.0006

were identified as a way to tell the story of the different aspects of the Hib infection: its effect in the population, the immune response and the effect from vaccinations.

iii) Then the Helsinki research group began to build the model. At this stage they had to choose the most applicable modelling method. This meant a set of choices that guided how the model assumptions were expressed in the model, that is, what was the appropriate model design, the parameter estimates to quantify the model, for example.

iv) In the fourth stage, the actual model building takes place. During the course of the Helsinki project, a *family* of models was built.[33] These models form a set or *family*, which means they *store* and *disseminate* information, parameter values, model assumptions, applicable algorithms or data sets throughout the project (and beyond). But this stage of model building benefited from interdisciplinary expertise brought into the project.

v) In the final stage (and this will be the topic of Chapter 3), the model-based evidence, that is model-output facts, estimates and computational templates are potentially disseminated back to the public health bodies that initiated the policy-driven questions motivating the project.

Through the stories of transmission we have become familiar with model building. Altogether, these five stages in the process of responding to a public health policy call show how models tell policy-relevant stories. Each of these stages also presents a challenge. When the timescale of this process is taken into account from the initial call to the policy-relevant outcome, the long chain of inference is not straightforward. In Helsinki, each of the stages had adjacent steps, so that a single model simulating transmission grew into a family of models explaining transmission, carriage and immunity. A focus on a single model or modelling project becomes dispersed. Uncertainties about continuous funding easily increase the socio-economic restrictions on the work environment. Ideally, we are looking at a description of a process that is identifiable in various fields of study. In practice, learning and analysing this process is a prerequisite for transparency, for greater access to the world of models. This world is not only the outer world of policymaking, usability or assessment. On the contrary, the inner world of models, their capacity to express transmission of infections in calculable and computable ways,

DOI: 10.1057/9781137298829.0006

is equally relevant. It is, after all, when both worlds come together that the openness and transparency of modelling are present. This is when models tell their stories in a comprehensible way.

2.4   Conclusion

We began with the idea of modelling as a style of reasoning, which is specific to epidemiology when it is seen as a chain of inference, as Hampton Frost suggests. Typical for a style of reasoning, in the sense in which Hacking (1992) discusses it, is that it is an elementary approach to shaping a disciplinary identity. Our observations about mathematical modelling and the broader development of mathematical techniques in epidemiology, however, show that epidemiology has an adaptable disciplinary identity. These techniques developed as responses to policy needs, they made their way, slowly but straightforwardly, into studies of transmission, and yet, their use is not unquestionably accepted. When we turn our attention to pandemic modelling, we will learn of the cautionary attitudes that accompany the application of modelling.

When looking at the uses of models in infectious disease epidemiology, both in the historical case and in the development of the family of models, we notice a common trait: the models tell us stories. These stories address the need to understand the infectious phenomenon in a way that is relevant to the policy process. The story has a purpose: to be used as evidence in the process that ultimately aims at benefiting public health. Yet, this may not be straightforward. As the story of a local modelling project shows, a quickly developed policy tool was not achieved as an outcome. What did evolve is a story of interconnected models. How this interconnectedness emerged can be summarised in a brief look at the *family of models*.

What the family of models reveals to us is a structured narrative of how Hib transmission happens, what the effective interventions are and how we can predict a possible outbreak. The models one after another addressed some of these aspects. When the answers were not directly acquired, the questions presented in the models were pursued to explore more details related to the dynamics of the infection. In the end, our narrative is not only a story of the transmission Hib, but contains elements that are useful to other infections that share similar features. It can also be read as a story of how interdisciplinary collaboration is

DOI: 10.1057/9781137298829.0006

formed and how that leads to the asking of more sophisticated questions in the models. The aspect of the interconnectedness of models, which has been expressed as a *family of models*, is useful when we try to understand how models disseminate knowledge and evidence across research and policy communities. This will be our focus in the next chapter.

Notes

1   For example, life-threatening diseases caused by *Haemophilus influenzae* type b bacteria were initially identified by Margaret Pittman in the 1930s (Pittman, 1931, 1933).

2   The intention and purpose in a story turn it into a narrative, according to Dry and Leach (2010).

3   Model building is aligned with storytelling, which captures their versatile, functional and mediating nature (e.g. Morgan, 2001; Gramelsberger, 2010).

4   Since the 1980s, modelling methods have been successfully applied to the study of various aspects of infections. This development has benefited from the increase in computational power. In recent years, the need to understand models among the groups that use model-based evidence has been recognised (e.g. Vynnycky and White, 2010; Daley and Gani, 1999; Anderson and May, 1992).

5   A similar development is known to have happened in climate research, where computational techniques were introduced in the form of large-scale differential models in the 1960s (cf. Gramelsberger, 2010; Gramelsberger and Mansnerus, 2012).

6   Ludwig Fleck identified thought styles and thought communities in the history of medicine. The continuation of them was analysed in Hacking (1992), who identified six styles of reasoning, extending the classification from A. Crombie. Most recently, Morgan (2012) studied styles of reasoning in relation to modelling in economics.

7   To provide a full history of the development of mathematical reasoning in epidemiology is beyond the scope of this book (cf. Anderson and May, 1992; Daley and Gani, 1999).

8   This was an assumption that became reality only 200 years later, in 1980, when Fenner announced the elimination of smallpox to the World Health Assembly (Gani, 2010: 233).

9   Variolation means inoculating a healthy person with pus from a person infected with smallpox. It was a new technique in Europe, which preceded modern-day vaccinations. In 1796, Edward Jenner applied the innovation of inoculating a healthy child with pus from cowpox blisters to prove his

DOI: 10.1057/9781137298829.0006

observations that milkmaids who got cowpox did not fall ill with smallpox. He then, after the child had had a mild case of cowpox inoculated the child with pus from a smallpox patient and the child proved immune to smallpox (Gani, 2010: 323).

10 Herd immunity means that partial vaccination coverage has an effect on the force of infection (Dietz and Heesterbeek, 2002: 17).

11 Cf. Worboys (2000) on the historical development of germ theory. The logical conditions of organism x being the cause of a disease y are known as Koch's postulates, although Louis Pasteur, Robert Koch and Robert Pfeiffer were the architects of germ theory (Bynum, 2006; Worboys, 2000).

12 These groups are pregnant women, children under 6 months of age and people who are immuno-compromised.

13 Cf. Amsterdamska (2001, 2005) on experimental epidemiology and William Topley; Amoss (1922) on experimental epidemiology.

14 Meeting at the National Public Health Institute, 17 November 2002.

15 The way in which a simulation tool developed into a simulation platform is examined in Mattila (2006b). The concept of a platform is informed by Keating and Cambrosio's analysis of the emergence of biomedical platforms (2000, 2003; Mattila, 2006c).

16 According to Auranen, 95% of all invasive diseases occur among children of less than five years of age. (Auranen, Ranta, Takala, and Arjas, 1996)

17 S-I-S pattern is typical for Hib infection, because the infection does not cause permanent immunity.

18 The stochastic process is known as the Markov process, which expresses the changes in the stages of carriage with random variables.

19 The concept of a platform comes from Keating and Cambrosio (2000, 2003). They analysed the development of *biomedical platforms*, which are conglomerates of sociomedical development that incorporate the environment within which the development happens.

20 Published in Auranen et al., 2004.

21 The earlier models were published in Auranen, Ranta, Takala, and Arjas, 1996; Auranen et al., 1999; Auranen, 2000.

22 For example, children in Finland go to school at the age of seven.

23 Cross-reactive bacteria, or CR, are antibodies that also react with some antigens other than with the ones they were produced in response to (Mäkelä et al., 2003).

24 Because immunity is 'controlled' or 'boosted' in individuals by vaccinations, I consider the vaccination model to be part of the immunity model. This also allows me to leave the detailed impact of different vaccination types aside, which clarifies the complex model to some extent.

25 These being conjugate and polysaccharide vaccines.

DOI: 10.1057/9781137298829.0006

26   A mathematical modeller and an epidemiologist said that 'we are able to play with models', which depicted their close collaboration and mutual understanding (cf. Mattila, 2006c).

27   For example, in England and Wales, the Hib campaign was introduced in 1992 (Heath and McVernon, 2002); in Finland 1998 (Peltola, Salo, and Saxén, 2005).

28   This varies according to the infection and vaccine. Some infections require that only one-third of the population be vaccinated (as the modellers estimated being the case for Hib infections); whereas measles requires 97.5% population coverage.

29   Natural immunity is an individual's immunity against infections that can be strengthened when an individual has other infections.

30   GAVI Alliance is the Global Alliance for Vaccines and Immunizations (www.gavialliance.org)

31   Interview with a modeller at the Health Protection Agency (2007).

32   For example, Health Protection Agency in the UK; the Institute for Health and Welfare in Finland.

33   Altogether 15 models during 1996–2001, see Infobox 2.2.

DOI: 10.1057/9781137298829.0006

3
Kinship Relations of Models

Abstract: *In order to show how models are interconnected, Mansnerus focuses on a family of models, built in Helsinki in the 1990s. This interconnectedness has a broader reach, which can be conceptualised as 'kinship relations', a notion initially used by Hoover (1991) in relation to economic models. Mansnerus argues that the interconnectedness of models shows how modelling methods, parameter values and estimates, and model-based evidence are stored and disseminated within and across research communities. By understanding the evolving relations of models, the nature of model-based evidence on its journey through public health research networks is made clear.*

Mansnerus, Erika. *Modelling in Public Health Research: How Mathematical Techniques Keep Us Healthy.* Basingstoke: Palgrave Macmillan, 2015. DOI: 10.1057/9781137298829.0007.

How are models capable of disseminating reliable knowledge? In this chapter we will shift the focus from models as narratives, which served as anecdotal 'birth stories' of models describing how modelling methods became commonly used in mathematical epidemiology, to the relatedness of models, through the notion of the *kinship relation of models*. A starting point for this exercise is the Good-night kiss model, built in Helsinki 1994/1995. The Good-night kiss model will serve as an ancestor, a great-grandma model, if you like. By analysing its 'family tree' we will begin to see how well model-based outputs are disseminated across different models within and outside the initial 'family' context in which the model was built. Once the 'family tree' is known to us, we will look more deeply into the 'characteristics' of model-based findings in order to assess what makes a model output easily adaptable into a new 'model family'. We are particularly interested in the differences that can be identified in these characters, as this will help us to see what facilitates the adoption of model-based outcomes and what may hinder it. In the concluding observations, we will elaborate the notion of kinship relations in terms of what it tells us about model-based evidence. The relatedness, iteration and attachment in model communities suggest that models may not be easily 'released' into an independent expert life, but need these 'family ties' to support them.

3.1   Models and kinship ties

'Models and theories are united by ties of kinship and consanguinity'. (Hoover, 1991: 375)

The increase in the use of modelling techniques overlooked a fascinating aspect: how modelling methods and techniques relate to each other or, perhaps, evolve together. I will conceptualise the relations between models as *kinship* relations. Kevin Hoover (1991) initially introduces this notion in his analysis of how economic research programme develop. Hoover builds his idea of the kinship relations of models and consanguinity on anthropological terminology. He claims that

When the model is used as an exemplar for another model, usually by another modeller, not every feature of the exemplar is transferred. Key features or methods or assumptions are transferred, while others are neglected. In choosing which features to borrow, however, the modeller already provides

DOI: 10.1057/9781137298829.0007

an interpretation of what is important – an interpretation which in turn may be adopted by still other modellers. (1991: 373)

What Hoover points out is that models combine *programmatic*, i.e. systematic, accepted and commonly used ways of approaching phenomena, as well as *adventitious*, unplanned or perhaps surprising uses. He then carries on discussing that a model usually serves as an example used by another modeller. In this new context, models can be used in both programmatic and adventitious ways. In this chapter, the exemplary uses of models are discussed through the analogy of *kinship* relations. This relates to the literature that has acknowledged how models function as tools and measuring instruments in scientific work (Morgan and Morrison, 1999). The most recent trend is to ask how we use models within and across various domains (in research and policy, for explanatory and predictive purposes).

For Hoover, the kinship relations of models are a way to respond to the Lakatosian idea of research programmes and their development. As a source for finding similarities between models, I will use the notion of kinship in the analysis of infectious disease models that were initially built to predict the transmission of *Haemophilus influenzae* type b bacteria. In Hoover's analysis, kinship relations are formed through a shared foundation myth. These relations may have a specific scope and range, by which he means that place and time are important. He also discusses social structures and the division of labour, and communication within and between tribes. He remains on a fairly general level in his use of an anthropological metaphor, and my interest is in using the metaphor in a more detailed manner, expanding it to depict how *communication* happens within family relations.

The process by which a family tree of the Good-night kiss model emerges and what forms of relatedness can be identified through the kinship lineage of models give us an idea of the characteristics of model-based outcomes and show us why modelling methods can be useful when disseminating evidence. Model-based outcomes refer to estimates and predictive scenarios, for example. In the third section, the focus is on model-based outcomes as facilitators for the formation of networks across research and policy contexts. And finally, special attention is given to relatedness, iteration and how model-based outcomes are attached to modelling communities, which may indicate that models have a painstakingly difficult path to grow into their expert positions that those in the working life outside academia expect.

DOI: 10.1057/9781137298829.0007

3.2   Kinship: evolving relations and links between models

Just as we have our ancestors – and most of us share a fascination for our origins as a way to make sense of who we are – we can apply the *metaphor* of kinship relations in order to map the relatedness of models. This metaphor sheds light on our leading focus on what models are. In the previous section, I introduced Hoover's account of economic models that inspire us to think about how models are related, how they form 'kinship relations' and why this is a useful way to look at modelling work.

As a notion, kinship can be easily thought of as an anthropological concept, a way to organise human histories. But in our daily lives we relate to our families, we name our *next of kin*, and we become aware of family histories through stories, traditions, habits or inheritance. Something tells us that we belong to a kin – whether that is a positive or a negative experience is another matter. And equally, something is disseminated through kinship relations. When we place this metaphor within the modelling context, the key idea is to learn to see how singular models are actually part of a 'family' and how that family then grows and disseminates model-based outputs to other modelling groups. Perhaps these became new distant relatives?

The following Figure 3.1 is our starting point. We are familiar with some of the members of this family. The Good-night kiss model was a starting point for modelling activities in Helsinki.

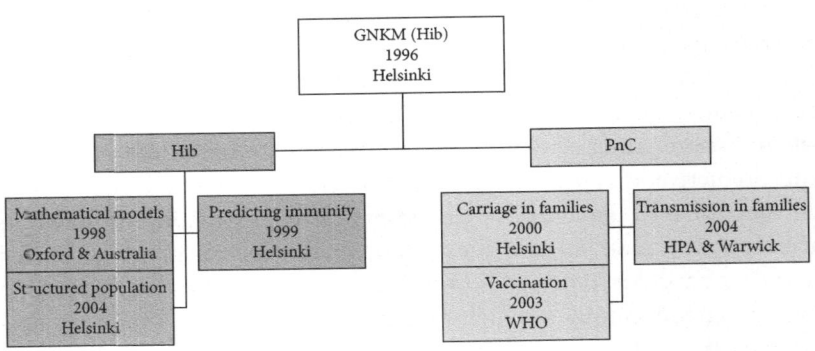

FIGURE 3.1   *The family tree of Helsinki models*

DOI: 10.1057/9781137298829.0007

Let us first analyse the family tree, and then, in the next section, look into the ways in which evidential claims are disseminated across the family tree.

Family tree of Helsinki models

The family tree of Helsinki models grows from the early Hib (*Haemophilus influenzae* type b) models to cover models built later in Britain and which not only address Hib infection but also provide evidence for vaccination planning in PnC (Streptococcus pneumoniae).

The family tree of Helsinki models, as depicted in the Figure 3.1 has its 'ancestor', the Good-night kiss model, which we discussed in detail in Chapter 2. Based on this model, and especially its capacity to depict transmission, a model that would *predict immunity to Hib* was built in 1999 in Helsinki. The Good-night kiss model effectively disseminates model-based assumptions, outcomes and parameter values to two other Hib models built by a joint international group based in Oxford and Australia. And particular transmission structures and estimates for transmission rates are adopted the *Structured population model* built in Helsinki by the same research group who composed the Good-night kiss model. Because Hib as a bacterial infection is similar to PnC (*Streptococcus pneumoniae*), researchers interested in estimating carriage of PnC, transmission and contact rates and optimising a vaccination programme, were led to the then-Health Protection Agency, currently Public Health England, and WHO, to look for published Hib modelling. This effort helped translate Hib-based findings into PnC research.

The family tree of Helsinki models shows how model-based outputs, findings or evidential claims establish links between different modelling communities. The Good-night kiss model was published in Auranen 1996 as an individual-based model built to describe Hib infection in a family with small children, when the infection is symptomless (see Infobox 2.1). The aim of the model was to estimate family and community transmission rates simultaneously by studying the spread of Hib infection via good-night kisses between family members. The model was fitted with data sets collected in Finland 1985–1986 and in the United Kingdom 1991–1992, just before these countries introduced Hib vaccinations into their immunisation programmes. This model was the first one built by the Helsinki group.

If we see the Good-night kiss model as the 'ancestor', the family tree then demonstrates how model-based evidential claims were adopted into

DOI: 10.1057/9781137298829.0007

other models built by the Helsinki group or by other research groups. I will first introduce a couple of models from the family tree and show how family ties are formed between them when model-based evidential claims are adopted into new models. This will help us to understand why the *characters* of these evidential claims are important.

In order to illustrate this process of forming the family tree and all its ties, we might think of the Helsinki model as being the nuclear family. What then forms the family ties? If we think of the relationship between the Good-night kiss model and the Hib models built at a later stage of the Helsinki project: a model predicting immunity to Hib (Auranen et al., 1999) and a structured population transmission model (Auranen et al., 2004), we can identify two model-based outputs. The Good-night kiss model estimates force of infection for Hib in a family. This estimate is adopted by the model that predicts immunity to Hib, which was built and published in 1995. We will call this model a direct offspring of the Good-night kiss model.

In 2000, a model depicting the carriage of Hib in families was published (Auranen, 2000). This model adopts from the Good-night kiss model the assumptions on microbial transmission, estimation of the average duration of carriage, estimation of transmission parameters and the effect of the pathogens' mechanism on carriage and transmission. Later, a model of indirect protection, built in Helsinki in 2004, adopted the assumptions on microbial transmission from the model depicting the carriage of Hib in families (Leino et al., 2004). In this sense, the family ties from the Good-night kiss model or the 'ancestor model' lead into the offspring. Of course, family ties cannot be said to have been established only on the basis of adopting model-based or produced evidential claims. What creates this family of models is naturally that all these models are built by the Helsinki group. All these models share some aspects of design, structure, computational solutions and perhaps mathematical algorithms. Earlier I discussed that these models can be talked about as *tailor-made*, they were purpose built to address research questions initially formulated in Research Plan 1994 by Arjas and Takala:

▸ Does vaccination alter the age distribution of Hib disease and incidence?
▸ Does natural immunity vanish from the general population, which would indicate the need for revaccination?
▸ How high must the vaccination coverage be in order to prevent the transmission of Hib disease in the population?

DOI: 10.1057/9781137298829.0007

Even though these questions address broader issues of the dynamics of Hib infection and have implications for vaccination policy as well, these interests did not remain only within the Helsinki group. While Hib vaccinations were introduced into the Finnish vaccination policy in the late 1980s, and in this sense the modelling was a post-assessment of the decision, WHO addressed the need to persuade developing countries to introduce Hib vaccinations. Late, PnC (*Streptococcus pneumoniae*) vaccination policy was to be discussed. This created wider interest in the epidemiological community towards these infections for two reasons. The fact that these bacterial infections behaved in a similar way and that their vaccinations induced similar carriage and immunity patterns increased the use of these early Hib models in early 2000 in regard to PnC modelling. In this sense the Hib model family grew into a kinship of infectious disease models. What facilitated the expansion of the family of models towards the kinship, or the growth in using model-based outputs beyond the immediate remit of Helsinki models, was not only the urge to implement vaccination policies on Hib and PnC. These evidential claims had a 'character' that facilitated their successful use in other contexts. What then is the nature of model-based evidence as an approach to discussing the ways in which evidential claims were adopted in a broad range of models outside the initial Helsinki group, reaching towards a policy context?

3.3   Nature of model-based evidence

Model-based evidence itself has a specific nature. It has been regarded as less robust and reliable, as it lacks the standards of experimental knowledge, which are the well-known backbone of scientific knowledge. Models (and computer simulations especially) are likened to experiments, but whether we can call them experiments is debatable.

Computational models (which are often simulation models) can be seen to represent experimental practice or experimenting (cf. Morgan, 2003, 2005; Fox Keller, 2003). Experimenting is the 'controlled manipulation of elements in a material world', as Morgan (2003: 216) claims. In this sense, a model experiment faces the challenge of materiality. To what extent can we conduct non-material experiments? Morgan (2003) offers two ways to conceptualise this: virtual experiments are those in which

DOI: 10.1057/9781137298829.0007

we conduct non-material experiments, such as model experiments, with semi-material objects. Virtual experiments are those in which we conduct non-material experiments by imitating material objects to some extent. Simulations are likely to represent *virtual* experiments, whereas model experiments can include semi-material objects that can be manipulated (e.g. data sets to calibrate or parameterise a model).

Despite the fine-grained distinctions of the degree to which models are or are not experiments, something of that experimental nature of modelling is worth bearing in mind. Experimentation itself, as understood since the scientific revolution initiated by Thomas Hobbes, Francis Bacon and Robert Boyle, among others in the 16th and the 17th centuries, indicates two aspects. First, experimenting is 'laying questions before Nature' (Oersted in Sintonen 2004). This is of course only beneficial if one knows what to ask. As we discussed in Chapter 2, modelling enables us to ask questions that were not previously thought of, reach beyond the bounds of direct observation, as Hampton Frost characterised of epidemiology. The second aspect is the instrumentality of experimenting. This has been highlighted in studies of the three-dimensionality of models (Griesemer, 2004; Hopwood and Chadarevian, 2004). For our purposes, the instrumentality of models, the very building and parameterisation of them, seeing them as instruments of investigation, as Morgan argues, is one of the reasons why model-based evidential claims are adopted through 'family ties'. Why is that?

As instruments for measuring, experimenting and testing, models require fine-grained understanding of the instrument itself. How has it been built? What is the correct model design? Which parameter values can depict the typical pattern of transmission? All these questions point to the underlying concern of model-based evidence: reliability. Just like an instrument is evaluated not only based on the successful measures it is capable of producing but also on the basis of the 'instrument maker', the reliability of model-based evidence depends on the credibility of the modeller as well as the validity of the data, model design and parameterisation (Boumans, 2004). This is what Boumans (2004) discusses as instrumental reliability in relation to the 'instrument maker'. In other words he incorporates the role of experts, the practice of calibration, with the procedures executed with the instrument. In terms of model-based evidence, the reputation and skills of the modelling group, the availability and quality of data to parameterise the model, and the simulations run, all form the reliability of the model in question. Yet, these elements do not come together automatically. To follow

DOI: 10.1057/9781137298829.0007

our analogy of the family ties of models, we can characterise model-based outputs and observe how they are received and used in different environments. This helps us understand the nature of model-based evidence in broader terms than within the context of scientific research and experimentation.

"She's got quite a character" is a common phrase. However, when we look at the characteristics of evidential claims, we do not expect character to be 'innate'. On the contrary, we consider character as socially formed in the context in which the evidential claim is received, used, adopted and modified. With this in mind we can think of two ways to characterise evidential claims: the claims can be *stubborn* or *flexible*, *enriched* or *simplified*. The aim of this exercise of characterising evidential claims is to show how the context plays a part in the process of accepting or ignoring the evidence they provide.

The multifaceted nature of evidential claims[1]

Stubbornness refers to evidential claims that are relatively resistant to change. These claims are unchangeable, inflexible or, we might say, robust. Good examples of these are assumptions and findings from epidemiological studies that show details of not only the pathogen but also of its circulation in specific age groups, its capacity to hide in symptomless carriers and its incapability to enforce permanent immunity. Common to these *stubborn* claims is that they are not easily moulded into models. They are robust in delivering their message, however.

The opposite pole of stubborn is *flexible*. These are evidential claims that can be easily adopted into new models. An example of flexibility is a constant recovery rate that was first established in the Good-night kiss model and later accommodated and modified to a PnC transmission model, built by Melegaro et al. in 2004.

Another pair of characteristics is *enriched* and *simplified* evidential claims. This time the evidential claim is either incorporated into a new model so that its information content is 'enriched' or broadened with other elements of knowledge. Or an initially sophisticated claim can be simplified in order to be useful in a new model. An example of this is a model-based numerical estimate for Hib transmission in a family that was first established as an outcome of M1 (Good-night kiss model) and later *simplified* into a comparative reference point in McVernon et al., 2004, which meant that the claim lost its initial numerical reference point. These examples are clarified in the following Table 3.1.

DOI: 10.1057/9781137298829.0007

TABLE 3.1   *Summary of the analysis of characteristics of evidential claims*

Characteristic of the evidential claim	Example	Demonstration of the characteristic
Stubborn[a] A claim that is resistant to change and may require auxiliary measures to be quantified in a model.	'Transmission of Hib occurs through asymptomatic carriers. Most episodes of Hib carriage pass without clinical symptoms and only in rare cases does carriage proceed to invasive disease' (Auranen et al., 2004).	The claim on general epidemiological knowledge on the dynamics of Hib transmission is standard epidemiological knowledge. It supported (but remained unchanged) claims of Hib transmission produced in the Good-night kiss model.
Flexible A claim that can be accommodated well in a new model.	'[as in Auranen et al., 1996], we set the transition from C to S to be dependent on a constant recovery rate' (Melegaro et al., 2004).	This claim refers to the SIS-structure or model design. It shows that the dynamics of Hib transmission patterns were easily adopted and modified to fit into the Melegaro model of PnC. This was also possible because PnC and Hib have similar immunity dynamics.
Enriched A claim that gathers further meaning and enriched information content in a new model.	'In the previous study on Hib carriage in families (1996) the force of infection is probably related to [the] different nature of data. In that article data on antibodies was not included' (Auranen, 1999).	This claim about the force of infection was enriched in the destination model with data about antibodies. This model (M2) discusses the importance of estimating the force of infection in relation to all the transmission dynamics details.
Simplified A claim that becomes simplified, usually a reference point in a new context.	'For example, Hib transmission rate is thought to be greater within families whose members have experienced Hib disease' (McVernon et al., 2004).	This evidential claim shows how the initially sophisticated estimate for a transmission rate in a family was simplified to a comparative 'thought to be greater than' claim in a model on trends in Hib infections.

Note: [a] This notion is also used by Daston (1991/1994) in relation to evidence (Daston, 1991a).

DOI: 10.1057/9781137298829.0007

These characteristics of evidential claims: *stubborn* and *flexible*, *enriched* and *simplified* offer a new dynamic way of understanding the nature of evidence. Instead of accepting evidence as something monolithic and stable, the characteristics reveal its changing nature. Especially in the context of modelling, these changes are important. Modelling is a relatively sophisticated activity, which involves highly specialised knowledge. Not all parameter estimates can be extracted from given data sets. It is not always reasonable to start from scratch with the model structure. Evidence of the infection, its transmission dynamics or the ways it conveys to immunity are not easily available. These claims can be adopted from other models. This is how the family tree grows towards kinship relations. Perhaps some of the stubborn relationships remind us of caricatures of mothers and daughters in an 'in-law' relationship in which habits and customs are stubbornly held onto. Sometimes new members of the extended family enrich the existing customs. Perhaps our metaphor of *kinship* relations of models underlines the observations that even model-based outcomes are subject to change.

Along with the characteristics of evidential claims, we can elaborate the ways in which these claims are put into use in the new environments. I have chosen to describe these functions in terms of evidential claims functioning as *brokers*, *mediators* or *containers*. What this means in the context of our kinship metaphor is that we can identify different ways of relating to new members in our family, or perhaps seeing these as ways to relate to new, extended families.

When we think of *brokers*, evidential claims function by helping open up and support new research areas, perhaps expanding and challenging aspects of existing or given research themes. For example, when evidential claims on Hib carriage and transmission in a family were adopted into a PnC model, we could see them functioning as brokers as they encouraged further PnC research on carriage and transmission in a population.

Mediators are evidential claims that bridge the gap between different areas of study, different approaches and that have the quality of reconciling different strands of research. An evidential claim that describes the indirect effects of Hib vaccinations (how conjugate vaccines reduce carriage of Hib and boost immunity levels) is a mediator by bridging Hib and PnC studies (as PnC vaccines are also conjugates).

Finally, evidential claims can store information as *containers*. It can be a claim that is later referred to or that moves on to a new study as

DOI: 10.1057/9781137298829.0007

TABLE 3.2   *Summary of functional roles of evidential claims*

Functional role and definition	Examples of functionality
Broker: A claim that is used to create and negotiate a space, to open new lines of research, ask new questions and expand ongoing processes.	A claim showing the Hib transmission rate in a closed population functions as a *broker* by opening new lines of research in PnC studies in a model by giving the direction and the estimated rate [of transmission]. 'Following the work by Auranen and colleagues, the model considers transmission of PnC within the household' (Melegaro, Gay and Medley, 2004).
Mediator: A claim that is used to reconcile different approaches, techniques, methods, data sets, parameter values; functions as an intervening claim that enables reconciliation.	A claim about the indirect effects from Hib conjugate vaccines showing their capacity to reduce colonisation of Hib in the nasopharynx. This claim bridges the gap between Hib and PnC studies: 'How much vaccine coverage (for PnC) is needed for indirect effects remains a key question. A model evaluating this in Hib conjugate vaccine showed that much of the decline in invasive disease could be attributed to indirect effects of the vaccine, even at relatively low levels of vaccine coverage' (Lexau et al., 2005).
Container: A claim that is used to enclose and contain information which can be picked up as a new input.	A claim that predicts the decline rate of immunity of Hib functioned as a container in McVernon et al. (2004): 'Our data shows that the reduction in opportunities for boosting natural immunity has resulted in a decline in specific Hib antibody titres among adults'.

Source: Adopted from Mansnerus, 2011.

a factual claim. A good example of that is an estimate of the predicted decline rate of natural immunity of Hib. This estimate was contained in a study by another group that focused on levels of Hib antibodies.

The functioning of evidential claims shows that they have an effect on the new contexts in which they have been accommodated: opening up new research, providing mediating solutions, which are reliable because they have been tested in other contexts or containing usable information, such as parameter estimates. Functioning also shows how *kinship relations* are actually formed between models. Evidential claims which are produced, contained and disseminated within and across different model families are adopted into 'new families' based on their functions and characteristics. In this sense our understanding of the kinship relations of models is at the same time an understanding of evidence in use.

3.4   Conclusion

Model-based evidence is used effectively within research communities when it is transferred and disseminated across modelling groups. This has also been shown to be a way to create and establish research networks. When we saw that model-based outputs can be characterised based on their functions in the receiving research communities, we could see that these outputs can be used more flexibly than initially indicated. Model outputs can turn into parameter estimates or assumptions in another context, for example. In this sense, we are talking about evidence in use *within* research communities. Identifying the ways in which models transfer evidential claims and characterising these based on their functions in the receiving contexts demonstrates that evidence is malleable and usable.

Kinship relations of models rely on ties formed through the exchange and adoption of evidential claims. This is, in short, an example of evidence in use. We know that evidence for medical science and clinical practice is gathered by multiple methods and derived from various sources of knowledge, such as experiments (including randomised control trials), surveillance studies, bioinformatics and modelling. As we learned, modelling methods have gained particular importance due to their capacity to address indirect, population-level effects and assist in vaccination planning. *Kinship* relations show how models are related and what this relatedness tells us about the nature of evidence in use.

What do we actually understand by evidence? Daston (1991) suggests that 'facts are evidence in potential', that factual claims have the potential to turn into evidence, perhaps becoming solidified. It is helpful to follow Evelyn Fox Keller's distinction between evidence *for* and evidence *of*. Evidence *for* a phenomenon refers to evidence that is for the support of 'a theory, argument or hypothesis'. Evidence *of* refers more to the common 'detective-story' type elements (a particular item 'a' is evidence of a person 'x' being in a particular place 'y' at a particular point in time 'z'...). For our purpose, evidence *for* is more interesting, as it points forwards, but to *two* directions rather than one, as Fox Keller suggests: evidence for theoretical claims or evidence *for use* – for *action*. It may seem that evidence of something refers to the *production* domain, while evidence for use refers to the *use* domain.

But our examples of evidential claims forming kinship relations between models indicate that they can be used as evidence of a

DOI: 10.1057/9781137298829.0007

phenomenon (e.g. microbial transmission) or for further theoretical claims (e.g. transmission pattern in a population) and for action in terms of assisting in decision-making processes. What this actually suggests is that evidential claims, when forming ties between models, becoming members of the family, so to speak, and manifesting their character in that process demonstrate how these claims are embedded in both their 'ancestor' and their 'new families'. In this sense, we have shown that model-based evidence can be seen as interactional, experiential knowledge. In the next chapter, we will continue our discussing the ways in which models work and broaden our understanding through the notion of *working life of models*.

Note

1   This section adopts and revises the study presented in (Mansnerus, 2011).

4
Working Lives of Models

Abstract: *When models live their lives, they grow up and enter the working life. They leave behind the sheltered world of research where they serve as scientific instruments and measuring devices. They enter a new domain of use, and are no longer close to the modellers, researchers or instrument makers; rather, they stand on their own to give evidence for policy.*

Mansnerus uses this metaphor of the working life to show how modelling played a pioneering role in public health research in the United Kingdom through a case study on predicting a measles outbreak in the 1994. She analyses the wise use of modelling methods and how they can support a preventive vaccination campaign.

Mansnerus, Erika. *Modelling in Public Health Research: How Mathematical Techniques Keep Us Healthy.* Basingstoke: Palgrave Macmillan, 2015. DOI: 10.1057/9781137298829.0008.

4.1 Introduction

As models live their lives, they grow up and enter working life. They leave behind the sheltered world of research where they serve as scientific instruments and measuring devices. They enter a new domain of use, where they are no longer close to modellers, researchers or instrument makers. Rather, they stand on their own to give evidence to policy.

The working life of models evolves from the understanding that various groups of users form a discursive space in which models are in use, their evidence serves as decision aids and they may function as boundary objects which bridge together various communities of users. When focusing on the working life of models in a reassessment and evaluation of vaccination strategies, we will understand better how models 'collaborate' with other forms of evidence in the decision-making process. The working life as a concept continues the dynamic exploration of the stages in the life-cycles of models and shows how models can perform actions given to them.

Optimising vaccination programmes or introducing new vaccines to protect public health is a multilayered process that increasingly relies on model-based evidence. Numbers drive the reassessment of vaccination programmes. Indicating an increase in infected cases, pointing to an outbreak or providing estimates for predictions, numbers guide the way in which vaccination schemes are reassessed and implemented. Where do these numbers come from? The use of mathematical modelling and simulation techniques has grown to support vaccination policies, along with more traditional methods. Surveillance data collected from notifiable diseases, such as measles, and comparative data on vaccine uptake in various countries complement and give context to model-based estimates. In order to understand how models are used, how they contribute to the evidence base needed to renew vaccination policies and what the potential limitations are, I will develop the notion of the working life of models.

The working life of models represents a phase within the life-cycle when models are no longer 'captives' of their initial research context, developed and studied as examples of their potential uses. Rather, when entering the working life, models become decision aids. What does this mean? The working life of models implies that we take a particular interest in *how models relate to other sources of evidence in decision-making processes*. In this chapter we will focus on two questions:

DOI: 10.1057/9781137298829.0008

1   How did models became part of evidence when the MMR-triple (measles, mumps and rubella) vaccine was implemented in the United Kingdom in 1988 and

2   How well were they used as decision aids in that process?

What does the working life of models look like? If we think of modelling, we also need to relate to various groups of actors involved in the process: modellers, specialists in epidemiology, policymakers, for example. All these groups may have informed but different understandings of what models are. This is why we need to see models in use within the wider context of public health evidence.

As a concept, the working life[1] of models develops further the argument that economic models, when used in policy, create a *discursive space* in which modellers, economists and policymakers can engage with each other (Evans, 2000). Models are not 'truth machines', he claims. However, in the discursive space the users and producers of models create shared understandings of their context-dependent nature and learn to relate model-based evidence to other available sources.

Therefore, focusing on the working life of models conceptualises the processes and practices employed when models are in use, beyond the boundaries of academic research and usually within a policy context (cf. van Egmond and Zeiss, 2010). Sometimes this happens at a distance, when primarily research-oriented models generate evidence that eventually informs policy. This path may be contested, as studies on climate modelling have shown (e.g. Oreskes, 2011; Oreskes and Conway, 2010). When modelling is closely integrated with policy processes, the distance is diminished, and the results are taken into account prior to the final publication of the model, as our case on the implementation of the MMR-triple vaccine[2] will show. I will analyse the *working life* of infectious disease models by examining two predictive measles models in order to show how they function across research and policy domains. Neither of these models is a lonely hero. In the process of reassessing the measles and rubella vaccination policies, they became part of a broader evidence base to support the implementation of the MMR-triple vaccine.

In order to contextualise the development and use of models as decision aids in vaccination planning, I will first provide background on how the need to renew the vaccination programme faced the challenge of a measles outbreak. This began the development of modelling methods. Then, I will discuss how models, or preferably, model-based

DOI: 10.1057/9781137298829.0008

evidence, is best used as 'a member of a team', complementing other sources of evidence.[3]

4.2 Revising vaccination policy: from target groups to mass campaign

When measles cases steadily increased in the 1980s, along with the worrying figures on congenital rubella syndrome (caused by rubella infection during the first trimester of pregnancy), public health officials in the United Kingdom began negotiations to revise the existing vaccination policy. In that programme, the rubella vaccine was only given to target groups, and the measles vaccine suffered from a low uptake. Other countries reported the successful control of measles outbreaks, and a new triple vaccine, a combined vaccine that provided measles, mumps and rubella cover, was available on the market. In this process of reassessing and redesigning vaccination policy, mathematical modelling methods were at work. As (then) recently developed technical tools, they were used to assess surveillance data and predict increased susceptibility to measles. Successful prediction of an approaching measles outbreak following a revised vaccination policy shows how useful model-based evidence can be.

INFOBOX 4.1 *Measles*

Measles is a highly infectious, life-threatening disease that mainly affects infants and children. Its main complications are encephalitis, pneumonia and bronchitis. The primary transmission happens via respiratory routes, by a person's breathing in droplets infected by the virus. As a highly contagious infection, measles follows a seasonal cycle that has an impact on nearly every person in a given population in the absence of an immunisation programme. In the United Kingdom, predictive measles models were used in the late 1980s to support the introduction of the measles, mumps and rubella (MMR) vaccination to the national vaccination plan.

Reforming rubella vaccination policies

By 1988, an alarming increase in the number of cases of congenital rubella syndrome brought about a change in rubella vaccination policy. Until then, rubella vaccines were offered to 'target groups', which meant

DOI: 10.1057/9781137298829.0008

women of childbearing age. However, this campaign succeeded only in protecting the vaccinated and did not establish herd immunity that would have protected those who were not vaccinated.

In 1983, the aim of the rubella vaccination policy was defined as 'the control and ultimate elimination of congenital rubella infection and therefore of all rubella defects' (Miller, 1988b: 317). Neither the reduction of natural rubella nor the development of herd immunity was part of the early strategy.

These pre-1988 vaccination schemes did not succeed in effectively protecting the public health, however. Each year, 100–200 infections in pregnancy were reported from laboratories in England and Wales. Many of those women were infected during early pregnancy, which meant that the infection caused the highest risk of foetal damage, resulting in therapeutic abortion. Around the time of the renewal of the vaccination campaign, approximately 20 cases of congenital rubella syndrome (CRS) were reported annually (Miller et al., 1991).

The main concern that drove public health officials to recognise the risks of a rubella infection, based on surveillance data, was a constant fluctuation in the number of cases of CRS despite an ongoing target group vaccination strategy, as rubella vaccine was given to girls aged 11–13 prior to 1988. Why did this strategy fail to prevent CRS from increasing?

This evidence from surveillance reports underlined the insufficiency of the selective, target group policy on rubella that failed to reach all individuals within the group and left the disease uncontrolled in the child population. In the re-evaluation of the existing vaccination policies, the main focus, then, was on rubella and measles, partly because of the constant concern they caused for the public health, and partly because there were vaccination schemes covering them. This process of assessing the immunisation policy happened in a series of meetings with public health researchers and officials.

The aim of the meeting was 'to consider the scientific evidence concerning the effectiveness of current rubella vaccination policy in the control of congenital rubella. To consider whether on scientific and practical grounds on any changes or additions should be made to current UK policy and to make recommendations'.[4] The meeting itself was initiated by Dr M. who was a leading epidemiologist at the then-Central Public Health Laboratory Service (PHLS), currently Public Health England.[5] She gathered evidence to support the reformation of the vaccination scheme. She was in personal communication with other public health officials in countries that had already implemented the triple vaccine, such as Australia, and the United States. This 1985

DOI: 10.1057/9781137298829.0008

preparatory work led to a series of meetings in 1987 in which two alternative vaccination strategies were discussed: immunisation of all infants of both sexes to eliminate the risk of exposure of pregnant women to rubella by interrupting the transmission of infection among children, or selective immunisation of adolescent girls to eliminate the risk of rubella occurring in pregnancy. The second strategy did not aim to interrupt the transmission of infection within the population. It was based on the assumption that acquisition of natural immunity during childhood could be boosted if the virus was allowed to circulate in the population. This approach failed to alter the pattern of infection in the community, however. Dr M. summarised the problems with the vaccination policy in the United Kingdom:

> In the UK, rubella vaccine was introduced in 1970 for girls aged 11–14 years and for seronegative women of childbearing age in 1974. In 1983, the aim of the vaccination policy was defined as 'the control and ultimate elimination of congenital rubella infection and therefore of all rubella defects'. ~ Neither the reduction of natural rubella, nor the development of herd immunity was part of the strategy; indeed the continued circulation of rubella virus was considered a necessary contribution to maintaining the level of immunity in women of childbearing age. (Miller, 1988b: 317)

It was clear that a more effective intervention on rubella was well grounded on the given evidence. The particular meeting condensed the discussions, interactions and various sources of data, and hence, gave support for the process of reforming the whole of the vaccination intervention. The surveillance data clearly emphasised the need to change the existing policy as it showed an increase in the number of cases of CRS.

Despite the clear evidence of the increased risk of CRS, one further step was to be taken in order to implement the fully revised policy. As rubella infection is predominantly a risk for pregnant women, persuading boys to comply with the new vaccination policy needed to be taken into account. The third component, a mumps vaccine, was the newcomer in the policy for solving this problem.

INFOBOX 4.2   *Rubella*

Rubella, or German measles, is regarded as a mild, although highly contagious, viral childhood infection. Its main symptoms are slight fever, headaches, sore throat and a widespread pink rash.

DOI: 10.1057/9781137298829.0008

Rubella, although it is known as a mild childhood pox, can cause foetal malformations, which are now known as congenital rubella syndrome (CRS).

Introducing a mumps vaccine to increase the uptake of the vaccination campaign

At the time the MMR-vaccine was introduced, in 1988, there was no vaccine against mumps available in the United Kingdom. Mumps was then a newcomer to the programme. The evidence base for the implementation of a mumps component came only partially from scientific publications, mainly because the triple vaccine was relatively new on the market. The public health researchers who had actively worked over the years to renew the policies, engaged in a vast network of communication with colleagues in other countries.

Even though the vaccine was not a part of the British vaccination scheme, it was already in use in the United States and Australia. Three years before the final decision, Dr M. gathered via personal correspondence a large amount of information from public health experts in order to support the implementation plan in the United Kingdom. This correspondence includes references to epidemiological studies that were conducted, although not yet published, and observations from the implementation processes, experiences and concerning potential hindrances during the campaign. The correspondence between Dr M. (United Kingdom) and Dr F. (Australia), leading public health epidemiologists, during the autumn of 1985 shows how different aspects of the vaccine implementation were interwoven.

The main concern related to a vaccine campaign is how to reach the target level of coverage in the population. As I explained in relation to rubella, an adequate level of vaccine coverage is essential for a successful vaccination campaign. One reason to include the mumps component as part of the triple vaccine was to provide a more cost-effective scheme and to increase the uptake. As Dr F. wrote to Dr M, 'I cannot give you accurate figures of these rates but the data on vaccine distribution shows that when the combined vaccine was introduced there was an increase in the number of doses distributed from 322,338 to 409,700' (Source: archived correspondence; See endnote 4.) In the same letter, Dr F. also emphasised an epidemiologically important reason: 'The rationale for adding mumps vaccination depended on the published US data that the

DOI: 10.1057/9781137298829.0008

vaccine was effective and safer than natural infection'. In other words, the natural circulation of mumps was reduced significantly with the new vaccine. An artificially induced immunity against mumps is safer than acquiring immunity naturally from the infection itself. With the vaccine, the unpleasant and potentially threatening conditions that follow mumps infection are avoided.

However, the correspondence also reveals a growing concern related to the changes in the natural circulation of the virus in a population. Dr M. expressed opposition against the mumps vaccine. She mentioned that the long-term effects of the immunisation were pointed out, and the issue of an increase in the incidence of orchitis in adult men was raised. Interestingly, this 'prophesised doom', as she vividly describes the risk, was drawn from a 'crystal ball' of modelling. This supports previous observations that modelling enables indirect inference based on the given information. Furthermore, Dr M. reflected on the parallels between the British and Australian debates related to the MMR-vaccination campaign. There were similarities in the way in which the two countries managed their vaccination schemes. She also emphasised that including the mumps component in the scheme helped overcome the philosophical argument about giving a vaccine to boys who really did not need it (referring to a mass campaign with the rubella vaccine in an unpublished summary from a meeting held at the then-PHLS).

The public health officials who prepared the MMR campaign in the United Kingdom not only grounded their decision on model-based evidence but also engaged with their colleagues, gathered information from their experiences and discussed how to interpret and understand that information in a series of meetings. One mode of correspondence was also to communicate with the three Primary Care Trusts (PCTs) that had implemented the triple vaccine as an 'experiment'. These PCTs were asked to 'pre-run' the vaccination campaign, monitor the possible side effects and report the feedback from parents. These results ranged from general observations of how willingly parents engaged with the new vaccination campaign to letters from the general practitioners (GPs) asking for further advice or reporting adverse effects of the vaccine. The analysis also shows why the mumps component was needed in the national scheme: an economic drive to increase the cost-effectiveness of the campaign; an epidemiological rationale to reduce the circulation of the virus in the population; and a persuasive 'selling point' to smoothe the attitudes of the parents of boys, since rubella was a threat to women of childbearing age.

DOI: 10.1057/9781137298829.0008

What happened with the measles campaign?

Thus, in 1988 the combined triple vaccine for measles, mumps and rubella (the MMR-vaccine) was introduced as part of the UK vaccination strategy. Prior to that, a single measles vaccine was brought into the vaccination programme in 1968, when the number of annual notifications of measles cases varied between 160,000 and 800,000. The single measles vaccine had been developed already in 1960. The UK vaccination policy followed the general trend in Europe. The MMR-triple vaccine was introduced in the Netherlands in 1987, and in Finland and Sweden already in 1982 (Blume and Tump, 2010; Kainulainen, Nohynek, Pekkanen, and Turtiainen, 2014). The implementation of the MMR-vaccine and the following years of monitoring its efficacy create a context to analyse the working life of predictive measles models.

What triggered the modelling process and the revision of the 1988-implemented single-dose MMR-vaccination policy was the increased number of measles cases. These cases were identified through notification data.[6] At the same time, there was a growing interest in developing computational techniques for use in public health policy. By the time of measles modelling in the 1980s, modelling techniques were not a novelty, as earlier disease models for computational platforms had already been developed in the late 1960s. Increased computational power made the techniques more adaptable and useable, as we observed in Chapter 2. This interest can also be seen in the published models studied here. Both articles (Babad et al., 1995; Gay, Hesketh, Morgan-Capner, and Miller, 1995) emphasise how the models were examined against observational data and how they provided a good fit for what was observed. In a way, these two aspects created the context for developing predictive measles models in the early 1990s. This is what we can think of as the working life of models. Let us look more closely at how the working life is formed and what different aspects are present when predictive measles models are at work.

INFOBOX 4.3   *Mumps*

Even though mumps appears to be a seemingly mild childhood infection, it is still a disease worth preventing. It is commonly known that mumps causes painful swelling of one or both parotid glands. Mumps is caused by the paramyxovirus. The severity of mumps is

DOI: 10.1057/9781137298829.0008

related to the fact that it can cause viral meningitis and encephalitis. It occurs in cyclical and seasonal peaks, and is often transmitted via droplets of saliva (Parish 1965).

4.3   Insights into models at work

In 1994, Ramsey et al. wrote that 'an epidemic of between 100 000 and 200 000 cases of measles has been predicted in England and Wales. This prediction was based on epidemiological evidence from several sources' (R141). What had led to this prediction and how were the results and observations – or model-based scenarios – used?

A closer analysis of the models in question shows two complementary ways of producing evidence for renewed vaccination strategy and a needed booster campaign. This analysis provides insights into how a transmission matrix and a predictive scenario are first depicted as models and then translated into a chorus of evidence. What are the various routes of information built into the models? What are their apparent limitations? And how were their results received at the time the use of these technical tools was limited or regarded as a novelty?

In attempting to understand the rationale of the one-off measles vaccination campaign, Ramsey et al. discussed and reviewed the epidemiological evidence that led to the prediction of a large measles outbreak that would have occurred in 1995. Concern that this outbreak would happen was raised after a 1993 outbreak in Western Scotland, where 5000 cases were reported and 138 were hospitalised (Ramsey et al., 1994).

How did the other sources of evidence support the prediction of the potential outbreak? Data for measles surveillance in England and Wales come from statutory notifications and death certifications to the Office of Population Censuses and Surveys, microbiologically confirmed cases reported to the PHLS Communicable Disease Surveillance Centre and consultations for new episodes of measles conducted by the Birmingham Research Unit of the Royal College of General Practitioners. At the same time, serological (blood sample-based) surveillance takes place by using residues of serum specimens submitted to public health laboratories in England.

The notification data showed that the number of annual notifications fell between 1988 and 1991 (after the implementation of the new MMR-vaccine), but that the age distribution of the notified cases changed

DOI: 10.1057/9781137298829.0008

and measles began to occur in older children. In 1994, there was a substantial rise in case notifications. A similar jump was documented in laboratory reports. Compared to 84 infections in 1993, there were 345 cases reported during the nine months of 1994. Based on the antibody prevalence data, a rise in susceptibility to measles was documented as well.

How did the models then work with this data? Their key task was to *predict* the occurrence and magnitude of the major epidemic in the mid-1990s. These models, the RAS (a realistic age-structured mathematical model of measles transmission) and the 'Who Acquires Infection From Whom' (WAIFW), *interpreted* the details of the data. In a way, the data only showed a rise in the number of notifications or infections. The interpretation meant that the different sources of data were examined against the known age structures and contact patterns. Based on this, the models gave 'advanced warning' of the outbreak, and therefore allowed time to plan and implement preventive actions.

The modelling process, when we contextualise it in relation to the use domain (i.e. the policy context) has a broader focus than that of building a single model as an object of inquiry. The call for modelling may be initiated by a need to assess prevailing public health policy, for example a vaccination scheme. In the case of measles, the quest was to evaluate the efficacy of the 1988 MMR-policy and to respond to the increase in measles cases. It seemed that the policy was failing, and ways to address the situation and reverse it were to be taken into account.

Modelling, however, can rarely respond to a need for a policy-initiated or a driven call without a process of translation. As we learned through the general remarks on models presented earlier, the process of identifying elements and integrating them into a well-functioning mathematical model can be seen as a process of simplifying some of the available information in order to describe the situation. This means that the modellers translate and express more specifically the general policy interests and concerns as a set of research questions, which can be studied in the model. In practice, it means bringing together existing knowledge of the phenomenon to be studied, deciding on the structure and design of the model and identifying the available observational data so that the model can be parameterised. This process can be seen as choosing the most appropriate model and expressing it in mathematical terms by using or developing algorithms and estimating parameters that are suitable for the modelling task. What does this process look like in the two measles models in which we are interested?

DOI: 10.1057/9781137298829.0008

Working on measles susceptibility

An early measles model was built to represent the 'WAIFW'-structure, in other words to model 'Who Acquires Infection From Whom'. Based on the estimates from this model, the predicted measles outbreak in 1993 was prevented or at least mitigated by a booster vaccination campaign in the United Kingdom. This model (Gay et al., 1995) was built to interpret susceptibility data from the surveillance programme and evaluate the potential for an epidemic. The model estimated the level of susceptibility in the population by using a single parameter, the reproductive number.[7] In the model, the population was divided into several age groups. The transmission rates were based on pre-vaccination case notification data. These rates were combined with susceptibility data, and following from that a next generation WAIFW-matrix was generated. The matrix shows allocation of distinct transmission rates (β_{1-5}) for five age groups (represented in the columns and lines of the matrix). The matrix contains values of transmission between groups. Based on this matrix, different scenarios were modelled with different reproduction rates.

Patterns of mixing between and within different age groups are important in determining the transmission of a disease within a population. The transmission rates cannot be measured directly, as Gay et al. (1995) explain, but they can be calculated from the age-specific pre-vaccination force of infection. This is estimated on the basis of age-specific notification data and serological data (ibid.: 143). The matrix depicts age structure in terms of specific age groups (rows and columns in the matrix). The age groups are 0–1; 2–4; 5–9; 10–14 and 15+. Gay et al. used a generalised version of the matrix used in other studies. The matrix takes into account within group mixing of 5–9-year-olds in order to reflect the high transmission rates in primary schools (ibid.: 144).

The key outcome of this WAIFW-model was a predicted outbreak of measles, due to an increase in the susceptible population of schoolchildren. This prediction was confirmed with data derived from disease notifications from England and Wales 1993–1994. The message of the model was that the predicted outbreak could be prevented with a booster (secondary) vaccination campaign. In the published report of the model, the modellers also discussed how this model showed a new role for model use in a public health setting. When modelling is applied to interpret serological surveillance data, the epidemic can be identified early on, and this allows time to plan and implement appropriate interventions (e.g. vaccinations). This model with its recommendations

DOI: 10.1057/9781137298829.0008

became a reference point in the documentation process to implement the booster vaccination. At the same time another measles model, which studied a realistic, age-related measles transmission, was built.

Studying scenarios for potential vaccination policy

In order to develop a wider understanding of the effects of the booster or secondary vaccination campaign, the so-called RAS-model was built. The policy need behind the modelling was framed as a question: why did the single-dose MMR-policy not lead to the elimination of measles? The RAS-model is a realistic, age-structured mathematical model of measles vaccinations in England and Wales from 1968 to 1993. It was built to evaluate the merits of future policy options and to justify a policy change, because outbreaks continued to occur among older children. The predictions from the RAS-model were 'verified' against a variety of epidemiological observations. The researchers report a good agreement between the observations and prediction, and the model is used to explore measles epidemiology in the future under the existing vaccination strategy and a variety of alterations to that strategy.

In the RAS-model, the flow from maternally immune to susceptibles happens when the infant loses the protection of passive immunity (usually estimated at six months of age). Some of those who are susceptible to the infection may be vaccinated, but in case the vaccine fails, they may experience a latent infection and therefore remain as a part of the infectious 'flow'. With effective vaccinations, the susceptibles gain immunity.

So, why was this model needed? At the time the model was built, the incidence of measles in England and Wales had declined to 'an all-time

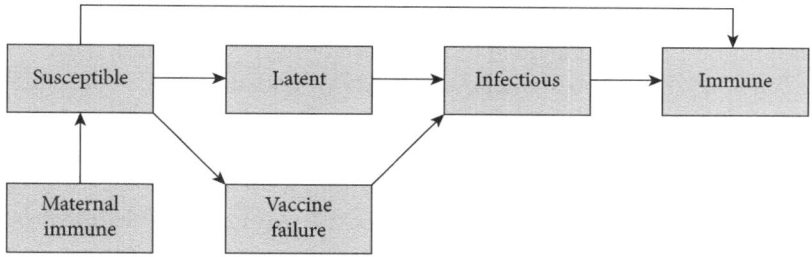

FIGURE 4.1   *The RAS-model as a flow diagram of transitions between population compartments*

Source: Adapted and simplified from Babad et al. 1995) describing effective vaccination.

DOI: 10.1057/9781137298829.0008

low', as Babad et al. (1995) discuss. It seems that the MMR-triple vaccine, implemented in 1988, had eliminated the seasonal and twice-yearly epidemic cycles with success. But measles persisted, and this raised the question of whether the current policy that offered a single dose was effective enough.

In a nutshell, the RAS-model employed a compartmental structure in order to depict transitions between the susceptible, the immune and the vaccinated groups in a population. It used a cohort-based age structure and adopted age-specific and seasonal contact rates from two WAIFW-matrices (one of which was developed in Gay et al., 1995). It received epidemiological parameters from age-structured case notifications for England and Wales.

By building a deterministic compartmental model, Babad et al. (1995) were able to assess more realistically the patterns of measles infection in England and Wales prior to mass vaccination. This RAS-model incorporated seasonality as a component that represented changes in contact rates during school terms and vacations. Another component built the cohort-based age structure into the model by placing individuals as they were born within yearly birth cohorts. This depicted more realistically how children moved from one school year to another in the educational system.

What did the RAS-model actually do? It simulated the impact of mass vaccination. First it gained a 'high degree of concordance' between its predictions and estimates that were available from seroprevalence[8] data. The model established a baseline policy and studied alterations in age groups. By doing so, it simulated various scenarios for short-term and long-term policy effects. Observations from the model suggested that in the short-term, the so-called 'catch-up' campaign would have improved the impact from the current single dose vaccination policy, increased herd immunity[9] and equalled out any variations in vaccine uptake.

Together these two models, the WAIFW and the RAS, represented pioneering efforts to provide model-based evidence for vaccination policy, although the final policy decision was not solely based on models. Examining how they contributed to the policy along with other sources of evidence will show that the step taken from within the modelling process to the policy domain requires an understanding of the heterogeneous context in which model-based recommendations are implemented. This is a translation process in its own right, similar to the process of simplification that led from the policy call to the model building.

DOI: 10.1057/9781137298829.0008

4.4   Conclusion

The working life of models implies that models become as if independent from their research contexts. They are working in the world, yet revealing aspects of the world. In this chapter, we have observed how modelling techniques were introduced into the context of vaccination strategies. What we learned through these observations was not only how models functioned and how they were able to predict the measles outbreak, but also how they were used and what kind of interpretations and misunderstandings were related to model-based evidence.

This chapter suggests that by studying the working life of epidemiological models, we can learn how models function outside the research context and complement available epidemiological evidence when renewing vaccination policy. The working life of the WAIFW and RAS-models reveal their nature as cross-boundary objects. Built to address a need to reassess an inefficient vaccination policy and to interpret available surveillance data, they predicted a measles outbreak and gave supporting evidence to the implementation of a secondary booster vaccination campaign in 1994 in the United Kingdom. As cross-boundary objects, they do not necessarily leave the research domain fully behind, in order to enter the policy domain. In our case, the modellers worked at the then-PHLS, currently the Public Health England, and gave advice on vaccinations to the Joint Committee of Vaccines and Inoculations (Miller, 1988a). These 'dual roles' of the modellers reflect the cross-boundary nature of the models themselves. In the discursive space created, the models brought together their producers and users. When the evidence from these models was combined with the surveillance data of increased risk of CRS, firm ground for revising the programme was established. The inclusion of the mumps component made the policy more attractive to treating boys and hence it became a stronger initiative for a mass campaign.

The predictive capacity of these models becomes one of the key ways in which they work for a vaccination policy. This is not a unique feature of infectious disease models. In climate research, the predictive capacity of models is shown to fulfil both social and epistemic functions. Even though the modelling exercise is thought to address the epistemic goals of research itself, the models provide predictions that allow them to be used in the quantitative future scenarios (e.g. in climate research (Dahan Dalmenico, 2007). The novelty of using models to predict the measles outbreak was that the predictive and preventive functions of modelling

DOI: 10.1057/9781137298829.0008

for public health became visible here. Due to the evidence from various sources and the clear indications from the models, the vaccination campaign was implemented as a preventive action, *prior to* the outbreak. It is far more usual to actually wait for an outbreak to occur before any action is taken, as Miller shows (1994).

The key lesson we can learn from the two measles models is that when models are working for a vaccination policy, they work best as members of a team. This case shows clearly that the model-based predictions were *interpretations* of the multiple sources of data available to observe the increase in measles cases. The models were not soloists, making bold predictions on their own. Their results were carefully related to what was already known, and yet these results documented something new: it is possible to prevent an outbreak; we do not need to wait for it to happen first. This careful and responsible way of using modelling methods became evident in the rhetoric the modellers used in the publications. They were clear about the limitations:

> In summary, it has not been possible fully to account for the discrepancies between the observed impact of vaccination on measles epidemiology in England and Wales and that predicted using the RAS-model. The causes are likely to be multiple in origin. (Babad et al., 1995: 341)

This is a realistic take on what happened in the model and how well it is able to stand behind its outputs. Again, it is not unique for this group of modellers to communicate the limitations. In my earlier studies, the understanding of model-based outcomes in relation to (and restricted by) the assumptions made in the modelling process has clearly been communicated. How well these restrictions then stay with the model-based evidence, when it is disseminated across other domains of research or policy, will be discussed in relation to pandemic risk modelling in the next chapter.

Notes

1　The idea of the working life is also influenced by the van Daalen analysis of the various roles of computer models in environmental policy, in which they suggest that environmental problems experience different phases in their *life-cycle*. Furthermore, the historical studies of *biographies* of scientific objects have given me inspiration to develop an organic concept of the working life of infectious disease models (Creager, 2002; Daston, 2000; van Daalen, Dresen, and Janssen, 2002).

DOI: 10.1057/9781137298829.0008

2   Measles, mumps and rubella triple vaccine.

3   This case study is based on archived material and documents (minutes from meetings, correspondence, scientific publications, policy recommendations) that are held at the Centre for Infections, Health Protection Agency, Colindale. Minutes from Working party meetings held between January–September 1987 (9 meetings). These minutes discussed in detail the reasons for the change in the vaccination policy, questions related to the licensing and supply of the vaccine, an educational programme related to the implementation, and targets in the vaccination coverage. Correspondence covers 15 letters between Dr M (HPA) and public health officials in England, Ireland and Australia between April and June 1987. The documents show how the MMR-vaccine was implemented in the UK vaccination programme. The process of informal discussions with epidemiologists at the Department of Immunisations has been most helpful to gain a broader understanding of immunisation campaigns, the history of the three MMR diseases and the need to renew the policies in the late 1980s. The models are analysed on the basis of skills I developed during an Introduction to Infectious Disease Modelling class at the London School for Hygiene and Tropical Medicine, 2007.

4   This case study presents quotations from the following documentation: Minutes from Working party meetings held between January–September 1987 (9 meetings). These minutes discussed in details the reasons for the change in the vaccination policy, questions related to the licensing and supply of the vaccine, educational programme related to the implementation and targets in the vaccination coverage. Correspondence covers 15 letters between Dr. M (HPA) and public health officials in England, Ireland and Australia between April–June 1987. Currently Public Health England, until 1 April 2013, the Health Protection Agency.

5   Measles is a notifiable disease, which means that when a general practitioner diagnoses a measles case, she needs to notify the public health laboratory (e.g. Public Health England in the United Kingdom) about the disease case for surveillance and monitoring purposes.

6   Reproductive number, or R_0, is the estimate of how many susceptible individuals will be infected by one infected person. Reproductive number is the estimate of the spread of the infection. Based on this rate the severity of the infection can be assessed. In the case of measles, the reproductive rate is nearly 10, as measles is highly infectious, whereas in the case of a pandemic influenza, the reproductive rate is between 2 and 3 (Fine, 1993; Giesecke, 2002; Nicoll and Coulombier, 2009).

7   Seroprevalence data are data collected from blood samples.

8   Herd immunity is the level of immunity that protects all members of population and is established when a particular level of vaccination coverage is gained (e.g. Fine, 1993).

DOI: 10.1057/9781137298829.0008

5
Encounters with Risks

Abstract: *Models can be built upon the available data from previous pandemics; thus, the past is modelled in order to predict the future. Modelling and simulation techniques were widely used during and prior to the 2009 'Swine flu' outbreak. Pre-pandemic modelling became a way to encounter possible pandemic risks and to assess effective mitigation strategies. Mansnerus defines two types of model-based predictions: explanation-based and scenario-building. By discussing their reliability, she highlights what kinds of limitations modelling techniques face.*

Mansnerus, Erika. *Modelling in Public Health Research: How Mathematical Techniques Keep Us Healthy.* Basingstoke: Palgrave Macmillan, 2015. DOI: 10.1057/9781137298829.0009.

DOI: 10.1057/9781137298829.0009

5.1   Introduction

In 2009, a pandemic outbreak caused by the A/H1N1 virus exposed the need for an immediate, urgent response. The outbreak's unpredictability, the lack of available data and the serious risk it posed to global public health were factors that invited groups of modellers to network, share resources and develop predictions and scenarios in order to deal with the risks from this potentially life-threatening pandemic influenza outbreak. In order to demonstrate how modelling can work for risky encounters such as disease outbreaks, I will first introduce the main approaches to clarify the risks and then discuss how we can have *modelled encounters with risks*.[1]

> Nothing is a risk in itself; there is no risk in reality. But on the other hand, anything can be a risk; it all depends on how one analyses the danger, considers the event. (Ewalds, 1991: 199)

Within the broad field of risk studies, we can identify resources from statistical-probabilistic, epidemiological and sociological approaches. The statistical-probabilistic approach emerged initially in the insurance industry as a way of enabling various estimates of personal benefits, the effectiveness of medical treatments and the use of risk calculations. The epidemiological approach applies risk calculations to human and animal health by turning them into an objective measure of how various health-related factors influence the probability of falling ill or encountering an infection, for example. These approaches can be broadened to include cultural and individual perceptions of risk, which sociological approaches to risk studies emphasise whilst still remaining in the realm of numerical calculations. Within the sociocultural approaches, we will encounter Michel Foucault's way of analysing risk as part of a larger set of questions pointing to societal governance and analysis of power relations. This approach is called *governmentality*, and it captures the idea that governance happens and is enabled through mentalities that subject us to power. Taylor-Gooby and Zinn (2006: 43) say that this type of analysis includes the 'construction of realities through practice and sense-making, encompassing the multitude of societal organisations and institutions producing social reality'.

In public health, what counts as a risk is a dynamic concept. As Ewalds suggests, 'nothing is a risk in itself'. Public health is concerned with 'long-standing and pervasive forms of risk rationality', as Dean (2010: 218) argues. This form of risk rationality is a way of thinking about and representing

DOI: 10.1057/9781137298829.0009

events through calculations. In Castel's (1991) example of mental health problems, risk rationality was formed through the classification of these problems ranging from being dangerous to posing a risk. Preceding this transition is an understanding of a population as 'the ultimate end of government', as Foucault (1991: 99–100) argues. He continues, saying that 'population has its own regularities, its won rate of deaths and diseases. ... [S]tatistics shows also that the domain of population involves a range of intrinsic, aggregate effects, phenomena that are irreducible to those of the family, such as epidemics'. This transition – from dangerousness to risk, from individuals to population as an object of governance reflects a conceptual shift towards *new risks*, which 'violate many assumptions of risk calculation', as Taylor-Gooby and Zinn (2006: 25) argue.

New risks are global and complex, and they share characteristics with catastrophes. They are 'mainly invisible and inaccessible by direct means', yet they challenge the statistical-probabilistic interpretation of risk (Taylor-Gooby and Zinn, 2006: 25). Infectious diseases can be seen as 'new risks' as they activate a sense of global threat and are not visible through regular statistical approaches. I will suggest that new risks can be encountered by accommodating the statistical-probabilistic approach of risk calculation (in the form of mathematical modelling) to the Foucauldian interpretation of risk rationality and governance. I call this approach *modelled encounters* with risks and apply it to two cases in which predictions of infectious risks play a central role.

The term *modelled encounters with risks* refers to the increased use of modelling and simulation techniques in predicting and preventing pandemic outbreaks. Encounters with risk, as Hutter and Power (2005: 1) clarify, are events of problematisation that 'place in question existing attention to risk and its modes of identification, recognition and definition.' 'Risk identification', they continue, 'is socially organised by a wide variety of institutions which support prediction and related forms of intervention around a possible course of future events'. Our encounters with public health risks are well mediated through surveillance and monitoring procedures, such as keeping records of notifiable diseases or participating in international collaboration to deal with outbreaks of emerging infections. Risks of emerging infections escape the networks of monitoring and challenge the preparedness planning that supports public health decision-making. In order to address unexpected risks or to revise and improve existing monitoring systems, statistical analysis and mathematical modelling are put in place.

DOI: 10.1057/9781137298829.0009

Computer-based modelling techniques are used to produce evidence for developing and assessing the preventive measures of public health. These *modelled encounters* provide predictions and scenarios that facilitate the assessment and management of infectious risks. Hutter and Power (2005) emphasise that risk identification requires social organisation across institutions. When we look at modelled encounters, social processes that identify, manage and assess risks need to be acknowledged. As we will learn, modelled encounters accommodate the social, which is embedded in modelling procedures, and thereby highlight that models are not 'truth machines' but 'a range of tools to explore future possibilities' (Hulme, Pielke, and Dessai, 2009: 127). What we are trying to understand is how to overcome uncertainties related to complex phenomena, such as infectious diseases, the climate or the economy. Modelling practices can help in forming a network that integrates available knowledge and introduces different expert communities to each other. This is one way of understanding what is meant by *modelled encounters with risk*.

The term *modelled encounters with risks* refers to events in which predictive simulations are used in urgent situations, for example, sudden outbreaks. Risks of major hazards are highly unlikely, yet anticipation and preparedness work require us to predict and plan for them. I will first expand our understanding of what kinds of predictions models are capable of performing. I use observations from *Haemophilus influenzae* type b dynamic transmission models. I discuss how these simulations can provide explanation-based predictions and scenario-building predictions. I will then move on to discuss how we can encounter infectious risks through these predictions. I will introduce the case of modelling pandemic outbreaks, as this will illustrate what happens when simulation models are in use prior to and during an emergency. In conclusion, I will discuss the limitations of simulated predictions, which will lead us to one of the key challenges in modelling – silent evidence.

5.2   Two types of model-based predictions

The predictive capacity of models is well established. In the early measles models, model-based predictions were the main drivers for initiating modelling as part of the evidence base to support the reassessment of vaccination programmes and policy. But those two measles models represent only a fraction of the variety of predictive models in use in

DOI: 10.1057/9781137298829.0009

infectious disease epidemiology. I conceptualise two types of predictions based on an analysis of *Haemophilus influenzae* type b bacteria. I call these two types, or modes of prediction, *explanation-based* and *scenario-building*. Explanation-based predictions can explain the transmission mechanisms captured in models. This increases the reliability of the models. Other factors that influence model reliability is the accuracy of their measurements and the credibility of the 'instrument makers', as Boumans (2004) claims, for example. Scenario-building predictions look forward; they depict future development or scenarios of what might happen. These future-oriented scenarios are 'thinking tools' that enable the assessment of different ways of responding to the outbreak. The term 'scenario' in this context means an outline of an imagined, possible situation that has been quantified through modelling. Thus, by understanding how predictions can be modelled in a common childhood infection, we can assess their use in encounters with infectious risks.

Explanation-based predictions in the case of Hib infections in the Finnish child population

Reassessing vaccination programmes lies at the heart of public health decision-making. A case of population-level transmission models of *Haemophilus influenzae* type b bacteria[2] provides an example of how modelling facilitates the renewal of vaccination strategies. This case shows how *explanation-based* predictions are at work. Explanation-based predictions inherently address 'what would happen if' questions. Answers to these questions derive their predictive capacities from available data sets and reach for short-term-predictions that are beneficial to predict outbreaks within a particular area. Dynamic transmission models are capable of addressing these short-term predictions effectively. In order to see how this happens in relation to Hib infections, I will show how Hib models address and formulate explanation-based predictions and what that means.

Generally speaking, when we seek answers to 'why' questions, we are attempting to explain a particular phenomenon, such as the cause of infection. When models address 'why' questions, they search for a particular mechanism that is responsible for the phenomenon. We could say that models capture epidemiological mechanisms and extrapolate explanations based on them. How do models then address mechanisms?

DOI: 10.1057/9781137298829.0009

Mechanisms anchor the explanations to available data sets, which form the epidemiological basis of the phenomenon. In philosophical terms, a mechanism can be defined as

> a structure performing a function in virtue of its component parts, component operations and their organization. The orchestrated functioning of the mechanism is responsible for one or more phenomena. (Bechtel and Abrahamsen, 2005: 423)

Bechtel and Abrahamsen show that a mechanism is involved with orchestrated functioning, that is, it is capable of bringing together specific properties, parts or operations of the phenomena. Mechanisms, from this perspective, are responsible for a phenomenon, for mobilising its cause, occurrence or development. In a way, mechanisms contain the generalisable properties of phenomena. With this in mind, we can look at disease transmission and how its mechanism becomes captured in models.

Disease transmission is a multiplex phenomenon, which is dependent on the frequency of contacts within a population group, the infectivity of the pathogen and the existing immunity within the population. When a mechanism of disease transmission is explained in a model, these aspects of transmission are taken into account. Let us focus on a specific example of how a mechanism is captured into a model and how this actually produces an answer to a 'what would happen if' question.

What would happen if a five-year-old child acquired an Hib infection and how likely would she be to infect the members of her family? This question motivated building of the population-simulation model that also studied disease dynamics and natural immunity. As we can see, the question itself ('what would happen if') has a predictive nature, and it was manipulated in a population-simulation model that has a three-part structure. In its structure we can identify a demographic model (covering the age structure of the Finnish population), an Hib transmission model (including a contact-site structure), and an immunity model (including the immunisation program and its effects).[3] In order to address the 'what would happen if' question and understand how transmission dynamics develop, the model studied three detailed questions:

1 How long does the immunity [against Hib] persist? (Auranen, Ranta, Takala, and Arjas, 1996)
2 How do we estimate the interaction between the force of infection and the duration of immunity? (Leino et al., 2000)

DOI: 10.1057/9781137298829.0009

3   What is the effect of vaccinations? (Auranen et al., 2004)

These questions address particular aspects that affect transmission dynamics in a population: length of immunity, estimates related to the force of infection and the impact of vaccinations.[4] These aspects form *mechanisms* of immunity and transmission. A mechanism of immunity can be defined as 'natural immunity that depends on repeated exposure to Hib bacteria resulting in production of functional antibody (Leino et al., 2000). This mechanism primarily sustains natural immunity in a population. In the population-simulation model, it was used for explaining what would happen to natural immunity when vaccinations were introduced to the whole of population. The reasoning behind this approach came from epidemiological studies that suggested that the Hib vaccine was itself capable of reducing carriage in a population, and that is was thereby likely to lead to a waning of natural immunity that had a protective effect on the population-level. What we are talking about here is known as *herd immunity*.[5] This indirect effect was documented in a model that studied the dynamics of natural immunity. The mechanism of immunity and its numerical estimate that showed the descending trend in serum antibody concentration was integrated into the population-simulation model. Hence the mechanism of natural immunity showed that if the bacterial circulation diminished (due to vaccinations), the natural immunity was likely to weaken and a potential increase in the risk of serious infections might affect those who were not vaccinated.

What can we say about explanation-based predictions? These micro-level observations of how models embody mechanisms and use them for predictions shows that the model can simultaneously produce an explanation of the phenomenon of interest (transmission dynamics) and predict its short-term development. In other words, by capturing the mechanisms of transmission and natural immunity, the population-simulation model was able to predict the course of Hib transmission in a population and explain how the underlying epidemiological mechanisms maintain the circulation of bacteria.

An interesting parallel can be found in economic modelling, in which den Butter and Morgan show how empirical economic models are linked with mechanisms as well:

> More general empirical models provide a consistent and quantitative indication of the net outcome of the various principal mechanisms thought to be at

DOI: 10.1057/9781137298829.0009

work based on the particular case and which might be affected by the policies proposed. (den Butter and Morgan, 2000: 296)

Explanation-based predictions are an ideal base for the short-term anticipation of public health risks, which are referred to as low-impact, high-frequency events in the risk literature (cf. Hutter and Power, 2005). These predictions allow estimations of risks by showing the short-term development of infections, explicating the optimal immunity levels within the community and sometimes providing unexpected results of the optimal vaccination coverage. However, these low-impact events do not compete for media attention on the same level as high-impact, low-frequency events, such as sudden outbreaks of infections that have the potential to spread as pandemics.

'Any events that may constitute a public health emergency of international concern' are to be reported to the World Health Organization (WHO), according to the International Health Regulations (IHR) (Dry and Leach, 2010). These regulations lead internationally coordinated activities and serve as an early warning, but they may not be able to anticipate or predict a pandemic outbreak. This is where *scenario-building* predictions become important. These are predictions that 'sketch, outline or describe an imagined situation or sequence of events, and outline any possible sequence of future events' (OED). In other words, scenario-building is a primary tool used to produce *qualitative* scenarios based on available, past data. Therefore, these scenarios are not based on data related to the anticipated future event (which does not yet exist), but on available sources of past data in order to anticipate the unknown, the risk. Thus, they function as modelled encounters with future or potential risks.

Building pandemic scenarios

Uncertainties about the severity of the pandemic outbreak of A/H1N1 in 2009, its geographical spread and the efficacy of vaccines raised questions about how to develop mitigation strategies to protect populations. Simulation models provided a way to predict a possible future course of the outbreak. They became tools for planning and testing intervention strategies.

Prior to the actual pandemic in 2009, pre-pandemic modelling had been employed in order to overcome the data limitations. In order to demonstrate and clarify how scenario-building predictions are produced

DOI: 10.1057/9781137298829.0009

by simulation modelling, I will focus on a recent pre-pandemic simulation model. This model is called an individual-based simulation model of pandemic influenza transmission for Great Britain and the United States (Ferguson et al., 2006). This model represents transmission in households, schools and workplaces, and the wider community, and is aimed at studying mitigation strategies for an outbreak. Mitigation covers all actions that aim at reducing the impact of a pandemic (Nicoll and Coulombier, 2009). I will examine two model-based assumptions that affect transmission: estimate for the reproductive rate and behavioural assumptions. This will lead us to see how *scenario-building* predictions encounter risks.

INFOBOX 5.1   *Pandemics, especially 2009 A/H1N1 outbreak*

Cycles of pandemics have caused concern for hundreds of years. The most famous pandemic, the 1918 Spanish flu, killed approximately 50 million people worldwide, according to older estimates. The most recent cycle of a pandemic began in April 2009 when a new influenza-type virus (A1H1) was identified and cases were confirmed first in the United States and Mexico. This new strain had been circulating in pigs, and hence the outbreak was named 'swine flu'. The strain spread rapidly as the primary contacts were amongst those who had travelled from Mexico. The World Health Organization (WHO) reacted to the potential threat by raising the pandemic alert level from 4 to 5, which meant sustained community outbreaks in a limited number of countries. Starting from this initial situation, the pandemic continued to spread, and an official declaration of a pandemic state was made in June 2009.

At the end of April 2009, human cases of a new influenza type A virus were confirmed. These cases were identified in the United States and Mexico. The virus, according to epidemiological evidence, had circulated in Mexico since February 2009, and may have already emerged earlier that year. It was also confirmed that the new human strain was identical to a strain of a virus that had been circulating in pigs in North America. The strain spread rapidly, and the first infections occurred through those who were or travelled from Mexico. WHO reacted to the situation based on their pandemic preparedness plan. Within a couple of weeks of the onset of the outbreak, WHO raised the pandemic alert level from 4 to 5, which meant that

DOI: 10.1057/9781137298829.0009

the epidemic was still being sustained in the form of local outbreaks in a limited number of countries by the end of April 2009. On 11 June 2009, WHO declared a pandemic and raised the alert level to phase 6, which meant wide geographical spread, but did not indicate the severity of the infection. According to the ECDC situation report on 14 September 2009, there were 50,892 confirmed cases and 137 deaths within the European Union/European Free Trade Association countries. In the United Kingdom, there were 13,322 cases, including 76 deaths.

5.3   Using models in risk assessment: simulating pandemic outbreaks

'Modelled encounters with risks' focuses on the development and use of modelling methods. In order to be successful in this task, the model development in 'peacetime', or in preparedness work, uses data from past outbreaks, develops reliable scenarios as quantitative thinking tools and serves as a decision aid. However, a pandemic outbreak, as we experienced in 2009, can change the situation. Now the scenario-building work loses its 'peacetime', exploratory nature, and comes under time pressure and faces a sense of urgency. Modelling groups network together rather than pursue their own independent models. The work is highly dependent on the availability of data, usually provided by surveillance sources. Yet, the data may give false estimates, as it is often rudimentary in the early days of a pandemic outbreak. In this section, we will dive into the pandemic simulation modelling in detail and discuss the predictive capacities of models that were built prior to and during the 2009 outbreak. Observations from these modelling practices will provide insight into how well modelling and simulation techniques serve in pandemic risk assessment.

In order to understand and develop effective mitigation strategies, key assumptions about transmission dynamics need to be modelled. As the Ferguson et al. population-simulation model (2006) is primarily interested in establishing the transmission dynamics and then assessing how to minimise the risk of the outbreak with effective mitigation strategies (such as travel restrictions, school closures or quarantine), it needs to express transmission as an estimate.

In general, transmission is quantified in epidemiological models as a basic reproductive rate, which is the rate that is used for estimating the spread of infection in a susceptible population based on the risk in a contact and how common the contacts are. It is defined as R_0, and known as the reproductive rate. The rate is determined by following four factors (Giesecke, 2002):

1   the probability of transmission in a contact between an infected individual and a susceptible one;
2   the frequency of contacts in the population;
3   how long an infected person is infectious;
4   the proportion of the population that is already immune.

All these characteristics can be expressed in mathematical terms, derived from empirical data used in earlier epidemiological studies or acquired through surveillance programmes. Yet, this rate carries a fingerprint of the pathogen. By this I mean that the reproductive rate is sensitive to the particular strain of the pathogen in question. This sensitivity introduces uncertainty into the model-based predictions. What if this particular strain is not as virulent as estimated?

If we think about pre-pandemic modelling, we are in a situation in which the future strain is unknown. All that is known is past pandemics that provided data for the modelling. This indicates variance in the reproductive rate, as it tends to be higher in crowded populations, and hence is sensitive to the density of population. Uncertainties about the virulence, infectivity and susceptibility of the populations are left into the pre-pandemic simulation models, as these will be addressed only when the actual pandemic virus is isolated. This level of uncertainty is very close to the model 'surface', as modelling itself is dependent on the availability and quality of the data.

Behavioural assumptions in pandemic models

The population-simulation model, which studies strategies for mitigating an influenza pandemic, assesses the effectiveness of behavioural interventions, which include movement restrictions, travel restrictions, quarantine and school closure, for example. What kinds of behavioural assumptions underlie the predictions?

Behavioural assumptions are challenging to model. In Ferguson et al (2006), a rather clear behavioural assumption is claimed when the model design is reported:

> We do not assume any spontaneous change in behaviour of uninfected individuals as the pandemic progresses, but note that behavioural changes that

increased social distance together with some school and workplace closure occurred in past pandemics.

Furthermore, the underlying assumption is that individuals will behave according to the guidelines, rules and restrictions given by the health authorities. In a way, the effectiveness of behavioural restrictions is based on the assumption of *rational agents*. But how reliable is this account of human behaviour? If pre-pandemic planning is based on a standardised view on human behaviour, mitigation strategies relying on compliance during the pandemic may fail. Yet, we need to keep in mind the technical and computational limitations of a pandemic model: behavioural observations can be introduced into the planning process without modelling them, as this has proven challenging.

Scenario-building predictions in pandemic risk assessment

What kinds of scenarios is this model capable of building? As we have learnt, both epidemiological and behavioural assumptions have their limitations. On the epidemiological level, the model-based assumptions represent the *fingerprint* of the pathogen, hence leaving some level of uncertainty when drawn to predictive scenarios. On the behavioural level, the assumption that individuals follow rational choices introduces uncertainty into the final scenarios: to what extent are these scenarios credible when predicting the efficacy of mitigation strategies?

The scenarios produced by the population-simulation model explored transmissibility of the pathogen and the efficacy of movement restrictions during an outbreak. It is possible to describe the way in which these scenarios serve and function as a 'playground', not in a pejorative sense, but rather pointing to their usefulness as a platform for examining and exploring particular features of the infection and its transmission (cf. Mattila, 2006c; Keating and Cambrosio, 2000, 2003).

In a sense, scenario-building predictions allow us to 'access the inaccessible' to use Naomi Oreskes's term (2007). As Hampton Frost suggests of epidemiology being capable of reaching beyond the bounds of direct observations, Oreskes's idea of accessing the inaccessible captures the benefit of applied modelling. Models provide qualitative tools and produce evidence of the unpredicted for use in decision-making. The challenge that remains is the challenge of communication. How can the particular nature of this evidence that is produced through these scenarios be made explicit? Ferguson et al. (2006: 451) point to the changing and mutable nature of this

DOI: 10.1057/9781137298829.0009

situation: 'The transmissibility of a future pandemic virus is uncertain, so we explored a number of scenarios here'. They argue that these scenarios depend on model validation and parameter estimation, which should be given a priority in future research. Transmissibility, which is based on an estimate of the reproductive rate, is considered to be on the level of the 1918 pandemic. If it actually follows the levels seen in the 1968 or 1957 pandemics, the global spread will be slower and all the non-travel-related control policies examined here will have a substantially greater impact. Ferguson and colleagues emphasise the importance of collecting the most detailed data on the clinical and epidemiological characteristics of a new virus. In other words, he is calling for research that allows us to base the scenario-building on a detailed understanding of the explanatory mechanisms of the phenomena. The fingerprint of the pathogen is important, as these pandemic simulations show.

5.4   Conclusion

Both explanation-based and scenario-building predictions fulfil the social functions of simulation models. Predictions inherently address the need to know what will happen in the future. Various scenarios help in allocating resources, achieving agreement on ordering and manufacturing vaccines, or stocking the antivirals during an outbreak. As our examples show, both types of predictive models have uncertainties built-in, due to the nature of the modelling process: the assumptions made may not provide accurate predictions of the scale of the outbreak, for example. Nor are they necessarily able to capture the variations in individual behavioural patterns. But what actually happens in predictive modelling is the process of testing out both assumptions and exploring them as part of various 'doable' scenarios. This indicates the usefulness of modelling, especially when focused on scenario-building. Scenarios are qualitative tools that help 'fill the gaps' in existing knowledge and allow reasoning to explore the 'unknown unknowns' (which will be analysed in Chapter 6). These functions are, it seems to me, both social and epistemic. In Amy Dahan Dalmenico's (2007: 126) work this tension is well explained. She argues that there is a continuous tension between the explanatory and the predictive functions of models, between operative and cognitive, understanding and forecasting. This tension, according to her, is a source of conflict and compromise in modelling.

DOI: 10.1057/9781137298829.0009

How beneficial are models for risk assessment of infectious diseases? In relation to scenario-building predictions, we discussed the idea that models provide a way to access the inaccessible. Models in this sense do more than epistemological work. In attempts to predict the future, models generate predictions to inform policy decisions. This, according to Oreskes, shows that models have primarily a social role. This is especially true in scenario-building, as these scenarios may not be able to satisfy the epistemic quest by explaining viral mechanisms of a pandemic, as explanation-based predictions can do with common infections.

Underneath the usefulness of model-based predictions lies the question of their reliability. The notion of instrumental reliability that incorporates both the instrument and the expertise required is introduced by Boumans (2004). Reliable predictions can be seen as a result of the quality of the model and the expertise of the modellers. In this sense, the calibration of the model is not indifferent to other factors, such as the expertise of building the model and the practice of using it when discussing instrumental reliability. In line with this form of reliability, Oreskes Shrader-Frechette, and Belitz (1994) argue that we should think of models as tools to be modified in response to knowledge gained through continued observation of the natural systems being represented. Therefore, when we estimate public health risks through modelling, instrumental reliability refers to the fact that these estimates, these predictions, are not accurate descriptions of reality, but rather the best available approximations of risks. They are not static either, but they can gain greater accuracy as more data are accumulated during the outbreak. Both types of predictions show that modelled encounters with public health risks depend on the complex chain of interactions between the experts and technologies, the users and producers of these predictions.

What are then the possible limitations of modelled encounters with risks? As we have seen, limitations in the availability of data are one of the most dominant challenges for reliable modelling. Data may be limited, collected for different purposes and may not accommodate relevant information for model parameterisation, as experienced in the Hib modelling case when part of the data used in modelling was gathered for statistical studies of the efficacy of the Hib vaccine. Computational capacity and lack of available expertise may limit model use for predictions. Along with technical and data-related limitations, models may face social and epistemic limitations. Are model-based findings accepted in the user community, well understood and interpreted? This

DOI: 10.1057/9781137298829.0009

all depends on the willingness of the users to broaden their knowledge of potential sources of expertise. Epistemic limitations refer to the 'built-in' uncertainties and the tension between predictions and explanations. However, as the cases show, both types of model-based predictions provide valuable access to the inaccessible. They are useful tools when employed in policymaking. Yet, uncertainties which arise from the lack of data and inadequate understanding of the nature of modelling need to be addressed. In the following chapter, I will discuss the dilemmas involved when evidence is silent during urgent pandemic modelling by focusing on the 2009/A1H1 outbreak as an example.

Notes

1   Some of the materials used in this chapter have been adapted from (Mansnerus, 2012).
2   Please see Infobox in Chapter 2.
3   As we discussed in Chapter 2, this model resulted after a ten-year period of modelling work, dominated by integrating practices that brought together the three parts that were built earlier in the project.
4   Vaccinations are primarily targeted to stop the infection from circulating in the population, but by doing so, they may also encourage other bacteria or competing strains of the bacteria (that are not covered by the vaccination) to become more dominant.
5   Herd immunity is known as the population-level protection against an infection (Fine, 1993).

DOI: 10.1057/9781137298829.0009

6
When Evidence Is Silent

Abstract: *During the 2009 pandemic outbreak, modelling took place in a time-pressured reality. A sense of urgency to make decisions was challenged by the lack of data. Evidence was silent and weak, and modellers did their best to bridge the gaps. In this chapter we analyse these 'known unknowns', factors of which we have very limited understanding at the beginning of modelling. These factors can be related to the microbiology of the pathogen or to the safety of the pharmaceutical interventions, for example. Mansnerus looks at how modelling methods alleviate unknowing in the context of pandemic risk assessment.*

Mansnerus, Erika. *Modelling in Public Health Research: How Mathematical Techniques Keep Us Healthy.* Basingstoke: Palgrave Macmillan, 2015. DOI: 10.1057/9781137298829.0010.

6.1   Introduction

When a pandemic occurs and affects people across the globe, its rapid development increases the need to know, predict, anticipate and guess. On an individual level, questions concerning personal health and well-being arise. What will happen to us? How does this affect me? What can I do to protect myself and my family? In cases like these, one's own ignorance in the face of the unpredictable nature of the pandemic itself is particularly hard to tolerate.

Let me reflect on two personal experiences that capture the difficulty of accepting the uncertainties concerning a pandemic. When the number of confirmed cases of A/H1N1 influenza rose rapidly in mid-July 2009 in the United Kingdom, the media reached out to researchers who might shed some light on the story. I had analysed simulation models that were developed to assess mitigation strategies as a part of pre-pandemic preparedness planning. My long-term research interest had been on analysing the use and application of modelling and simulation techniques in infectious disease epidemiology. On the basis of my research profile, when the A/H1N1 outbreak 2009 reached its height, a journalist from BBC4 News Hour called me. He was keen to know about the potential risks of the pandemic: How is the distribution of *Tamiflu*[1] organised? Who is actually at risk? What kinds of effects are anticipated from the spread of the pandemic? What will happen globally? Our discussion showed that uncertainties, which were inevitably attached to the course of the A/H1N1 v pandemic, were not welcome. 'We don't know for sure, but the models assume that', was not an acceptable answer. This experience led me to think about the limits of knowing. What do we actually know about the pandemic? What remains unknown? How could we effectively communicate the limits of evidence to various interest groups, such as decision-makers, researchers and the public, who may assume that we *should* know for sure, who may acquire robust, reliable evidence?

Another experience captures the scope of *unknowing* in the case of a pandemic. In August 2009, my sister flew from Helsinki to London. Before the flight she was concerned about the risk of catching the flu, since the A/H1N1 in the United Kingdom had a rather severe media image in Finland. She told me that the media kept repeating the rising number of cases and the number of lives lost in the United Kingdom. The Finnish health authorities gave a recommendation that the public

DOI: 10.1057/9781137298829.0010

should consider carefully whether to travel to the United Kingdom at all in late July 2009. On the plane she sat next to a couple who was seriously ill, coughing and sneezing for the best part of the flight. Five days later in London, she felt unwell and reported symptoms of headache, joint and muscle pains, cough and high temperature. I became a 'flu buddy'[2] for her. After a self-assessment of her symptoms with an online form, I got a designated code from the NHS Direct website and picked up a pack of *Tamiflu* from a pharmacy. But did she actually have the A/H1N1 viral infection? We do not know, since she was not clinically tested or diagnosed. The assumed microbial cause of her influenza remained unconfirmed. These experiences highlight how evidence is limited in the early days of a pandemic. We cannot know the severity of an infection in individuals or of its spread within a population.

Public health policymakers face uncertainties in their efforts to control emerging infectious diseases. During a pandemic outbreak, such as A/H1N1 in 2009, decisions are made urgently despite the limited data availability. In this sense, weak evidence causes tension in the process of decision-making: the uncertain and unpredictable nature of the event is not easily alleviated. This tension and uncertainty are addressed as *silent evidence* in this chapter.

Current sociological and philosophical discussions have increasingly focussed on the production of non-knowledge. Whether the production process is intentional or not, it is worth exploring how a lack of sufficient evidence can affect the risk assessment process. I will pay special attention to the use of mathematical methods and computational techniques in overcoming silent evidence and its shortcomings in an urgent situation.

Our focus is on the story of how silences in the evidence during an outbreak are managed and alleviated by mathematical modelling techniques. The notion of silent evidence is an elaboration of historian Michel Trouillot's (1995) work. Philosopher of archaeology Alison Wylie (2008) has used Trouillot's insightful work in her analysis of how the unknown manifests in archaeological studies, or how traces of evidence can detect silences. I will look at both personal experiences and analyses of risk assessment during a pandemic to uncover the ways in which 'silences' are built into the assessment process. I will begin with the personal experiences that reflect how unacceptable it is not to know, how we are dedicated to uncovering the uncertainties. I will then describe the

DOI: 10.1057/9781137298829.0010

process through which pandemic risk assessment progresses and how it shows the evaluation process for vaccination strategies.

The story of silent evidence progresses through four sections. First, I will clarify what is meant by evidence and what the seemingly contradictory term 'silent evidence' might mean. I will characterise Trouillot's work in light of the general understanding of evidence. Second, I will identify so called known unknowns in a pandemic outbreak situation based on European Centre for Disease Control (ECDC) risk assessment reports. I will show how these unknowns can be seen as 'silent evidence'. How the 'known unknowns' are addressed in mathematical models will be the focus of the third section. Finally, I will discuss how silent evidence conceptualises the uncertainties that are inevitably present when we try to make sense of a sudden outbreak and act upon it.

6.2   What is meant by silent evidence?

Silent evidence refers to evidence that is unfolding. It is evidence that must be confirmed and documented with data. It is evidence that at times can be weak and yet that is used to support decision-making processes.

The silence of evidence, as presented in historical studies, refers to the idea that there are past events, past narratives or ancient objects that have yet to tell their story. We know only *traces* about them (Wylie, 2008). Such traces are textual fragments of documents in historical studies or discovered pieces of pottery in archaeological studies, for example. On the basis of these traces, we are to reconstruct their histories, to tell their stories. Wylie builds her analysis on Trouillot's idea of silences in history. According to her, Trouillot argues that in historical studies, the narrative itself is produced at innumerable sites. Wylie claims, 'What we know, as much as we do know, tracks power as it operates in social contexts both past and present' (2008: 187). By broadening the discussion to the archaeological context, she argues that contextual, that is, socio-political, economic and cultural factors shape ignorance. She shows that ignorance is a function of the poverty of empirical data; perhaps the relevant evidence has not survived in the archives or on archaeological sites.

Trouillot's starting point is to understand how a historical narrative is constructed: what has happened and what is said to have happened? This distinction allows him to look at the different ways in which silence

DOI: 10.1057/9781137298829.0010

is left in the historical narrative. Trouillot's examples are drawn from the Haitian Revolution (1804) in Western historiography. He underlines that there are various forms of silencing that took place in the narratives. Silence was due to the poverty of sources; hence, silences became embedded in a story he was able to tell on the basis of his archival work. There were also events of general silencing, which were due to uneven power relations in the production of sources, archives and narratives. In that case, Trouillot made the silences speak for themselves by juxtaposing the available narratives of the event itself. Furthermore, he talks about the abundance of sources and materials. In this case, silences appear in the interstices of the conflicts between previous interpreters. According to Trouillot (1995: 26),

> Silences enter the process of historical production at four crucial moments: the moment of fact creation (the making of sources), the moment of fact assembly (the making of archives), the moment of fact retrieval (the making of narratives) and the moment of retrospective significance (the making of history in the final instance). These moments are conceptual tools, second-level abstractions of processes that feed on each other. [...T]hey help us understand why not all silences are equal and why they cannot be addressed – or redressed – in the same manner. To put it differently, any historical narrative is a particular bundle of silences, the result of a unique process, and the operation required to deconstruct these silences will vary accordingly.

As Trouillot points out, in historical studies silences arise in the generation of textual traces, the compilation of these traces as an archive, the retrieval of traces as facts to be built into historical narratives and the construction of narratives that have retrospective significance. I will apply these four stages in my exploration of the silence regarding how evidence is gathered and used in a pandemic risk assessment process.

Firstly, there is the moment of generation: traces of evidence are needed. In pandemic risk assessment, traces of evidence are, for example, reported cases of the infection or the number of fatalities caused by it. These traces are compiled, not into an historical archive, but collected at the centres that monitor the development and spread of a pandemic, such as national public health institutes (e.g. Public Health England in the United Kingdom) or international organisations (e.g. WHO, and the European Disease Control Centre). These two phases take place continuously. It is at the moment when evidence is needed for decision-making, when something emerges, that the traces are retrieved as facts and built

DOI: 10.1057/9781137298829.0010

into narratives. Later on, explanatory narratives are constructed so that they carry some retrospective significance, and perhaps capacity to predict the course of the pandemic. The poverty of empirical data, the fact that 'traces' of evidence are scarce when the behaviour of the phenomenon itself is complex, leaves space for silence. In this sense, traces of evidence are material. Think of the collection of surveillance data during a pandemic: various health authorities report the cases to the public health institutes; in this process each case leaves a material trace in the public health records that are then translated into a cumulative number of cases for further statistical analysis.

The wilful silencing of evidence may emerge from uneven power relations in the production of sources. But silence as a poverty of sources limits the narrative a historian is able to tell. Or it may be a result of conflicts between previous interpreters. These aspects of silent evidence broaden the idea of intentional or wilful silencing. At a particular moment, the silence of evidence may be a combination of these aspects. As Trouillot says, 'I walked in silence between the old walls, trying to guess the stories they could never dare to tell' (1995: 31). Trouillot's metaphorical silence in this statement reminds us of the plurality of silences. There are several sources that can create silence of evidence. In Michel Foucault's words, 'There is not one but many silences, and they are integral part of the strategies that underlie and permeate discourses' (1978: 27).

When these silences manifest, they challenge the very notion of evidence. Something that should be clear, accessible and manifest knowledge is not able to address the given problem. Standardising the production of knowledge that leads to evidence is one attempt to address this challenge.

Standardizing evidence and ignorance

The standardisation of knowledge production, in particular in the ways in which evidence is collected in experimental settings, is exemplified in the dominant model of evidence-based medicine (EBM). The systematic ways in which evidence is in use extend the tendencies of standardisation from production to decision-making processes. It seems intuitive that standardising practices are ways to work towards overcoming unknown factors. On the one hand, those favouring evidence-based approaches conceptualise the hierarchies of evidence, which arise from the mode of evidence production (e.g. Petticrew and Roberts, 2003). On the other

DOI: 10.1057/9781137298829.0010

hand, critical accounts suggest that evidence-driven knowledge production might have its pitfalls, such as the overvaluation of quantifiable knowledge or the diminished or ignored role of the actors involved in the process (Sismondo, 2007; Lambert, 2006). In other words, evidence is prone to manipulation through its preferred production mode. Or it is subject to excessive production because of the demand to form a base of solid evidence for decision-making. This can lead to distorted practices, such as 'ghost writing' as a mode of excess production of evidence in favour of marketing or product launch (Sismondo, 2007).

Generally speaking, the ideal of a solid, robust body of knowledge that is gained by synthesizing available sources of knowledge can be questionable. Current critiques emphasise that evidence becomes disconnected from intentionality, from the practices related to the production, application and evaluation of evidence. As studies have shown in the case of the standardisetion of medical knowledge and related care practices, medical practitioners are actively engaged with standards, procedures and facilitating tools. Standards were not imposed on them, but the process was managed through intentional practices[3] (Daston, 1991b; Hastrup, 2004; Timmermans and Berg, 2003). Furthermore, medical anthropologists argue that the 'ideal evidence' is exclusive to the heterogeneity of knowledge production by favouring, for example, randomised control trials (RCTs) as a main source of knowledge (Lambert, 2006). Therefore, within the evidence-based movement, standardised evidence is assumed to be detached from intentions and practices and to follow a hierarchical preference for how to produce and collect it. Interestingly, the current discussion on ignorance presents us with typologies of unknowing. Can we identify a joint tendency of standardisation in these two separate discussions?

Ignorance, as recently argued, is not merely a lack of knowledge – or being in 'want of knowledge'. Nancy Tuana suggests (2006: 2) that practices of *not knowing* should be understood in a similar way as the complex practices and processes of knowledge production. In her account, ignorance may result from five sources: as 'configurations of interests'; blocking knowledge; 'cultivating ignorance among particular groups'; 'wilfully not wanting to know', that is, 'an active social phenomenon of forgetting'; or 'loving ignorance', that is, acceptance of what we cannot know. To develop and nuance the notion of silent evidence, we might draw from Tuana's typology: Can we find aspects of forgetting and self-deception? Are we able to identify acceptance of the limits of our evidence in a

DOI: 10.1057/9781137298829.0010

particular moment? Proctor and Schiebinger (2008) introduce a broader frame to look at the various forms of *not knowing*, ranging from 'selective choice' to 'strategic ploy'. For them, ignorance could also be a naive state, a resource that invites us to gain more knowledge. It may also be a passive construct or a form of resistance. Taking the productive side of ignorance into account, I suggest that situating ignorance within the stages through which evidence cumulates allows us to explore the forms of unknowing further through the stages of emergence and maturation. Furthermore, this approach introduces us to temporality that is present in the processes of using evidence. In the following, I will analyse how unknown microbiological factors and their effect on population represent 'productive ignorance' in the pandemic risk assessment.

Who remains silent?

Evidence as standardised knowledge makes decision-making prone to contestations. By privileging some modes of knowledge production over others, evidence is, perhaps, wilfully or intentionally silenced. Exposing the manipulative practices which silence the evidence becomes more obvious. As Oreskes and Conways' study shows (2010), delays in accepting the evidence for climate change as an anthropogenetic process were based on prolonged disagreements about what counts as good, reliable evidence. Various interest groups within the oil industry, which benefited from the delays in sanctioning CO_2 emissions, maintained these disagreements. One source for disagreement was the mode of producing evidence. Simulations of the various scenarios of global warming were contested, as Oreskes argues. She shows that different interest groups manipulated the competing views by weakening each other's evidence. The scientific evidence, produced by computer simulations, was labelled weak and unreliable. This convinced the broader audience of the uncertainty of the evidence. At the same time, weakening the evidence was a selective choice. The lobbyist groups in the oil industry maintained and manipulated, for example through publicity campaigns on radio, the construct of the denial of the anthropogenetic origin of climate change. This case shows the manipulative and wilful action taken with evidence that aims at silencing it. Silenced evidence leaves someone uninformed or ignorant of the subject matter. If it is done wilfully, we may talk about strategic ignorance, as McGoey (2007) argues. In her analysis of the safety of anti-depressants, she shows that 'ignorance allows those in authority to deny knowledge of the truths which they are increasingly expected to

DOI: 10.1057/9781137298829.0010

share' (p. 217). This resembles ignorance as a maintained, manipulated, strategic or active construct (cf. Proctor and Schiebinger, 2008). But the picture is more complicated when we think of the risk assessment of population interventions that aim at mitigating a pandemic.

6.3   Identifying known unknowns

As the 2009 A/H1N1 pandemic spread, the main concern was to predict when the second wave of the pandemic was likely to appear, how severe it would be and how risk groups[4] could be protected. These uncertainties were summarised as follows by the ECDC (August, 2009):[5] 'Pandemic viruses are unpredictable, and can change their characteristics as they evolve and perhaps reassert with other influenza viruses.'

Along with uncertainties related to predicting the origin of the pandemic outbreak, there were other 'known unknowns' taken into account in risk assessment reports from the ECDC (25 September and 21 August 2009). I will divide these factors into three groups:

1   'known unknowns' related to or caused by the microbiological factors,
2   lack of *precise* parameters for modelling and forecasting purposes, and
3   effectiveness and safety of pharmaceutical interventions.

What do these factors mean? What kinds of risks they embody? Ortwin Renn (2008: 20) states, 'risks are mental constructions. They are not real phenomena but originate in the human mind'. It seems that these three groups of 'unknown factors' and the risks they represent are not purely 'mental constructions'. The microbiological factor, the virus itself exists, and it is unknown how it behaves in terms of infectiousness and mutability. When assessing the effectiveness of pharmaceutical interventions, that is, antivirals and vaccinations, these properties of the microbiological agent are taken into account. What remains unknown is the interaction between the virus and the population. Policies on antiviral distribution or the optimisetion of the dose for a pandemic vaccine aim at maximising the protection and minimising the risk from the viral infection on a population. The risk groups are carefully monitored, and extensive measures are taken to support their health and recovery. How do these three groups represent 'silent evidence'?

DOI: 10.1057/9781137298829.0010

First group: 'silent evidence' about the microbiological factors represents unavailability. It also highlights the productive aspect of ignorance. In the early days of a pandemic, the microbiological factors remain unknown, but they generate research and surveillance activities that aim at generating evidence about those factors. Second group: 'lack of precise parameter values for modelling purposes' represents a situation in which evidence remains silent, partly because of unavailability and partly because data are simplified or trimmed in order to be used in model parameterisation. Third group, 'effectiveness of pharmaceutical interventions' is potentially an example which manifests both 'silent' and 'silenced' evidence. All these groups of unknowns are affected by temporality. The sense of urgency may cause some of the evidence to remain silent at the moment when decisions are due. Think, for example, of the efficacy of vaccinations: the decision to begin vaccine production and to organise a mass campaign takes place with a sense of urgency – when a part of the evidence is absent and a part remains silent in order to produce a 'doable' plan to protect a population.

The ECDC assesses the overall evidence as *weak* at present as it comes mostly from early observations of the pandemic and reported cases (ECDC, 21 August 2009, emphasis mine). A risk assessment report on the recent pandemic A/H1N1, from July 2009, states that the available evidence is 'weak'. What is the weakness of the evidence in this case? The report explores what is known and not known about the various risk factors of the pandemic. In short, weak evidence is evidence not yet known, as in the case of unknown microbiological factors, not yet available, as in the lacking parameter values or estimates for modelling, or not yet tested, as in the case of pharmaceutical interventions. Instead of subscribing to an evaluative term, I suggest that the weakness of evidence, in this sense, could be regarded as silence. As silent, evidence is not yet 'comprehensible to all', or may not have 'a voice' yet. In a way, silent evidence has become evidence for *use*, say, for assisting a decision-making process, but there may remain 'gaps' in its capacity to represent a phenomenon, which requires further accumulation of factual knowledge (cf. Mansnerus, 2010).

> Our public health programs will not be effective if absolute proof is required before we act; the best available evidence must be sufficient. (Michaels, 2008: 91)

DOI: 10.1057/9781137298829.0010

The 'gaps' in evidence, as described previously, are captured in Michaels's notion of the best *available* evidence. It may not be possible to reach the absolute proof, as he mentions.

What kind of evidence is sufficient for decision-making in public health? How does ignorance, or 'unknown factors', emerge in the production of evidence? In order to explore this question, I shall analyse two aspects of silent evidence: its production and its use in pandemic risk assessment processes. Through these aspects, I will then ask whether we can identify processes and practices that standardise ignorance in a similar way as evidence-driven research standardises knowledge.

6.4   Analysing unknown factors

When the pandemic occurs, the antigenic type and phenotype are unknown until the virus is isolated and analysed. It remains unknown how well the virus will respond to available antivirals[6] and how this response will change when the epidemic matures. 'Known unknowns' related to the microbiological characteristics of the virus also indicate the likely risk of complicating conditions. The main concern is that some individuals who contract the virus will develop complicating and potentially life-threatening complications as a result of the infection. It also remains unknown whether the pandemic strain will dominate over the seasonal type A influenza.

How the silence of evidence manifests in case of the A/H1N1 influenza pandemic will tell us something about its magnitude and its function as a part of discourses of prediction and prevention, of risk and uncertainty. Only after the viral strain is identified, can evidence of its severity be assessed. The unknown parameter values and estimates are fully uncovered after some of the microbiological unknowns are detected. The nature of the microbiological factors again has an impact on the effectiveness of pharmaceutical interventions. It is worth asking how the quality of ignorance changes in all three of these groups. Microbiological factors present the constant risk of emerging infections, whereas the effectiveness of pharmaceutical interventions contains more variation from the governance of risks by human efforts. In other words, when assessing the risk of a pandemic through these factors, we can identify the silences within them. Silence as a part of the unknown nature of the microbiological phenomena seems not to be intentional. The unknown factors of

DOI: 10.1057/9781137298829.0010

the safety and efficacy of pharmaceutical inverventions urge us to ask to whom are they unknown following McGoye, 2007.

One characteristic of a pandemic is that it is more likely to affect children and young adults. The most recent observations confirm that so far, the highest number of cases has occurred within the age group of 10–29 year olds, and 89.6% of the cases are among those under 40 years of age (Gianella et al.: 1).

The severity of a pandemic is measured as estimates of the case-fatality rates, clinical attack and hospitalisation rates. Interestingly, the pandemic risk assessment report (ECDC, 21 August 2009: 7–8) describes the difficulty of estimating these rates in the following way:

> [On case fatality rate] This is difficult to estimate with great accuracy at this stage and it should anyway be remembered that it is a measure that is sensitive to social factors.

> [On clinical attack rate] In previous pandemics it was unusual to observe population clinical attack rates of less than 20%, while for seasonal influenza, rates are usually between 5% and 10%. However, this pandemic may be unusual since it seems that older people may be missing from those infected.

> [On hospitalisation rate] As this is a difficult figure to derive for Europe. A rate observed from reported cases for the United States (11%) is correct, but should not be used for planning, as it will be an overestimate.

What explains these difficulties in measuring estimates of these rates? Garske et al. (2009: 339) explain the potential bias of these estimates. By definition, 'the case-fatality ratio is the ratio of the total number of deaths from a disease divided by the total number of cases'. According to Garske et al., this simple method of estimation works perfectly in a 'fully ascertained (and complete) epidemic'. Often, this is not the case. They argue that in most infectious diseases, there is 'underascertainment' of cases. This means that people who have only a mild infection or remain asymptomatic are not likely to seek health care, and are not likely to be tested. In other words, the more severe cases are more likely to be diagnosed, which is a source of bias in the estimate. Another source of bias arises from the delay between disease onset and final outcome in severe cases. This effect is called *censoring*, and it means that the case-fatality ratio will be too low and will change (is likely to grow) during the epidemic. Similarly, Lipsitch et al. (2009: 113) mention two sources of uncertainty that 'critically affect severity estimates': overestimation of the proportion of the cases (i.e. 'underascertainment', mentioned by Garske et al.), and the downward bias, because these estimates are calculated

DOI: 10.1057/9781137298829.0010

as simple ratios, (i.e. the bias caused by *censoring*). Common to these biases is a lack of observation and a lack of data, which is profound at the beginning of the pandemic, but which changes when the epidemic matures. However, variation in surveillance practices and differences in policies of the distribution of antivirals may prevent the accumulation of data of confirmed clinical cases. For example, the UK policy to distribute antivirals on the basis of self-assessment was likely to lead to a lack of confirmed clinical cases and to maintain the bias in the estimates, and may have had a potential effect on viral mutations.

Assessing predictions and interventions

Most common population-level interventions to prevent transmission of a pandemic or to mitigate its effects are mass vaccinations and antiviral treatments. The ECDC report (21 August 2009) mentions two 'known unknowns' related to these interventions: 'the effectiveness of interventions and counter-measures including pharmaceuticals' and 'the safety of pharmaceutical interventions'. What does this mean in terms of evidence? Firstly, the effectiveness of these interventions is dependent on the microbiological characteristics of the virus that causes the pandemic. Its responsiveness to antivirals may vary and is subject to change during a pandemic. Secondly, the development of vaccine against the pandemic strain can only begin when the strain is identified. In order to prepare the vaccine development, there are two types of vaccines developed as 'a rehearsal': so-called mock-up and pre-pandemic vaccines. Mock-up vaccines are those vaccines that contain 'a strain of the influenza virus that has been specifically chosen because the population has never been exposed to it'. The idea of a mock-up vaccine is to allow a company to develop and test a vaccine with a 'look-alike' strain that can easily be changed once the pandemic strain is identified. This procedure shortens the time taken to produce the vaccine. A pre-pandemic vaccine contains a strain of virus that is assumed to cause the pandemic. It is a vaccine that is prepared on the basis of a 'best guess' in the current situation; pre-pandemic vaccines contain the strain of the A/H5N1, 'avian flu', which was expected to cause the next pandemic (European Medicines Agency, Pandemic influenza preparedness website).

The European Medicines Agency (EMEA) has approved two pandemic vaccines: Pandermix, produced by GSK, and Celvapan by Baxter. The GSK vaccine is a split virion[7] vaccine, whereas the Baxter vaccine contains a whole, inactivated virion. These vaccines are brought to

DOI: 10.1057/9781137298829.0010

market and will be given in a mass vaccination campaign in the United Kingdom to the risk groups. The vaccination will be given in two doses at an interval of three weeks. A similar policy has also been adopted in Finland. The document from the Department of Health (2009) recommends the following prioritisation of the groups to be vaccinated.

1   individuals aged 6 months and up to 65 years in the current seasonal flu vaccine clinical at-risk groups;
2   all pregnant women, subject to licensing conditions on trimesters;
3   household contacts of immunocompromised individuals; and
4   people aged 65 and over in the current seasonal flu vaccine clinical at-risk groups.

The same document discusses all aspects of the vaccine. One concern related to the A/H1N1 vaccine is the risk of Guillain-Barré Syndrome (GBS), which is a rare, but is a serious neurological condition. There are two reasons for discussing this concern. Firstly, an increased risk of GBS was associated with the 1976 swine influenza vaccines used in the United States. Secondly, the syndrome itself is documented to follow after an influenza-type illness. However, the documentation from the Department of Health underlines that there is no evidence to suggest that either of the licensed vaccines will carry an excess risk of GBS (Department of Health, 30 September 2009).

But the use of vaccinations easily raises other concerns when they are offered to the population. Leach and Fairhead (2007) name various factors that are present in what they call 'vaccine anxiety'. These 'anxieties' are grounded in experiential knowledge. They may not be rational nor can they be addressed only rationally. In Leach and Fairhead's account, 'anxieties' arise in relation to the body, to various social processes and practices that influence thinking about the vaccination, and to wider political concerns. It seems to me that these dimensions are at least partially represented in the concerns of safety related to the pandemic vaccine. A document from the Department of Health explores the safety aspects of the vaccines. It raises the question whether there is evidence that the pandemic vaccine with A/H1N1 component increases the risk of GBS syndrome. This concern bothers those who remember something from the 'past'. However, a recent incident in which a teenager collapsed and died after being given an HPV (human papilloma virus) vaccination at school[8] may also cause people to remember the 'bad side effects' of vaccinations. The notorious case in this regard is of course the MMR

DOI: 10.1057/9781137298829.0010

(measles, mumps and rubella) vaccination and the false claims that the vaccine causes autism or other adverse conditions. Looking at vaccinations from this perspective reminds us how a lack of evidence may maintain risk. This aspect of silent evidence may not be easily communicated. Individuals assess their personal risk, often without a wider, communal or altruistic perspective.

One way to give voice to this silent evidence is through modelling and forecasting activities. As we learned, these activities embody one set of 'known unknowns', since modelling and forecasting purposes rely on available data in order to estimate parameter values. For example, there are difficulties in estimating the precise parameters needed for modelling and forecasting. These parameters estimate, for example, the numerical value of transmissibility, as a basic reproductive rate. Again, we can see a link with the 'known unknowns': the moment at which the models are built for estimation purposes, the microbiological factors remain undetected. The case of estimating precise parameter values[9] can be linked with the broader discussion on model calibration and its problems. In this context, however, it is worth noting that modelling exercises begin at the moment when evidence is 'silent', when only available estimates are derived from past data. Yet, these estimates are used in scenarios to look at the various mitigation strategies, of which pharmaceutical interventions form a significant group.

Therefore, during a pandemic, such as recent A/H1N1, decisions are made with a sense of urgency. This may, indeed, result in difficulty in decision-making processes. By exploring a middle ground in pandemic risk assessment, I have shown that despite the lack of definitive knowledge, we can nevertheless find a fruitful way to operate. This is a central characteristic of the evolution of risk assessment. As Lipsitch et al. (2009: 112), claim: 'a combination of urgency, uncertainty, and the costs of interventions makes the effort to control infectious diseases especially difficult'. This uncertainty raises the question of how to provide evidence for decision-making processes. One way of approaching these questions is to take into account the environment in which the decisions are made, as Boumans (2008) suggests. His account supports the idea that the ways in which evidence is obtained should be assessed as rational throughout the process of decision-making. It may not be straightforward to gain evidence of an emerging situation. Lipsitch et al. (2009: 112) argue that 'in practice, decisions have had to be made before definitive information was available on the severity, transmissibility or natural history of the

DOI: 10.1057/9781137298829.0010

new (H1N1)v virus'. It seems that the unpredictability of viruses, in terms of their capacity to mutate – uncertainties related to 'known unknowns' – diminishes once human intervention in the form of increased control, the predictive power of computational tools, surveillance, and monitoring practices are introduced into pandemic planning. This implies that risk assessment is an unfolding process, in which unknown factors mature once more evidence is gained. Hence, by regarding unknowing as 'silent' in the maturation of evidence, we can accommodate temporality and degrees of uncertainty that are inevitably present within the risk assessment processes.

6.5   Conclusion

This chapter studies the unknown factors within a pandemic risk assessment process and conceptualises the process through a notion of ignorance as silence of evidence. This notion shows that silences may remain intentional or unintentional, depending on the source of unknown factors. In this way, this notion highlights the idea that ignorance is both productive and produced, that unknowing can be regarded as a positive factor, and not only as a negative, intentionally manipulated state of affairs. This means that the unknown microbiological factors represent a risk that is not only a mental construct, as the risks related to the safety of pharmaceutical interventions indicate the role of agents in the assessment process. This raises the question of who remains silent. The chapter elaborates the notion of silence of evidence on the basis of Trouillot's approach to historical narratives. This is seen as useful, since it includes two meanings of silent evidence: 'silenced', that is, intentionally manipulated, and a 'silent' absence of inaccessible evidence. Ortwin Renn (2008) defines the purpose of risk assessment as 'the generation of knowledge linking specific risk agents with uncertain but possible consequences' (p. 24). By exploring this process of 'generating knowledge' and acknowledging the silences embedded in it, we will have a more accurate idea of the limits of evidence that is to be used within the assessment processes.

Ignorance as silent evidence, as shown, can manifest in the following ways. First, a 'poverty of sources', the fact that 'we know that we do not know', as it is commonly phrased, limits the available evidence. This dimension of silence may not necessarily imply the intentional silencing of evidence, but simply acknowledges the lack of microbiological certainty, especially

DOI: 10.1057/9781137298829.0010

in the early days of a pandemic. The intentional silencing of evidence is more likely to happen when there is uneven power in the production of evidence, whether manipulative practices of 'ghost writing' in the evidence production are used in order to secure fast access to markets within the pharmaceutical industry, or whether there remain conflicts of interest that direct the interpretation of the available evidence. Thus, silence of evidence is not to be seen as something merely undesirable. Or in Trouillot's terms, 'Facts are not created equal: the production of traces is always creation of silences' (p. 29). How do these silences manifest themselves in decision-making processes, in which they are considered as unknown factors?

This chapter describes three groups of 'known unknowns', the factors that cannot be fully supported by evidence in the case of a pandemic. These groups are unknown in relation to the microbiological charac-teristics of the pandemic, parameter-estimation in modelling exercises, and the effectiveness and safety of pharmaceutical interventions. I have shown that each of these 'known unknowns' can be identified as silent evidence. In other words, these are not seen as manipulative or strategic ignorance, maintained wilfully, but as a lack of robust evidence. As Wylie summarises,

> Ignorance is atlantic, to be sure, but focusing on how it is produced and main-tained holds the potential for systematic, empirically and theoretically well-informed calibration of what we know. The greatest challenge lies in resisting the pressure to assume that when comprehensive, definitive knowledge lies out of reach, the result is undifferentiated ignorance. (2008: 199–200)

Following Wylie's suggestion, when considering ignorance as silence of evidence and seeing it as a productive condition that generates further inquiries, we are enriching the notion of ignorance with positive quali-ties. This becomes important when evidence matures over time, as the case of pandemic shows.

Through the concept of silent evidence, we have developed an under-standing of the uncertainties within outbreak modelling. Silent evidence highlights the challenge of gradually overcoming the 'known unknowns'. This happens when the unknown factors are seen as productive during the outbreak. Silent evidence creates a conceptual contrast by showing how numerical evidence can be weak, uncertain and offer limited deci-sion support. Yet, numerical evidence is easily relied on. How this mani-fests in the current use of models and other forms of quantification will help us contextualise model-based evidence in a more balanced way.

DOI: 10.1057/9781137298829.0010

Notes

1   Tamiflu is the market name for oseltamivir, an antiviral medicine manufactured by Roche.

2   NHS information on pandemic flu advises us to name 'flu buddies' who will fetch antivirals from a pharmacy.

3   In a similar way, when evidence is 'silenced', intentionally withheld, we might ask whether ignorance becomes 'standardised'. This might be one way of reading McGoey's (2007) study on the wilful suppression of evidence in the case of SSRI anti-depressants.)

4   For public health professionals, risk groups are those who suffer from chronic conditions, are pregnant or immunocompromised. The ECDC lists the following population groups as risk groups: 'chronic respiratory diseases, chronic cardiovascular diseases, chronic metabolic diseases, chronic renal and hepatitic diseases, persons with deficient immunity, chronic neural or neuromuscular conditions, any other condition that impairs a person's immunity or prejudices their respiratory function, including severe or morbid obesity, pregnant women, children (especially those under two years)' (25 September 2009).

5   The European Centre for Disease Control.

6   Antivirals that are authorised for use in the EU are Tamiflu (oseltamivir) and Relenza (zanamivir).

7   A virion is a complete infective form of a virus outside a host cell.

8   BBC News online, 29 September 2009: 'Schoolgirl Dies after Cancer Jab'.

9   The predictive use of models in public health risks assessment is studied in Mansnerus (2009b and 2010).

DOI: 10.1057/9781137298829.0010

7

Governing by Numbers

Abstract: *How do numbers govern the world? How is the authority of computational techniques shaped? Model-based evidence is an important part of the whole body of evidence upon which pandemic predictions or vaccination strategies are based. Models, when functioning as an evidence-base, turn into instruments of governance. Their authority is likely to make us believe in the numerical representations they produce. They act as senior experts that guide and govern public health.*

Mansnerus argues that models, along with other measurement and assessment tools form a techne *of governance (the technical rationality of governance). Models, in this sense, are recontextualised, and their use in policy-making processes is brought to the centre of the analysis. A case study on the use of modelling techniques to improve animal health illustrates this.*

Mansnerus, Erika. *Modelling in Public Health Research: How Mathematical Techniques Keep Us Healthy.* Basingstoke: Palgrave Macmillan, 2015. DOI: 10.1057/9781137298829.0011.

'One need no longer have recourse to magic means to master or implore the spirits, as did the savage, for whom the mysterious powers existed. Technical means and calculations perform the service.' (Max Weber, in Gerth and Wright Mills, 1958: 117)

7.1   Introduction

How do numbers govern the world? How is the authority of computational techniques shaped? Model-based evidence, as shown in previous chapters, is an important part of the whole body of evidence upon which pandemic predictions or vaccination schemes are based. Models, when functioning as evidence-base, turn into instruments of governance. Their authority is likely to make us believe in the numerical representations they produce. They act as senior experts that guide and govern public health.

One way of gaining critical distance from their authority is to recontextualise modelling with the help of recent studies in the sociology of quantification. This discourse sees models as 'machinery' used to calculate risk. Models, along with other forms of measurement and assessment tools (e.g. auditing procedures), form a *techne* of governance (Dean, 2010). This Foucauldian concept refers to the development of technical tools for the purpose of governance. When we recontextualise models, as suggested, we will learn more about the ways in which modelling or, more broadly, practices of quantification affect policy processes. We begin to see how models gain the position of expert – or at times are ignored as 'senile elders', preferably forgotten.

In order to demonstrate 'governing by numbers' in action, I will use a case study of foot-and-mouth disease (FMD) modelling as an example. I will briefly show the development of modelling activities related to FMD during and after the 2001 outbreak and the follow-on improvements that led to the development and improvement of in-house modelling at a government department,[1] such as the introduction of an Intelligent Customer Function, ICF (Gauntlett, Sharpe, Birch, and Scanlan, 2012).[2] These developments indicate that 'governing by numbers' requires a carefully planned and managed communication and collaboration between modellers and various groups of stakeholders. The FMD case will show how this communication can be improved when a Policy Feedback Loop (PFL)[3] is put in place. The PFL knits together the *evidence cycle* and the

DOI: 10.1057/9781137298829.0011

policy cycle[4] from the modelling point of view. It is a communication platform on which models can stand as senior experts, giving their advice,
if we follow the metaphor of the life-cycle that informs this narrative.
Through the concrete case of FMD, we will learn how best to use modelling methods in the context of governance and what are the limitations
that arise. This will lead us to develop a broader perspective on the use
of modelling techniques in policy and an understanding of how to strike
a balance between overreliance on and underestimation of model-based
outputs.

7.2   Governing by numbers

We are obsessed with numerical evidence, fascinated by numbers, and
we hand over our own critical judgement as soon as we are approached
by *probabilities* or *likelihoods*. Are we perhaps over-reliant on numbers?
Quantification provides us a 'technology of distance', to use Porter's (1995)
terminology. As a technology of distance, quantification relies on mathematics and produces knowledge that is independent of the particular
people who produce it. These observations, which are based on historical
studies on the development of the insurance industry, suggest that trust
in numbers was shaped by the industry's need to create standards for
deciding who could be insured and who would pose a significant financial risk (Porter, 1995). Porter's interest is in finding out how numbers
are made valid, how they relate to the political and bureaucratic context
and how they potentially feed back into the academic context (1995).
Expanding the role of statistics in politics, Desrosières (1998) argues
that statistics enables us to approach phenomena quantitatively (in his
studies, examples are unemployment, inflation, growth). While doing so,
we tend to forget that these numbers, or social facts as it were, are also
political. This is what he calls the 'double role of statistics'. Both Porter
and Desrosières point towards what is known as the 'co-production of
statistics and society', as Rudinow Saetnan, Lomell, and Hammer (2011)
recently formulated in their research. What enables this 'co-production
of statistics and society' is the formation of *quantitative authority*, as
Espeland and Stevens (2008) argue, based on Desrosières:

> Authority of numbers can be investigated through their practical uses;
> describing how they become embedded in networks of people who make

and use them, and the techniques and routines that facilitate this embedding. (p. 421)

In other words, quantitative authority is built on the persuasiveness of numerical information. When we are governing by numbers, this 'dual role' of numerical representations, their quantitative authority, whether derived from statistical analysis or mathematical modelling, is worth a closer examination.

How do models then gain quantitative authority? Modelling, if seen as a set of mathematical techniques, can be characterised as a way to produce scientific evidence, but perhaps not to be part of the broader discourse of quantification. I would suggest the opposite. Computations translate uncertainties into the tangible, the numerical and the quantitative. As such they gain authority and become 'forms and tools of calculation', as Dean (2010) argues. This is the formation of technical rationality, or *techne*, in Dean's terms. *Techne* refers to the processes and practices of calculation that transform and produce knowledge in order to organise, govern and perhaps even to anticipate risks and uncertainties by numerical means. This is possible, because of the flexibility of modelling techniques. These techniques offer a variety of functions when producing and disseminating scientific evidence, for example, by enhancing predictive and scenario-building capacities, as we explored in relation to their use in risk management.

As technologies of distance, modelling facilitates in the making of inferences that 'extend beyond bounds of direct observation'. This idea primarily addressed to describe epidemiological reasoning by Hampton Frost (in Snow 1965, ix), but it is also applicable to modelling when we are interested in recontextualising modelling methods and identifying how they gain quantitative authority. Models in the policy context can bridge the gap between theory and practice (den Butter and Morgan, 2002). In this sense a model is not only a scientific object but it also constitutes expertise and enables normative knowledge to be gained. This means that models occupy a dual role: they produce scientific evidence and provide that evidence to policy processes (cf. Landström, Whatmore, and Lane, 2011; van Egmond and Zeiss, 2010; Yearley, 1999).

What is it in models that allows us to use them in policy? When examining epidemiological models in both human and animal health, the concept of *framework* comes up. They are 'frameworks that allow us accurately conceptualise and communicate our ideas about the behaviour of a particular system', as Keeling suggests (2005: 1195). As frameworks,

DOI: 10.1057/9781137298829.0011

however, models can be applied either within the context of knowledge production or, as the focus of this chapter suggests, in the policy context, where they are used as quantitative authority. We can extend our metaphor of the life-cycles of models and say that models become *senior experts* in the policy world. Mary Morgan (2012) provides a way to look at this duality of models by arguing that they can be used as an 'enquiry into the world of models' or 'enquiry with the models into the world'. By this, she means that models can be used to develop theories or they can be targeted to application-oriented and policy-driven work. This is when they become frameworks or platforms.[5] And only when they act as such frameworks, can they gain dominance by virtue of their numerical representations, by becoming technologies 'in distance'. In the following, we will examine a case in which epidemiological models informed animal health policy during a FMD outbreak in 2001, and how their quantitative authority was later subjected to more informed and integrated way into the policy cycle.

7.3   Using models as senior experts

Our metaphor of life-cycles of models highlights how models become senior experts when used in policy. This means that models have left their academic, research-oriented environment and gained enough independence so that they can facilitate policy work as decision aids. Their role as senior experts is in emphasising the specific nature of policy research. This means they have the capability to address specific questions, develop a reliable evidence-base and support decision-making.

As senior experts, models are capable of forming a discursive space in which expert knowledge is brought together, as suggested by Evans (2000). The capacity of models to turn into senior experts requires that we revise the modelling process and see it as an interactive, communicative enterprise. This may not always be the case. Model-building can be left to the technical experts, mathematicians and statisticians, which may undermine the importance of communication with the customer. In order to understand the importance of communication and to integrate it into the model-building process within the policy process, I will introduce the concept of the Policy Feedback Loop (PFL).

The PFL is a way to identify the different stages of the modelling process and explain what kind of expertise and communication are

DOI: 10.1057/9781137298829.0011

required when developing models as decision aids. The PFL understands modelling as a focused or *tailored* activity that responds to a specific policy call or an urgent situation, such as an infectious outbreak. In this sense, modelling becomes an iterative process, which happens when an interdisciplinary team identifies and incorporates model ingredients such as data, theoretical assumptions and mathematical or computational solutions into an appropriate model or a simulation framework. The PFL introduces to the modelling process a deeper understanding of the dynamic interaction and communication that takes place between experts from epidemiology, policy, natural, veterinary and social sciences. In this sense the PFL aims at increasing transparency at various stages of the modelling process (cf. Keeling, 2005; Boumans, 1999; Auranen, 1999; Mansnerus, 2013; Mattila, 2006a, 2006c).

Although the use of modelling in policy has been widely acknowledged, this multilayered process has not been conceptualised in a dynamic way (Louz, Bergmans, Loos, and Hoeben, 2010; van Egmond and Zeiss, 2010). An early account of model use in zoology introduces a stepwise process of model-building (Habbema, De Vlas, Plaisier, and Van Oortmarssen., (1996). In this account, modelling progresses from a question, through design and parameterisation, to model-based predictions and their use in policy. These steps indicate the development and use of models. As a linearly represented progression, these steps lack communication with various model users. The process covers eight consecutive steps (Habbema, De Vlas, Plaisier, and Van Oortmarssen, 1996):

1   identification of questions to be addressed,
2   investigation of existing knowledge,
3   model design,
4   model quantification,
5   model validation,
6   prediction and optimisation,
7   decision-making, and
8   transfer of a simulation program

The points of interaction and communication are missing in this description of modelling. As suggested, the PFL introduces this into the dynamic, iterative and communicative modelling process. The PFL follows the process from the initial call for research to the engagement with user groups, and in this way integrates the social and technical

DOI: 10.1057/9781137298829.0011

aspects of modelling into one framework. The PFL is comprised of the following stages:

I) initial policy call,
   PFL: Communication between the policy goals and what can be modelled
II) identification and clarification of a question to be modelled and translation of it to model assumptions,
III) model design and parameterisation,
   PFL: Communication of the initial model outcomes and policy outputs, allowing them to affect the parameterisation; increased availability of data that feeds back to parameterisation as well
IV) initial outcomes, and
V) model-based outcomes: predictions, scenarios,
   PFL: communicating the policy needs and strategy, being explicit about the outcomes that are needed for policy.
VI) translation of these outcomes to policy recommendations

As we can see in this Figure 7.1 which illustrates the PFL, the general cycle of modelling is expanded to include the stages at which communication with the group(s) of expert(s) is recommended. Usually, the modelling cycle would simply take the initial policy call as a starting point, complete the task and report the key outcomes back to the policy customer. However, this is likely to lead to a situation in which the model does not deliver the outcomes the policy customer is expecting and, we could say, the model is not functioning as a decision aid. Why are these three 'feedback loops' identified?

A policy call refers to the process in which a clear need for evidence to support, revise or renew a policy strategy is needed. Once the modelling project is on its way, the policy customer needs to develop a way to communicate and influence the modelling process. The question here is that modelling is not only an academic exercise. When addressing policy, it becomes part of the evidence cycle as a decision aid. This is how communication is established between the first and the second stage of the modelling cycle, hence forming the first feedback loop.

When the modelling progresses, the model design and parameterisation (stage III) and the communication of initial outcomes (stage IV) become important. At this stage, data accumulates and supports model parameterisation. Communicating initial outcomes helps clarify what is expected from the model, reassess its design and identify potential policy

DOI: 10.1057/9781137298829.0011

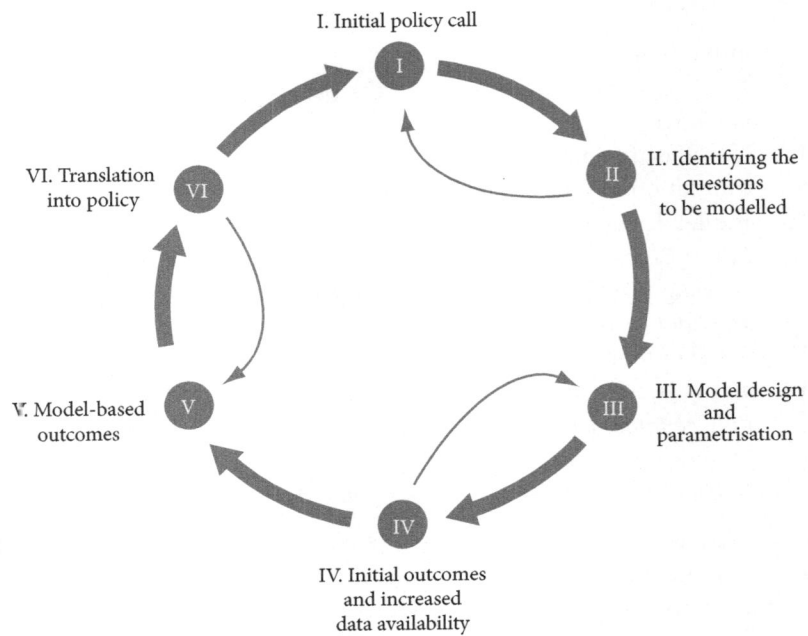

I. Initial policy call

VI. Translation
into policy

II. Identifying the
questions
to be modelled

V. Model-based
outcomes

III. Model design
and
parametrisation

IV. Initial outcomes
and increased
data availability

FIGURE 7.1   *Policy Feedback Loop of modelling for policy and its stages*

needs that the model is not able to satisfy. This is the second feedback loop.

The process of translating the model outcomes to policy offers the third feedback loop, which is needed for a more interactive and communicative modelling process. When model outcomes are ready at stage V, they are not necessarily directly transferrable to policy at stage VI. They need to be translated, related back to the initial policy call or communicated in a way in which they respond to the strategy to be developed. Communication at this stage means that the modellers need to be able to explain the outcomes in an understandable way and show how the outputs relate to model assumptions. The challenge is that model outcomes embody degrees of uncertainty. The policy customer is concerned with how reliable the outcomes are, and how firmly they can base their decisions on these outcomes.

There, each of these feedback loops within the modelling cycle creates an iterative process of modelling. Iteration in the modelling context

DOI: 10.1057/9781137298829.0011

means that each stage in the process is compared against the previous one or against existing knowledge and expertise. In dynamic transmission models applied in human infections (*Haemophilus influenzae* type b), iteration served as a way to increase the reliability of the model-based predictions, for example. By relating back to the notification data, to the observations, the model-based predictions were validated. They were said to be a good fit between the observed and the estimated. The reliability of a model in this case was attributed to its capacity to mimic the observational data (Auranen, 1999). As I suggest, in the PFL model iteration is closely related to increased communication and interaction between the experts. This is in line with what Evans (2000) suggests as creating a *discursive space* through modelling. However, iteration as part of the model-building can be time consuming, and thus the most suitable time for it is during the contingency planning, or the so-called peace-time modelling work, instead of in an urgent situation during outbreaks. In the following, I will assess how the PFL can be integrated into modelling FMD.

7.4 Quantitative authority of modelling of foot-and-mouth disease (FMD)

The 2001 FMD outbreak was unpredicted and required urgent responses. The main goal for these early predictive outbreak models was to find out how quickly the outbreak would affect the UK farming industry. When the outbreak ended, mathematical models were further used to analyse the mechanics of it and learn as much as possible about the specific aspects of disease transmission and outbreak response. Finally, models were further developed for current use to assess the effects of disease control measures on systems that are too intractable to undergo experimental procedures. This means that modelling FMD outbreaks takes place as part of outbreak response. In the 2001 FMD outbreak, three models were in use: the Imperial Model (TIM), the Cambridge-Edinburgh model and InterSpread (Ferguson, Donnelly, and Anderson, 2001a, 2001b; Keeling, 2005; Keeling et al., 2003). After the outbreak, the EXODIS-FMD™ model was commissioned by Defra in response to a 'lessons to be learnt' inquiry (I. Anderson, 2002). One of the key points highlighted was the increased need for transparency, which means facilitating communication and understanding of models throughout the process, as suggested in the PFL.

DOI: 10.1057/9781137298829.0011

Epidemiological modelling has a long history of using susceptible-infected-recovered(SIR)-type simple transmission models, as we learnt in Chapter 2. This type of model shows the changes in SIR states of the infected agent, or in this case, the farm. Basic SIR-models ignore spatial variation, as they only address the transmission dynamics. In 2001, the Imperial model (TIM) was formulated based on the SIR-model (Ferguson et al., 2001a, 2001b). According to Keeling, the initial model was built shortly after the outbreak and as 'necessarily a crude approximation, ignoring farm differences and only differentiating between local and long-range transmission' (p. 1199). Contrasting the TIM model with InterSpread, Keeling points out that the TIM was not able to accommodate the level of detail that the InterSpread model addressed. The key shortcomings of the Imperial model were the lack of ability to address spatial structure and stochasticity in the transmission dynamics, as SIR-models are deterministic. The advantage of this model was that it provided rapid responses during the early stages of the outbreak.

In the 2001 FMD outbreak, the modelling of the initial response came from simple transmission models that are commonly used in epidemiology. These SIR-type simple transmission models show the changes in the SIR states of the infected agent, or in this case, the farm. Basic SIR-models ignore spatial variation, as they only address the transmission dynamics. The Imperial model that was developed during the outbreak took this format (Ferguson et al., 2001a, 2001b). The basic assumptions were based on homogeneous mixing and left the farm differences unidentified. These assumptions ignored the farm differences, but differentiated between local and long-range transmission, which gave rough estimates as model outputs (Keeling, 2005: 1199). The analysis based on this model showed that in order to significantly slow down the epidemic, slaughtering on farms within 24 hours of case reporting (without laboratory confirmation) was needed (Keeling, 2005: 1157). This recommendation was confirmed by a later model (Ferguson et al., 2001b: 542). The key benefit of this model was the quick response it provided through the rough outbreak estimates, even though the spatial estimates were lacking. After the initial response to the 2001 FMD, outbreak with the SIR-model, spatial simulation models were built independently.

The InterSpread modelling framework was the only spatially explicit disease transmission model used at the time that accommodated complex stochastic simulation (Keeling, 2005: 1197). It was able to incorporate the complexity of geographical locations of farms and animal movements between the farms and to the market, for example. InterSpread was developed outside the UK policy user community, as part of New Zealand animal disease management policy (Stevenson et al., 2013).

Sharing similar initial conditions with InterSpread, the Cambridge-Edinburgh model is another spatial model, which includes all the location data of the UK farms and livestock as documented in the census. Yet the Cambridge-Edinburgh model includes a simpler and more transparent transmission mechanism with fewer parameters, which gives it an advantage over the InterSpread model (Keeling, 2005: 1198). Simplification of the assumptions implied increased transparency and openness to scientific scrutiny, according to Keeling. In managing an epidemic, such as the 2001 FMD outbreak, modelling can be a useful tool for making predictions that shows the number of infected farms and identifies the expected effects of control strategies (Morris, Stern, and Stevenon, 2001: 137). The benefits of simulation models are best developed when decision-makers can evaluate the strengths and weaknesses of model-based outcomes (Stevenson et al., 2013).

INFOBOX 7.1 *Foot-and-mouth disease (FMD)*

Foot-and-mouth disease (FMD) is an infectious disease that affects cloven-hoofed animals. The transmission can be airborne or come through contact with fluid from the blisters it causes in the animals. FMD is usually not fatal to adult animals, but causes severe losses in productivity and can have a very high economic impact during an outbreak in a disease-free country (Defra).

Criticising FMD models

Primarily, data are scarce or non-existing at the beginning of an outbreak. Often the lack of data is the motivation to build a model that can provide predictions or long-term scenarios. However, a lack of data does not necessarily affect the model design. It usually steps in when the model is parameterised. As we discussed earlier, some models are useful as theoretical 'thinking tools' that provide quantified scenarios of 'what might happen if' situations during an outbreak. In this way, predictive models function as decision tools for various preventive actions and assist in evaluating their efficacy.

DOI: 10.1057/9781137298829.0011

Being based on 'highly improbable biological assumptions', as Mansley, Donaldson, Thursfield, and Honhold (2011) criticise the FMD models, reveals that communication or collaboration with veterinary experts and modellers was not strong enough during the model-building process. What can be modelled often differs from the plausible biological or epidemiological assumptions that the model needs to be based on. This can create a situation in which modellers must rely on epidemiological understanding, as documented in a study of interdisciplinarity in infectious disease modelling (Mattila, 2006). Again, a way to improve the situation is to form an 'in-house' modelling team or a team that closely collaborates if modelling is outsourced to research groups. This may require the forming of close collaboration and engaging multidisciplinary expertise for the modelling process, as was done when the EXODIS-FMD™ model was built.

Building the EXODIS-FMD™ model as a response to criticism

The EXODIS-FMD™ model was able to assess different control measures on disease spread and take into account the economic impacts of outbreak scenarios. EXODIS-FMD™ was commissioned on the basis of the need for increased model transparency after the 2001 FMD outbreak. Although an external company built and developed the model, the modelling process was monitored through a Defra-led steering group, which included academic peer review during the model-building process. The lessons from the 2001 outbreak: increased dispersion of model-related questions, miscommunication of the policy needs and decreased transparency in communicating the model-based outcomes were addressed in the steering group and during the modelling process. The need for improvement, an increase in transparency and greater availability of modelling tools were emphasised in several reviews (Macpherson, 2013).

EXODIS-FMD™ is a stochastic simulation model that can simulate a large number of possible outbreaks. As a transferable framework, it can be optimised to different infections. It uses farm census data that can be updated based on individual farm information in the event of an outbreak. In general, EXODIS-FMD™ is comprised of two models: the epidemiological model and the economic model, which runs a cost-benefit analysis of the efficient use of resources. The starting point for the epidemiological part of EXODIS-FMD™ is a compartmental transmission

DOI: 10.1057/9781137298829.0011

model: SEIR.[6] In the compartmental core, EXODIS-FMD™ has a spatial model that uses the census data of farm locations, and the number and kinds of animals on the farm. The idea is that EXODIS-FMD™ is not only modelling the disease transmission but also its national and local management as the model allows the UK landscape of farming to be as detailed as possible. This means, for example, that farm size, location, number of dangerous contacts and infected premises, protective zones and travel restrictions can be parameterised in the model, along with the details of the resources (human veterinary workforce needed to identify and document the outbreak).

Developing quantitative authority through FMD modelling

The 2001 FMD models, the Imperial model, the Cambridge-Edinburgh model were built by academic research groups, and InterSpread was developed for the New Zealand policy community, whereas EXODIS-FMD™ was tailored for Defra use and its development was overseen by a steering group that involved veterinary experts and model users from Defra. The development of EXODIS-FMD™ in collaboration with its policy users enhanced its flexibility but also increased the complexity and length of the development cycle. However, this is a crucial differ-ence between the models. We suggest that some of this transparency has been achieved with EXODIS-FMD™ both in the stages of the PFL when a policy initiative is revised into a research question, and when model-based outcomes are fed back into policy. The key characteristics of three of these models can be summarised in Table 7.1 overleaf.

The development of EXODIS-FMD™ in collaboration with its policy users enhanced its flexibility but at the same time increased its complex-ity. This is a crucial difference between the models. As identified, the feedback loop has had elementary success in the policy context. It seems to me that EXODIS-FMD™ achieved some of this.

7.5   Conclusion

The PFL accommodates iteration by identifying the stages of modelling in relation to communication modellers, epidemiologists, social scientists and decision-makers. The initial policy (I) call will be simplified into a question that can be modelled. This simplification process is required as

DOI: 10.1057/9781137298829.0011

TABLE 7.1   *Comparison of the three models developed to predict foot-and-mouth disease outbreaks in order to highlight main differences between the modelling approaches*

Characteristics of the FMD models	The Imperial Model (TIM) (Ferguson, Donnelly, and Anderson, 2001)	InterSpread (Keeling 2005)	EXODIS-FMD™ (RiskSolutions, 2009)
Description	Homogeneous mixing, no spatial element, a SIR-model.	A spatial stochastic simulation model.	A spatial stochastic transmission model.
Model design and assumptions	No farm differences identified in the model. Clustering of infection is included into this model; hence, it is more comprehensive than a standard SIR-model.	A large, complex and very flexible model to predict the spread of infection, taking into account multiple factors.	Flexible platform to alternate control strategies and task/resource combinations. Provides a transferable framework that can be adjusted to different infections or updated with individual farm data.
Summary	Provides quick, but rough, estimates of the outbreak.	Flexible spatial modelling tool, slow to provide results and complexity of the model may prevent replication by independent groups.	'Tailored' on the basis of specific modelling needs. Provides flexibility and parameter variation for accurate representation of the outbreak scenario.

Note: The Cambridge-Edinburgh model mentioned in the text is close to the InterSpread model as a stochastic simulation model.

a policy initiative can be too broad to be modelled due to lack of data or available computational tools. Within the context of the FMD outbreak in 2001, the initial questions during the outbreak were specific and driven by a direct policy need for the answers to those questions (stage II). Subsequent to the outbreak, the policy questions become vague as the focus changes to lessons learnt rather than needing specific forecasts. Finally, in the years following the large outbreak, the focus changes to

DOI: 10.1057/9781137298829.0011

the prevention and management of outbreaks in a livestock industry that is vastly different from what it was during previous outbreaks due to the passage of time.

The existing knowledge based on the literature, experimental data, experiences of existing models and data from surveillance programmes is integrated as a part of the assumptions about models (stage III). The UK livestock industry can change quite dramatically during a short space of time in which multiple government agencies are involved in developing and applying modelling in collaboration with the industry. These changes may be very subtle and not immediately clear from information routinely collected. Therefore, in order to capture these changes, it may be necessary to consult closely with stakeholders. The effects of these changes may be that the questions originally asked become inappropriate or impossible to answer without excessive data collection. This highlights the first stage of the PFL, when the modeller must return to the identification of the questions to be answered and modify them in light of the new information.

Model design follows the existing understanding of how the phenomenon of interest behaves, and is often represented through a compartmental structure. Model quantification is the process of estimating the optimal parameter values and setting the algorithms to run the simulations. At this stage the model is structured to represent transmission dynamics. Once this is taken into account, parameterisation will describe a particular infection that takes place in a particular context (stage IV). This will later on make the generalisation of the simulation framework challenging. In the case of FMD models, the initial working group may have dispersed, and new users may be keen to question the choices made for specific parameter values, for example. In this case, generalisability may meet the loss of institutional memory, due to changes in personnel involved with model use (stage V). The challenge for translating the model-based outcomes into policy is in the continuation of institutional memory (stage VI), which is also identified as an important part of the effective use of models in policy (cf. HMT's review of modelling).

The PFL can establish and maintain communication between modelling and user communities in order to facilitate focused modelling that responds to the initial policy call. These are the two functions of the PFL. Different stakeholder groups can be engaged with at the different stages in the model-building. Once the model-building is on its way, initial model outcomes and predictions can inform further the model design

DOI: 10.1057/9781137298829.0011

and parameterisation. This requires flexibility in the model design, which is built into the EXODIS-FMD™ platform, for example. Thus, the PFL incorporates the need for accurate predictions, plausible testing of outbreak scenarios and the need to involve model users with some level of technicalities (e.g. model assumptions, problems with data, limits in model design) during the modelling process. All this, ideally, increases the transparency of the model-building process, which helps the model-based outcomes be documented and communicated back to the policy processes.

Especially in policy-initiated modelling, the PFL can ensure that the transparency of the process is maintained throughout. The starting point for successful modelling is that all the actors involved, those who commission the modelling and those who build the models, become owners of the modelling assumptions.[7] Emphasising the ownership and engagement with the modelling process is vital for the life-cycle of the model, which covers the process from the commissioning of the modelling to its policy delivery. This increases confidence in the model-based evidence.

The core challenge addressed by the idea of the PFL is to establish and maintain communication between modelling and user communities. Furthermore, in the policy context, user communities become a broad category, reaching from scientifically trained researchers to decision-makers. One of the key features of the feedback loop is to engage these different stakeholder groups with the different stages in the model-building. Modifying the research questions and clarifying what can be modelled may mean simplifying the initial policy call. Once the model-building is on its way, the initial model outcomes and predictions can inform further the model design and parameterisation. This requires flexibility in the model design, which is well presented in the EXODIS-FMD™ platform. Therefore, a feedback loop takes into account the need for accurate predictions, the plausible testing of outbreak scenarios and the need to involve model users with some level of technicalities (e.g. model assumptions, problems with data, limits in model design) during the modelling process. All this, ideally, increases the transparency of the model-building process, which helps in documenting and communicating the model-based outcomes back to the policy processes.

When modelling for policy, we face the challenge of increasing and maintaining transparency that allows a deeper understanding of model assumptions, model design and model parameterisations. The

DOI: 10.1057/9781137298829.0011

availability of data, inaccuracies in biological or epidemiological assumptions, and urgency when modelling is conducted during an outbreak have an effect on model reliability. Even when models may satisfy the criteria of usability within research communities, policy needs and the use of models as decision aids during an outbreak increase the need to identify and communicate the degrees of uncertainty that are built into the model.

It seems to me that the FMD models did gain quantitative authority. Perhaps we could say that they reached the position of a 'senior expert' too soon, as the pressure from the 2001 outbreak was tangible. This instant availability of models is likely to create an 'overreliance' on models, as if models were giving one the answer one wished to hear. When I talked to a developer involved in the process, he pointed out that a model cannot give one an answer. It is the process of modelling that forms the expertise and understanding of the process. In the later development of EXODIS-FMD™, the collaborative and communicative aspects of the process became important. Experts from different fields met, discussed and critiqued the model. This was the way to create a framework that is able to provide evidence for the policy cycle. By creating this level of close communication around modelling, we can see how models no longer can hold 'magic', but that they become experts. They are as if there were an extra person in the room, as the developer emphasised. Thus, in order to understand what is a balanced way of relating to modelling processes and their use in policy, I would suggest that letting the model become an expert is the way forward. How this can happen in a productive way, will be explored in the concluding chapter.

Notes

This chapter has grown out of collaboration with Francesca Gauntlett and Charlotte Cook (AHVLA). The case study was conducted during a research fellowship funded by Defra and hosted by AHVLA during 2013–2014. RiskSolutions is acknowledged as the developer of the EXODIS-FMD™ model.

1   Department of Food, Environment and Rural Affairs, UK.
2   Intelligent Customer Functions means that a group of officials with the technical, policy and logistical knowledge oversees the modelling work and ensures it is fit for the purpose.
3   The concept of Policy Feedback Loop was jointly developed with Francesca Gauntlett and Charlotte Cook.

DOI: 10.1057/9781137298829.0011

4   Evidence cycle and policy cycle are defined in Defra's strategy (2010–2013). They illustrate the processes through which evidence is produced to respond to policy needs and how policy uses this evidence. Cycle refers to the progressive, iterative nature of the process.

5   Keating and Cambrosio 2000 and 2003.

6   This SEIR model stands for Susceptible, Exposed, Infected, Recovered or Removed, as four compartments of the transmission process.

7   This was also emphasised in the context of epidemiological modelling of human infections in a presentation by Auranen, AHVLA Workshop 6 February 2013.

DOI: 10.1057/9781137298829.0011

8
Lives of Models in the World of Policy

Abstract: *When models gain seniority as experts in public health, their lives become intertwined with ours. They provide estimates and predictions, turning them into action. Mansnerus argues that this can lead to the renewal of vaccination policies or improvement in animal health. Policy needs are simplified, and the model-based evidence faces a heterogeneity in which their recommendations may be resisted and disputed. Mansnerus concludes by discussing the critical voices that warn us about overreliance on model-based evidence, and the supportive ones that remind us of their beneficial use. We use models to overcome the ethical and financial restrictions we face when making sense of infectious risks that affect us all.*

Mansnerus, Erika. *Modelling in Public Health Research: How Mathematical Techniques Keep Us Healthy.* Basingstoke: Palgrave Macmillan, 2015. DOI: 10.1057/9781137298829.0012.

When models gain seniority as experts in public health, their lives become intertwined with ours. They not only provide estimates and predictions but also turn them into action. Models help renew vaccination schemes or improve foot-and-mouth disease predictions, as we learned through the case studies. Yet we know that the modelling process can be described as fluctuation between simplicity and diversity. The policy needs are simplified, so that they can be successfully addressed in models, and the model-based evidence faces varied responses that may resist or even dispute the given. This fluctuation is best captured in the life span of models. This framework accommodates both the critical voices that warn us about overreliance on model-based evidence and the supportive ones that remind us of their beneficial use. After all, we use models to overcome ethical and financial restrictions we face when making sense of infectious risks that affect us all.

How public health research uses modelling techniques has been the guiding question in the studies presented in this book. The answer unfolds through the case studies in which modelling has been brought to bear on decision-making processes in public health or animal health. These cases also highlight when modelling is at its 'best', part of a broader base of evidence. However, in order to assess the use of models, we need to understand how they are developed in the first place.

8.1   Understanding models through their lives

The life-cycles of models is a metaphor that captures the sense of emergence, development, maturation, professional or working life as an expert, seniority and perhaps passing away. As a concept, it helps make sense of the whole process of modelling. Even if models appear to be a new development in human and animal epidemiology, we have traced back their life-cycles, their development, a good hundred years ago, to the early observations from measles outbreaks that were skilfully compiled into graphs and calculations of measles 'cycles' which oscillated between England and France (Hamer, 1906). Later, if we follow the life span of epidemiological models, compartmentalised models introduced in the 1950s and the dynamic transmission models in the 1960s–1970s can be seen as the predecessors, perhaps the real 'ancestors' of the Helsinki models, with which we became familiar in Chapters 2 and 3. The organic metaphor of the *life-cycle* shows that we are not dealing with a fixed set

DOI: 10.1057/9781137298829.0012

of techniques, but rather, once invented, they will then be brought into use more and more broadly. The life-cycle of the Helsinki models shows how one model (Good-night kiss model) that managed to depict Hib transmission in a closed family in a successful way provides evidential claims for other models that are built within the same research group or by other research groups altogether. There is maturation and growth within the family of models through the ways in which they were used and amended to depict other infections than Hib. But, as our narrative suggests, the general picture of how modelling methods become part of public health policymaking processes can be seen through the idea of 'growing up'. Yet, at times of urgent outbreaks, modelling methods may appear to be more 'senior' than they actually are. This was partly the challenge for the 2009 A/H1N1 pandemic outbreak modelling and the early estimates derived from the models. Likewise, in the 2001 foot-and-mouth disease outbreak, the early models built by academic groups delivered demanding advice that led to quick decisions on the mass culling of infected animals.

The appearance of models' expert position is referred to in terms of their 'quantitative authority'. The co-production of statistics and society implies that there will remain 'paradoxes' between the model-based outputs and the modelled phenomena. The co-production does not necessarily clarify our understanding of the phenomena, but shows the societal interests that penetrate into the models. Sometimes the paradox may be simple and solvable, such as a model-based outcome that recommends vaccinating every third child[1] and its apparently impossible nature of being a basis for a country-wide vaccination policy. Sometimes, however, the paradox ties in with the quantitative authority. When facing model-based scenarios with limited understanding of the method or the communication with the modellers, the lure of the numbers, their quick applicability as evidence-based, wins the judgement and backs up the decision. In order to increase awareness, especially in current times when numbers tend to govern the world, particular recommendations for policy environments are in place.

The metaphor of the lives of models shows how modelling methods are developed and used, built and applied in current endeavours to produce and employ scientific evidence within research and policy contexts. The capacity of models to encounter risks is a good example. In the pre-pandemic period and during the 2009 outbreak, the capacity to produce predictive scenarios was one of the key reasons to use

DOI: 10.1057/9781137298829.0012

modelling methods. In these situations models lived their lives, encountered the challenge of 'silent evidence' and helped overcome the 'known unknowns' more efficiently during the outbreak. Let us now look more closely at the ways in which models have been functioning on all these occasions.

8.2   Predicting, preventing and keeping us healthy

Through the variety of functions, models are capable of performing both in the production and use of scientific evidence. What is vital is to understand that the ways in which models function is not restricted to or contained within the scientific domain. The studies discussed here emphasise the importance of crossing the boundaries between knowledge production and use, and highlighted the use of models in the domain of human and animal health policy. This means that models employed in the study of infectious diseases cross boundaries, which means that they are built for certain purposes, often initiated by health-policy questions, but that they can simultaneously be used for the further development of statistical or modelling methods. Health-policy questions influence and guide the choice of model building and hence blur the boundaries of research and policymaking. This has been addressed as *tailoring* a model to solve specific research problems. An example of this is the broader interest in planning and executing cost-effective vaccination strategies.

But models do more than cross or blur the boundaries between research and policy. And at times these blurred boundaries may cause challenges for policy, which requires robust evidence for urgent decisions. This plurality and diversity of models in decision-making is acknowledged in Evans (2000), who incorporates the development of new models, in his case economic models, into new ways of using them. This, he claims, forms a 'discursive space' in which 'users and economists can develop shared understandings Evans, 2000: 223.' This fresh account of models-policy interaction focuses on the 'end point' or application stage, when political tides may influence the model choice. In this sense models seem to allow a special kind of interaction between policymakers and modellers. In the case of the Helsinki models, the interaction with policy processes was less direct, as the group was formed for research purposes. However, the initiative to form the group and start modelling activities at the then-National Public Health

DOI: 10.1057/9781137298829.0012

Institute in Helsinki in the mid-1990s came from the Department of Vaccines. The thinking behind this was that modelling could function as a general tool for health-policy processes, such as vaccination planning. Building this general tool was more laborious and time consuming, but nonetheless it moved the modelling work forward. Along with directing the modelling work, the Helsinki group acknowledged the importance of models functioning as a media for communication. These functions have been explored through the idea of the kinship relations of models, in Chapter 3. The family and kinship relations of models show that evidential claims can be adopted into new modelling environments, either academic or policy based. And when this adoption happens, new forms of research or collaborative networks may also emerge. On the other hand, in the context of using models in the context of governance, the need to increase communication within the modelling cycle seemed to be important. This is amended by a suggestion to establish the Policy Feedback Loop to increase transparency and feedback opportunities when modelling process takes place in the policy context for policy needs. In light of these functions of models, we can develop our initial call to explore the benefits and limitations of modelling methods.

8.3   Benefits and limitations of modelling techniques

What are then the benefits and limitations of modelling techniques? Through their evolution, we have seen how methods of quantification become accepted, how their influence spreads across different areas of study and how they make their way into the policy context. To what degree this is a beneficial development?

Chapter 2 showed how, when identifying the kinship relations of models, this allowed factual knowledge to be adapted and accepted in different modelling contexts. Techniques, modelling methods, established information on how the infection can be transmitted within a population moved from one model to another, creating kinship ties. The main benefit of this approach is that in relying on other models and solutions they carry to new contexts, the models become more reliable. The estimates have already been used in other contexts. This exchange also facilitates connections and the formation of networks between the different modelling groups.

DOI: 10.1057/9781137298829.0012

When we follow models in their working lives, we can see how they complement other forms of evidence that is available in order to renew and revise vaccination policies around the MMR (measles, mumps and rubella) diseases in the United Kingdom. This is an observation that tells us something about the limits of the models. Yet, as in the case with MMR modelling, the predictive capacities of models are welcomed, as they provide ways to encounter risks.

When modelling is trusted as the sole source of evidence, as was the case in some of the early models used in the foot-and-mouth disease 2011 outbreak, their message may be taken too seriously. This may lead to interpretations or recommended actions that will not result in a satisfactory outcome. In a similar way, evidence can remain silent, as in the early days of the 2009 A/H1N1 outbreak. Were this the case, the modelling process may not be reliable. Data are scarce, and estimates from the models can change rapidly as the outbreak develops. Overall this highlights the challenge of building trust in numerical evidence but maintaining a critical distance to it. Are we willing to accept that we are governed by numbers? When models are used as senior experts, as in the case of foot-and-mouth disease modelling, these questions become important to address. Currently, critical assessment of models us increasingly in place; the use of models as decision aids is strongly guided through quality assurance processes. In a sense, the processes are acknowledging how models can be beneficial, yet increasingly acknowledging their limitations.

8.4   Conclusions

Exploring the building, development and adoption of models into the policy context, this study opens new avenues to studying and conceptualising modelling. In the policy context, the most rewarding work would be to conduct empirical research into the implementation and use of the Policy Feedback Loop in a modelling project for either animal or human health issues. Through such a study, we would be able to indicate how well models function as decision aids, what factors can facilitate and improve the use of models in a policy context. As this study shows, it may not be straightforward to commission modelling, maintain close communication during the process and utilise the expertise gained through the collaboration as well as through the models themselves.

DOI: 10.1057/9781137298829.0012

Another aspect that might be helpful to highlight, and which this study is only able to allude to, is the differences between research-oriented, exploratory modelling and modelling as a decision aid. Identifying how the nature of research changes when utilised in a policy context can be helpful, especially if the time frame for deliverables is tight. These themes would shed new light on the questions of how to define the boundaries between basic and applied research, for example.

Silent evidence, questions of knowing and not knowing, of ignorance have gained more attention recently (e.g. McGoey, 2012). As suggested in relation to the dilemmas raised of 'known unknowns' during a pandemic outbreak, we are eager to find certainty through standardising knowledge and producing evidence. Perhaps further research into the details of how modelling can alleviate the pressure that arises from not knowing is a new avenue to explore.

This study completes a long-term research interest in the nature of model-based evidence, its dissemination, evaluation and utilisation. At the same time it opens new questions to explore: improved model use in policy; in-depth understanding of how we can manage situations in which we do not know; how objects of research manifest a malleable nature in different contexts, and how the idea of narratives, the stories we tell with technical, mathematical objects, such as models, help us see the ordinary in what is generally thought of as highly technical and inaccessible. If anything, this study has been an attempt to make the inaccessible accessible by broadening our understanding of what models are.

Note

1   Discussed at the British Academy Conference, Modelling for Policy by Auranen, May 2012.

DOI: 10.1057/9781137298829.0012

Glossary

AHVLA: Animal Health and Veterinary Agencies Laboratory

bTB: Bovine Tuberculosis

Defra: The Department of Environment, Food and Rural Affairs

ECDC: European Centre for Disease Control, Stockholm

FMD: Foot-and-mouth disease

ICF: Intelligent Customer Function

▶ **Model:** A model is a quantified representation of reality or, in technical terms, of a system.

Model developer: A person who can access the source code of the model and develop the model by coding.

Modelling as decision-aid: Modelling that responds directly to the need for new evidence within a policy cycle.

Multidisciplinary: Several disciplinary approaches and backgrounds in collaboration with each other, approaching a problem or subject from several angles; there is no integration of these approaches.

Policy Feedback Loop or PFL: A concept that identifies three stages within the modelling cycle in which increased communication between modellers and the policy customer should take place.

Reliability: Reliability of models refers to their capacity to measure accurately as instruments. When we focus on the reliability of models, we are interested in how well

DOI: 10.1057/9781137298829.0013

they function as instruments, how well they are 'calibrated' and how knowledgeable the modellers are (Boumans, 2004). Oreskes, Shrader-Frechette, and Belitz (1994) dispute the idea that we can talk about model validation or verification, and they argue that the primary value of models is heuristic (Oreskes, Shrader-Frechette, and Belitz, 1994).

Simulation: A computer simulation is any computer-implemented method for exploring the properties of mathematical models where analytic methods are unavailable (Humphreys, 2004).

DOI: 10.1057/9781137298829.0013

References

Amoss, Harold L. (1922). Experimental Epidemiology I: An Artificially Induced Epidemic of Mouse Typhoid. *The Journal of Experimental Medicine*, 36(1), 25–43.

Amsterdamska, Olga. (2001). Standardizing Epidemics: Infection, Inheritance and Environment in Prewar Experimental Epidemiology. In Jean-Paul Gaudillère & Ilana Löwy (Eds), *Heredity and Infection: The History of Disease Transmission* (pp. 135–181). London: Routledge.

▶ Amsterdamska, Olga. (2005). Demarcrating Epidemiology. *Science, Technology and Human Values*, 30, 17–51.

Anderson, Ian. (2002). *Foot and Mouth Disease 2001: Lessons to be Learned Inquiry Report*. London: The Stationary Office.

Anderson, Roy, & May, Robert. (1992). *Infectious Diseases of Humans: Dynamics and Control*. Oxford: Oxford University Press.

Arjas, Elja, & Takala, Aino. (1994). *Research Plan*. Rolf Nevanlinna Institute.

Arjas, Elja, & Takala, Aino. (1996). *Research Plan*. Rolf Nevanlinna Institute.

Auranen, K., Eichner, M., Kayhty, H., Takala, A. K., & Arjas, E. (1999). A Hierarchical Bayesian Model to Predict the Duration of Immunity to Haemophilus Influenzae Type B. *Biometrics*, 55(4), 1306–1313.

Auranen, K., Ranta, J., Takala, A. K., & Arjas, E. (1996). A Statistical Model of Transmission of Hib Bacteria in a Family. *Statistics in Medicine*, 15(20), 2235–2252.

DOI: 10.1057/9781137298829.0014

Auranen, Kari. (1999). *On Bayesian Modelling of Recurrent Infections.* (Doctor of Philosophy), University of Helsinki, Helsinki.

Auranen, Kari. (2000). Back-Calculating the Age-Specificity of Recurrent Subclinical Haemophilus Influenzae Type B Infection. *Statistics in Medicine,* 19, 281–296.

Auranen, Kari, Arjas, Elja, Leino, Tuija, & Takala, Aino. (2000). Transmission of Pneumococcal Carriage in Families: A Latent Markov Process Model for Binary Longitudinal Data. *Journal of the Americal Statistical Association,* 95(452), 1044–1053.

Auranen, Kari, Eichner, Martin, Leino, Tuija, Takala, Aino, Mäkelä, Pirjo Helen, & Takala, Tapio. (2004). Modelling Transmission, Immunity and Disease of Haemophilus Influenzae Type B in a Structured Population. *Epidemiology and Infection,* 132(5), 947–957.

Babad, H. R., Nokes, D. T., Gay, N. J. , Miller, Elizabeth, Morgan-Capner, P., & Anderson, R. M. (1995). Predicting the Impact of Measles Vaccinations in England and Wales: Model Validation and Analysis of Policy Options. *Epidemiology and Infection,* 114(2), 319–344.

Bechtel, William, & Abrahamsen, Adele. (2005). Explanation: A Mechanistic Alternative. *Studies in History and Philosophy of the Biological and Biomedical Sciences,* 36, 421–441.

Blume, Stuart, & Tump, Janneke. (2010). Evidence and Policy-Making: The Introduction of the MMR-Vaccine in the Netherlands. *Social Science & Medicine,* 71, 1049–1055.

Bolton, Gillie. (2010). *Third Edition: Reflective Practice: Writing and Professional Development.* London: Sage Publications.

Boumans, Marcel. (1999). Built-in Justification. In Mary Morgan & Margaret Morrison (Eds), *Models as Mediators: Perspectives on Natural and Social Sciences* (52nd ed., pp. 66–96). Cambridge: Cambridge University Press.

Boumans, Marcel. (2004). The Reliability of an Instrument. *Social Epistemology,* 18, 215–246.

Boumans, Marcel. (2008). Battle in the Planning Office: Field Experts versus Normative Statisticians. *Social Epistemology,* 22(4), 389–404.

Brauer, Fred. (2009). Mathematical Epidemiology Is Not an Oxymoron. *BMC Public Health,* 9(S2), 1–11.

Burchell, Graham, Gordon, Colin, & Miller, Peter. (1991). *The Foucault Effect: Studies in Governmentality.* Chicago: University of Chicago Press.

DOI: 10.1057/9781137298829.0014

Bynum, William F. (2006). *The Western Medical Tradition: 1800–2000*. Cambridge: Cambridge University Press.

Castel, Robert. (1991). From Dangerousness to Risk. In Graham Burchell, Colin Gordon, & Peter Miller (Eds), *The Foucault Effect: Studies in Governmentality* (pp. 281–298). Chicago: Chicago University Press.

Creager, Angela. (2002). *The Life of a Virus*. Chicago: The University of Chicago Press.

Dahan Dalmenico, Amy. (2007). Models and Simulations in Climate Change: Historical, Epistemological, Anthropological and Political Aspects. In Angela Creager, Elizabeth Lunbeck, & M. Norton Wise (Eds), *Science without Laws: Model Systems, Cases, Exemplary Narratives*. Durham and London: Duke University Press.

Daley, Daryl & Gani, Joe. (1999). *Epidemic Modelling: An Introduction* (Vol. 15). Cambridge: Cambridge University Press.

Daston, Lorraine. (1991a). Historical Epistemology. In J. Chandler, A. Davidson, & H. Harrotoonian (Eds), *Questions of Evidence: Proof, Practice, and Persuasion across the Disciplines* (pp. 243–274). Chicago: The University of Chicago Press.

Daston, Lorraine. (1991b). Marvelous Facts and Miraculous Evidence in Early Modern Europe. In J. Chandler, A. Davidson, & H. Harrotoonian (Eds), *Questions of Evidence: Proof, Practice, and Persuasion across the Disciplines*. Chicago: Chicago University Press.

Daston, Lorraine (Ed.). (2000). *Biographies of Scientific Objects*. Chicago and London: The University of Chicago Press.

Dean Mitchell. (2010). *Governmentality: Power and Rule in Modern Society*. London: Sage.

Defra: http://www.defra.gov.uk/animal-diseases/a-z/foot-and-mouth/

den Butter, Frank & Morgan, M. (2000). *Empirical Models and Policy-Making: Interaction and Institutions*. London: Routledge.

Department of Food, Environment and Rural Affairs (8.4.2011): Defra's Evidence Investement Strategy: 2010-2013 and beyond. https://www.gov.uk/government/publications/defra-s-evidence-investment-strategy-2010-to-2013-and-beyond (accessed 1.11.2014).

Desrosières, Alain. (1998). *The Politics of Large Numbers: A History of Statistical Reasoning*. Cambridge, MA: Harvard University Press.

Dietz, Klaus & Heesterbeek, J. A. (2002). Daniel Bernoulli's Epidemiological Model Revisited. *Mathematical Biosciences*, 180, 1–21.

Dry, Sarah & Leach, Melissa (Eds). (2010). *Epidemics: Science, Governance and Social Justice*. London: Earthscan.

DOI: 10.1057/9781137298829.0014

Espeland Nelson, Wendy & Stevens, Mitchell. (2008). A Sociology of Quantification. *European Journal of Sociology*, 49(3), 410–436.

European Centre for Disease Control and Prevention. (2009). ECDC Interim Risk Assessment Pandemic (H1N1) 2009 infl uenza. Stockholm: ECDC.

Evans, R. (2000). Economic Models and Economic Policy: What Economic Forecasts Can Do for Government. In F. Butter & M. Morgan (Eds), *Empirical Models and Policy-Making: Interaction and Institutions*. London: Routledge.

Ewalds, François. (1991). Insurance and Risk. In Graham Burchell, Colin Gordon & Peter Miller (Eds), *The Foucault Effect: Studies in Governmentality* (pp. 197–210). Chicago: Chicago University Press.

Farr, William. (1885/2000). Vital Statistics: Memorial Volume of Selections from the Reports and Writings. *Bulletin of the World Health Organisation*, 78(1).

Ferguson, Neil M., Cummings, Derek A. T., Fraser, Christophe, Cajka, James, C., Cooley, Philip, C., & Burke, Donald. (2006). Strategies for Mitigating an Influenza Pandemic. *Nature*, 442, 448–452.

Ferguson, Neil M., Donnelly, Christl, & Anderson, R. M. (2001a). The Foot-and-Mouth Epidemic in Great Britain: Pattern of Spread and Impact of Interventions. *Science*, 292(5519), 1155–1160.

Ferguson, Neil M., Donnelly, Christl, & Anderson, R. M. (2001b). Transmission Intensity and Impact of Control Policies on the Foot and Mouth Epidemic in Great Britain. *Nature*, 413, 542–547.

Fine, Paul. (1993). Herd Immunity: History, Theory, Practice. *Epidemiologic Reviews*, 15(2), 265–302.

Foucault, Michel. (1978). *The History of Sexuality:1. The Will to Knowledge*. London: Penguin Books.

Foucault, Michel. (1991). Governmentality. In G. Burchell, C. Gordon & P. Miller (Eds), *The Foucault Effect: Studies in Governmentality*. Chicago: University of Chicago Press.

Fox Keller, E. (2003). Models, Simulation and 'Computer Experiments'. In H. Radder (Ed.), *The Philosphy of Scientific Experimentation* (pp. 198–215). Pittburgh: University of Pittburgh Press.

Gani, J. (2010). Modelling Epidemic Diseases. *Australian & New Zealand Journal of Statistics*, 52(3), 321–337. doi: 10.1111/j.1467-842X.2010.00586.x

Garske, Tini et al. (2009). Assessing the Severity of the Novel Influenza a/H1N1 Pandemic. *British Medical Journal*, 339, 220–224.

DOI: 10.1057/9781137298829.0014

Gauntlett, Francesca, Sharpe, Kate, Birch, Colin, & Scanlan, Simon. (2012). *Modelling into Policy: How Can an 'Intelligent Customer' Ensure Appropriate Use of Evidence.* Paper presented at the Appliance of Science in the Progressive Control of FMD, Jerez de la Frontera, Spain.

Gay, NJ, Hesketh, M., Morgan-Capner, P., & Miller, Elizabeth. (1995). Interpretation of Serological Surveillance Data for Measles Using Mathematical Models: Implications for Vaccine Strategy. *Epidemiology and Infection*, 115, 139–156.

Gerth, H. H. & Wright Mills, C. (1958). *From Max Weber: Essays in Sociology.* Abingdon: Routledge.

Gianella, A., Walter, A., Revollo, R., Loayza, R., Vargas, J., & Roca, Y. (2009). Epidemiological Analysis of the Influenza a(H1N1)V Outbreak in Bolivia. *Eurosurveillance*, 14(35), 1–3.

Giesecke, Johan. (2002). *Modern Infectious Disease Epidemiology* (2nd ed.). London: Arnold.

Gramelsberger, Gabriele. (2010). Story Telling with Code. In Andrea Gleininger & Georg Vrachliotis (Eds), *Code: Between Operation and Narration* (pp. 29–40). Basel: Birkhauser.

Gramelsberger, Gabriele & Mansnerus, Erika. (2012). The Inner World of Models: Case of Climate and Infectious Disease Modelling. In Chris Bissell & Chris Dillon (Eds), *Ways of Thinking, Ways of Seeing.* Milton Keynes: Open University Press.

Griesemer, J. (2004). Three-Dimensional Models in Philosophical Perspective. In S. Chadarevian & N. Hopwood (Eds), *Models: The Third Dimension of Science.* Stanford: Stanford University Press.

Habbema, J. D., De Vlas, S. J., Plaisier, A. P., & Van Oortmarssen, G. J. (1996). The Microsimulation Approach to Epidemiologic Modeling of Helminthic Infections, with Special Reference to Schistosomiasis. *American Journal of Tropical Medicine and Hygiene*, 55(5 (supplement)), 165–169.

Hacking, I. (1990). *The Taming of Chance.* Cambridge: Cambridge University Press.

Hacking, Ian. (1992). Style for Historians and Philosophers. *Studies in History and Philosophy of Science*, 23(1), 1–20.

Hacking, Ian. (2010). Inaugural lecture: Chair of Philosophy and History of Scientific Concept at the Collège de France, 16 January 2001. *Economy and Society*, 31(1), 1–14.

DOI: 10.1057/9781137298829.0014

Hamer, William H. (1906). Epidemic Disease in England. *The Lancet*, 733–739.

Hampton Frost, W. (1965). Introduction. In J. Snow (Ed.), *Snow on Cholera; A Reprint of Two Papers*. New York: Hafner.

Hastrup, K. (2004). Getting It Right: Knowledge and Evidence in Anthropology. *Anthropological theory*, 4(4), 455–472.

Health, Department of. (2009). Cabinet Office. The H1N1 swine flu vaccination programme 2009–2010.

Heath, P. T. & McVernon, J. (2002). The UK Hib Vaccine Experience. *Arch Dis Child*, 86, 396–399.

HM Treasury Review, known as Macpherson Review 2013: Review of Quality Assurance of Government Analytical Models, final report. www.gov.uk/government/publications/review-of-quality-assurance-of-government-models (accessed 3.5.14).

Hoover, Kevin. (1991). Scientific Research Program or Tribe? A Joint Appraisal of Lakatos and the New Classical Macroeconomics. In M. Blaug & N. De Marchi (Eds), *Appraising Economic Theories: Studies in the Application of the Methodology of Research Programs* (pp. 364–394). Aldershot: Edward Elgar.

Hopwood, N. & Chadarevian, S. (2004). Dimensions of Modelling. In S. De Chaverian & N. Hopwood (Eds), *Models the Third Dimension of Science*. Stanford: Stanford University Press.

Hulme, Mike, Pielke, R. A. Jr, & Dessai, S. (2009). Keeping Prediction in Perspective. *Nature Reports Climate Change*(11).

Humphreys, Paul. (2004). *Extending Ourselves: Computational Science, Empiricism, and Scientific Method*. Oxford: Oxford University Press.

Hutter, Bridget M. & Power, Michael. (2005). *Organizational Encounters with Risk*. Cambridge, UK ; New York: Cambridge University Press.

Kainulainen, Katariina, Nohynek, Hanna, Pekkanen, Eeva, & Turtiainen, Pirjo. (2014). Matkailijan terveysopas: Tuhkarokko, sikotauti ja vihurirokko Retrieved 7.8.2014, 2014, from http://www.terveyskirjasto.fi/terveysportti/ktl.mat?p_artikkeli=mato0048

Keating, Peter & Cambrosio, Alberto. (2000). Biomedical Platforms. *Configurations*, 8, 337–387.

Keating, Peter & Cambrosio, Alberto. (2003). *Biomedical Platforms: Realigning the Normal and the Pathological in Late-Twentieth Century Medicine*. Cambridge, MA; London: The MIT Press.

Keeling, Matt, J. (2005). Models of Foot-and-Mouth Disease. *Proceedings of the Royal Society of London. Series B.*, 272, 1195–1202.

DOI: 10.1057/9781137298829.0014

Keeling, Matt, J., Woolhouse, E. J., May, R. M., Davies, G., & Grenfell, B.T. (2003). Modelling Vaccination Strategies against Foot-and-Mouth Disease. *Nature*, 421.

Kermack, W. O. & McKendrick, A. G. (1927). A Contribution to the Mathematical Theory of Epidemics. *Proceedings of the Royal Society of London. Series A, Containing Papers of a Mathematical and Physical Character*, 115(772), 700–721.

Lambert, Helen. (2006). Accounting for EBM: Notions of Evidence in Medicine. *Social Science & Medicine*, 62, 2633–2645.

Landström, Catharina, Whatmore, Sarah, & Lane, S. N. (2011). Virtual Engineering: Computer Simulation Modelling for Flood Risk Management in England. *Science Studies*, 24(2), 3–22.

Langmuir, Alexander. (1976). William Farr: Founder of Modern Concepts of Surveillance. *International Journal of Epidemiology*, 5(1), 13–18.

Leach, Melissa & Fairhead, James (Eds.). (2007). *Vaccine Anxieties: Global Science, Child Health and Society*. London: Earthscan.

Leino, T. (2003). *Population Immunity to Haemophilus Influenzae Type B - Before and After Conjugate Vaccines*, Publications of the National Public Health Institute A23/2003. Helsinki, Finland.

Leino, T., Auranen, K., Makela, P. H., Kayhty, H., & Takala, A. K. (2000). Dynamics of Natural Immunity Caused by Subclinical Infections, Case Study on Haemophilus Influenzae Type B (Hib). *Epidemiology and Infection*, 125(3), 583–591.

Leino, Tuija, Takala, Tapio, Auranen, Kari, Mäkelä, Pirjo Helen, & Takala, Aino. (2004). Indirect Protection Obtained by Haemophilus Influenzae Type B Vaccination: Analysis in a Structured Population Model. *Epidemiology and Infection*, 132(5), 959–966.

Lexau, Catherine A., Lynfield, Ruth, Danila, Richard et al. (2005). Changing Epidemiology of Invasive Pneumococcal Disease Among Older Adults in the Era of Pediatric Pneumococcal Conjugate Vaccine. *JAMA*, 294(16), 2043–2051.

Lipsitch, Marc, Riley, Stephen, Cauchemez, Simon, Ghani, Azra, & Ferguson, Neil M. (2009). Managing and Reducing Uncertainty in an Emerging Influenza Pandemic. *New England Medical Journal*, 361(2), 112–115.

Louz, Derrick, Bergmans, Hans, Loos, Birgit, & Hoeben, Rob. (2010). Emergence of Viral Diseases: Mathematical Modeling as Tool for Infection Control, Policy and Decision-Making. *Critical Reviews in Microbiology*, 36(3), 195–211.

DOI: 10.1057/9781137298829.0014

Macpherson, Nicholas. (2013). *Review of Quality Assurance of Government Models*. London.

Mäkelä, Pirjo Helen, Käyhty, Helena, Leino, Tuija, Auranen, Kari, Peltola, Heikki, Lindholm, Niina, & Eskola, Juhani. (2003). Long-Term Persistence of Immunity after Immunisation with Haemophilus Influenzae Type B Conjugate Vaccine. *Vaccine*, 22, 287–292.

Mansley, L. M., Donaldson, A. I., Thursfield, M.V., & Honhold, N. (2011). Destructive Tension: Mathematics versus Experience – the Progress and Control of the 2001 Foot and Mouth Disease Epidemic in Great Britain. *Reviews in Science and Technology*, 30(2), 483–498.

Mansnerus, Erika. (2009a). *Acting with 'Facts' in Order to Re-Model Vaccination Policies: The Case of MMR-Vaccine in the UK 1988*. Working papers on the Nature of Evidence: How Well Do 'Facts' Travel? Economic History Department, LSE, (37/2008). London.

Mansnerus, Erika. (2009b). The Lives of Facts in Mathematical Models: A Story of Population-Level Disease Transmission of Haemophilus Influenzae Type B Bacteria. *BioSocieties*, 4(2/3), 207–222.

Mansnerus, Erika. (2009c). *Modelled Encounters with Public Health Risks: How Do We Predict the Unpredictable?* Discussion papers from the Centre for Analysis of Risk and Regulation. Centre for Analysis of Risk and Regulation. London School of Economics and Political Science. London.

Mansnerus, Erika. (2010). *Ignorance and Uncertainty in the Life-Cycles of Evidence: The Case of Pandemic Influenzae Preparedness Planning*. Discussion papers from the Centre for Analysis of Risk and Regulation. Centre for Analysis of Risk and Regulation. London School of Economics and Political Science. London.

Mansnerus, Erika. (2011). Using Models to Keep Us Healthy: The Productive Journeys of Facts across Public Health Research Networks. In Peter Howlett & Mary Morgan (Eds), *How Well Do Facts Travel? The Dissemination of Teliable Knowledge* (pp. 376–402). Cambridge, MA, New York: Cambridge University Press.

Mansnerus, Erika. (2012). Understanding and Governing Public Health Risks by Modeling. In Rafaela Hillerbrandt, Martin Peterson, Sabine Roeser, & Per Sandin (Eds), *Handbook of Risk Theory*. Dordrecht: Springer.

Mansnerus, Erika. (2013). Using Model-Based Evidence in the Governance of Pandemics. *Sociology of Health and Illness*, 35(2), 280–291.

DOI: 10.1057/9781137298829.0014

Mansnerus, Erika & Wagenknecht, Susann. (2014). Feeling with the Organism: A Blueprint for Empirical Philosophy of Science. In Hanne Andersen (Ed.), *Empirical Philosophy of Science: Workshop Proceedings*: Springer.

Mattila, Erika. (2006a). Interdisciplinarity in the Making: Modelling Infectious Diseases. *Perspectives on Science: Historical, Philosophical, Sociological*, 13(4), 531–553.

Mattila, Erika. (2006b). *Questions to Artificial Nature: A Philosophical Study of Interdisciplinary Models and Their Functions in Scientific Practice* (Vol. 14). Helsinki.

Mattila, Erika. (2006c). Struggle Between Specificity and Generality: How Do Infectious Disease Models Become a Simulation Platform. *Simulation: Pragmatic Constructions of Reality – Sociology of the Sciences Yearbook 25*, 125–138.

Marcy, Kenneth (Ed.). (1941). *Papers of Wade Hampton Frost, M.D. A Contribution to Epidemiological Method*. New York: The Commomwealth Fund.

McGoey, Linsey. (2007). On the Will to Ignorance in Bureaucracy. *Economy and Society*, 36(2), 212–235.

McKenzie, F. Ellis. (2004). The Role of Mathematical Modeling in Malaria Control. *Am J Trop Med Hyg*, 71(2S), 94–96.

McVernon, Jodie, Trotter, Caroline L., Slack, Mary P. E., & Ramsey, Mary E. (2004). Trends in Haemophilus influenzae type b infections in adults in England and Wales: surveillance study. *British Medical Journal*, 329, 655–658.

Melegaro, A., Gay, N. J., & Medley, G. F. (2004). Estimating the Transmission Parameters of Pneumococcal Carriage in Households. *Epidemiology and Infection*, 132(3), 433–441.

Michaels, D. (2008). Manufactured Uncertainty: Contested Science and the Protection of Public's Health and Environment. In Robert Proctor & Laura Schiebinger (Eds), *Agnotology: The Making and Unmaking of Ignorance*. Palo Alto, CA: Stanford University Press.

Miller, E., (1988a). Measles, Mumps and Rubella Vaccine. [Editorial]. *British Journal of Hospital Medicine*, 40(October), 247–249.

Miller, E , (1988b). Measles, Mumps and Rubella: Present and Future Immunisation Policy. *Public Health*, 102, 317–321.

Miller, E.. (1994). The New Measles Campaign. *British Medical Journal*, 309, 1102.

Miller, E., Waight, P. A., Vurdien, J. E., White, J. M., Jones, G., Miller, B. H. R., Tookey, P. A., &

DOI: 10.1057/9781137298829.0014

Peckham, C. S. (1991). Rubella Surveillance to December 1990: A Joint Report from the pHLS and National Congenital Rubella Surveillance Programme. *Communicable Disease Review*, 1(4), 29 March 1991, ISSN 0144-3186.

Morgan, Mary. (2001). Models, Stories and the Economic World. *Journal of Economic Methodology*, 8(3), 361–384.

Morgan, Mary. (2002). Model Experiments and Models in Experiments. In L. Magnani and N. Nersessian (Eds), *Model-Based Reasoning: Science, Technology, Values*. Kluwer Academic Publishers/Plenum Publishers: New York.

Morgan, Mary. (2003). Experiments without Material Intervention: Model Experiments, Virtual Experiments and Virtually Experiments. In Hans Radder (Ed.), *The Philosophy of Scientific Experimentation* (pp. 216–235). Pittsburgh: University of Pittsburgh Press.

Morgan, Mary. (2005). Experiments versus Models: New Phenomena, Inference and Surprise. *Journal of Economic Methodology*, 12(2), 317–329.

Morgan, Mary. (2012). *The World in the Model*. Cambridge: Cambridge University Press.

Morgan, Mary & Morrison, Margaret. (1999). *Models as Mediators. Perspectives on Natural and Social Sciences*. Cambridge: Cambridge University Press.

Morris, R.S., Stern, M. W., & Stevenson, M. A. (2001). Predictive Spatial Modelling of Alternative Control Strategies for the Foot-and-Mouth Disease Epidemic in Great Britain 2001. *Veterinary Record*, 149(137–144).

Nicoll, A. & Coulombier, D. (2009). Europe's Initial Experience with Pandemic (H1N1): Mitigation and Delaying Policies and Practices. *Euro Surveillance*, 14(29).

Oersted, Christian. On the Spirit and Study of Universal Natural Philosophy, London 1852, quoted in Sintonen 2004.

Oreskes, Naomi. (2007). From Scaling to Simulation: Changing Meanings and Ambitions of Models in Geology. In Angela Creager, Elizabeth Lunbeck, & M. Norton Wise (Eds), *Science without Laws. Model Systems, Cases, Exemplary Narratives*. Durham, London: Duke University Press.

Oreskes, Naomi. (2011). My Facts Are Better Than Your Facts: Spreading Good News about Global Warming. In Peter Howlett & Mary Morgan (Eds), *How Well Do Facts Travel? The Dissemination of Reliable Knowledge* (pp. 136–166). Cambridge, MA.: Cambridge University Press.

DOI: 10.1057/9781137298829.0014

Oreskes, Naomi, & Conway, Erik. (2010). *Merchants of Doubt: How a Handful of Scientists Obscured the Truth on Issues from Tobacco Smoke to Global Warming*. London, New York: Bloomsbury.

Oreskes, Naomi, Shrader-Frechette, Kristin, & Belitz, Karen. (1994). Verification, Validation and Confirmation of Numerical Models in Earth Sciences. *Science*, 263, 641–646.

Peltola, Heikki, Salo, Eeva, & Saxèn, Harri. (2005). Incidence of Haemophilus Influenzae Type B Meningitis during 18 Years of Vaccine Use: Observational Study Using Routine Hospital Data. *British Medical Journal*, 330(7481), 18–19.

Pettigrew, Mark, & Roberts, Helen. (2003). Evidence, Hiearchies and Typologies: Horses for Courses. *Journal of Epidemiology and Community Health*, 57, 527–529.

Pittman, Margaret. (1931). Variation and Type Specificity in the Bacterial Species Hemophilus Influenzae. *The Journal of Experimental Medicine*, 53(4), 471–492.

Pittman, Margaret. (1933). The Action of Type-Specific Hemophilus Influenzae Antiserum. *The Journal of Experimental Medicine*, 58(6), 683–705.

Porter, Theodore. (1995). *Trust in Numbers: The Pursuit of Objectivity in Science and Public Life*. Princeton, NJ: Princeton University Press.

Proctor, Robert & Schiebinger, Laura (Eds). (2008). *Agnotology: The Making and Unmaking of Ignorance*. Palo Alto, CA: Stanford University Press.

Ramsey, M., Gay, N. J., Miller, Elizabeth, Rush, M., White, J., Morgan-Capner, P., & Brown, D. (1994). the Epidemiology of Measles in England and Wales: Rationale for the 1994 National Vaccination Campaign. *Communicable Disease Report*, 4(12), R141–146.

Renn, Ortwin. (2008). The risk handling chain. In F. Bouder, D. Slavin, & R. Löfsted (Eds), *The Tolerability of Risk. a New Framework for Risk Management*. London: Earthscan.

Ross, Ronald. (1911). *The Prevention of Malaria* (2nd ed.). London: Murray.

Rudinow Saetnan, Ann, Lomell, Heidi, & Hammer, Svein. (2011). *The Mutual Construction of Statistics and Society*. New York: Routledge.

Sintonen, M. (2004a). The Two Aspects of Method: Questioning Fellow Inquirers and Questioning Nature. In M. Sintonen (ed.), *The Socratic Tradition: Questioning as Philosophy and as Method*. Kluwer Academic Publishers: Dordrecht.

DOI: 10.1057/9781137298829.0014

Sismondo, Sergio. (2007). Ghost Management: How Much of the Medical Literature Is Shaped behind the Scenes by the Pharmaceutical Industry? *PLoS Med*, 4(9).

Stevenson, M. A., Sanson, R. L., Stern, M. W., O'Leary, B. D., Sujau, M., Moles-Benfell, N., & Morris, R.S. (2013). InterSpread Plus: A Patial and Stochastic Simulation Model of Disease in Animal Populations. *Preventive Veterinary Medicine*, 109(1–2), 10–24.

Taylor-Gooby, P. & Zinn, J. (Eds). (2006). *Risk in Social Science*. Oxford: Oxford University Press.

Timmermans, Stephen & Berg, Marc. (2003). *The Gold Standard: The Challenge of Evidence-Based Medicine and Standardization in Health Care*. Philadelphia, PA: Temple University Press.

Trouillot. (1995). *Silencing the Past: Power and the Production of History*. Boston, MA: Beacon Press.

Tuana, Nancy. (2006). The Speculum of Ignorance: The Women's Health Movement and the Epistemologies of Ignorance. *Hypatia*, 21(3), 1–19.

van Daalen, C. Els, Dresen, Leen, & Janssen, Marco. (2002). The Roles of Computer Models in the Environmental Policy Life Cycle. *Environmental Science and Policy*, 5, 221–231.

van Egmond, Stans & Zeiss, Ragna. (2010). Modelling for Policy: Science-Based Models as Performative Boundary Objects for Dutch Policy Making. *Science Studies*, 23(1), 58–78.

Vynnycky, Emilia & White, Richard G. (2010). *An Introduction to Infectious Disease Modelling*. Oxford: Oxford University Press.

Worboys, Michael. (2000). *Spreading Germs: Disease Theories and Medical Practice in Britain 1865–1900*. Cambridge: Cambridge University Press.

Wylie, Alison. (2008). Mapping Ignorance in Archaeology: The Advantages of Historical Hindsight. In Robert Proctor & Laura Schiebinger (Eds), *Agnotology: The Making and Unmaking of Ignorance*. Palo Alto, CA: Stanford University Press.

Yearley, Steven. (1999). Computer Models and the Public's Understanding of Science: A Case-Study Analysis. *Social Studies of Science*, 29(6), 845–866.

DOI: 10.1057/9781137298829.0014

Index

A/H1N1 (Swine Flu), 9, 61, 68, 76, 83, 85, 116
Abrahamsen, Adele, 65
asymptomatic carrier, 16

Bacon, Francis, 36
Baxter, 87
Bechtel, William, 65
behavioural assumptions, 70
Berg, Marc, 81
Bernoulli, Daniel, 11
Boumans, Marcel, 15, 36
Boyle, Robert, 36

Celvapan, 87
characters, 34
climate change, 82
computational techniques, authority of, 94
congenital rubella syndrome, 47
co-production of statistics and society, 95, 113
cross-disciplinary, 20

Daston, Lorraine, 41
data, 4
Dean, Mitchell, 61, 96
den Butter, 66
Desrosières, Alain, 95
De Vlas, 98
discursive space, 45
disease transmission, 14
Dry, Sarah, 67

ECDC, 78
economic modelling, 66
EMEA, 87
Espeland, Wendy, 95
Evans, Robert, 45, 114
evidence, 75, 85
    cycle, 94
    hierarchies of, 80
    silencing of, 80
    silent, 84, 90
evidential claims, 37
    as brokers, 39–40
    as containers, 39–40
    as mediators, 39–40
    enriched, 37–9
    flexible, 37–9
    simplified, 37–9
    stubborn, 37–9
Ewalds, François, 61
experiments, 35
experiments, virtual, 36
expertise, 20

Farr, William, 11
foot-and-mouth disease (FMD), 94, 97, 101, 102, 103, 106, 116
Foucault, Michel, 4, 61, 61
Fox Keller, Evelyn, 35, 41

'ghost writing', 81
Good-night kiss model, 14
governing by numbers, 94
governmentality, 61

DOI: 10.1057/9781137298829.0015

Guillain-Barré Syndrome, 88
GSK, 87

Habbema, 98
Haemophilus influenzae type b
  bacteria, 13, 15, 18, 23, 33
Hamer, William, 12
Hammer, 95
Hampton Frost, Wade, 10, 36
health policy, 114
Helsinki modelling project, 14, 17
herd immunity, 11, 12, 66
Hib, *see Haemophilus influenzae* type b
  bacteria
Hobbes, Thomas, 36
Hoover, Kevin, 30
Hutter, Bridget, 62

ignorance, 81, 90, 91
ingredients, 14
instrument maker, 36
Intelligent Customer Function (ICF), 94
interdisciplinary collaboration, 20
International Health Regulations
  (IHR), 67
interventions, 87
invasive infection, 16

Kermack, A.G., 16
kinship relations, 29, 30, 31, 32
'known unknowns', 78

Lambert, Helen, 81
Leach, Melissa, 67
life-cycle, 3, 44, 95, 112
Lomell, 95

magic, 94, 109
malaria, 12
mathematical methods, 13
McGoey, Linsey, 82
McKendrick, W.O., 16
measles, 12, 46
measles campaign, 51
measles, mumps and rubella (MMR),
  49, 50, 116

mechanisms, 65, 66
model
  Cambridge-Edinburgh, 101
  compartmental, 19, 56
  computer-based simulation model, 2,
    17, 35
  demographic, 17, 18
  EXODIS-FMD™, 101, 104, 106
  family of, 24, 25, 32
  Helsinki models, family tree of, 32,
    33, 114
  immunity, 17
  Imperial Model (TIM), 101, 106
  individual-based stochastic
    simulation, 17
  as instrument, 36
  InterSpread, 101, 106
  life-cycle of, 3, 44, 95, 112
  as playground, 20
  policy-initiated, 108
  predictive capacity of, 57, 63, 96
  Realistic Age-Structured Model of
    Measles Transmission (RAS), 53,
    55, 56
  Reliability (of model-based
    predictions), 73
  as senior expert, 97
  S-I-S, 15–16
  simulation, 35
  SIR, 102
  stories, 22
  structured population, 33
  transmission, 17
  'truth-machines', 63
  WAIFW, 53, 54, 56
  working life, 44
model-based evidence, 13, 41, 56, 94, 116
modelled encounters with risks, 61, 62,
  63, 69
modelling, 53
modelling exercise, 14
modelling methods, 2, 9–10, *see also*
  mathematical methods
modelling techniques, use in public
  health, 112
Morgan, Mary, 22, 35, 66

DOI: 10.1057/9781137298829.0015

multidisciplinary, 20, 104
mumps, 49, 51

national public health institutes, 23
non-carrier, 16
not knowing, 81, 82

optimal vaccination coverage, 22
Oreskes, Naomi, 82
Ortwin, Renn, 83, 90

pandemic outbreak, 9, 61, 68
pandemic scenarios, 67
pandemic severity, 86
    case fatality rate, 86
    clinical attack rate, 86
    hospitalisation rate, 86
pandemic risk assessment, 71
Pandermix, 87
Petticrew, Mark, 80
PnC, *see* Streptococcus pneumoniae
policy call, 21, 22
policy context, 35
policy cycle, 95
policy feedback loop (PFL), 97, 99,
    100, 116
policy instrument, 17
Power, Mike, 62
predictions, 64
    assessing, 87
    explanation-based, 64, 72
    immunity to Hib, 33
    scenario-building, 64, 68, 71, 72, 96
preventive measures, 14
probabilities, 95
Public Heath England, 47

quantification, 95
quantitative authority, 101, 113

reasoning, styles of, 10, 25
reproductive number, 54

reproduction rates, 54
risk, 61, 62
    assessment, 90
    statistical-probabilistic approach, 61
    epidemiological approach, 61
    sociological approach, 61
risk groups, 83
Roberts, Helen, 80
rubella, 46, 48, *see also* congenital
    rubella syndrome
Ross, Sir Ronald, 12
Rudinow Saetnan, Ann, 95

seniority, 111
silent evidence, *see* evidence
simulation platform, 17, 19
Sismondo, Sergio, 81
Stevens, Mitchell, 95
stochastic simulation, 102, 104
Streptococcus pneumoniae, 35
Swine Flu, *see* A/H1N1

Tamiflu, 77
Taylor-Gooby, Peter, 61
techne, 94, 96
    of governance, 94
technology of distance, 95
Timmermans, Stefan, 81
transmission, 11, 16
Trouillot, Michel, 78

unknown factors, 85, *see also* 'known
    unknowns'
vaccination policy, 46, 56

World Health Organization (WHO),
    21
'what would happen if' question,
    65
Wylie, Alison, 78

Zinn, Jens, 61

DOI: 10.1057/9781137298829.0015

Personal Media and Everyday Life

DOI: 10.1057/9781137446466.0001

Other Palgrave Pivot titles

Nikolay Anguelov: Policy and Political Theory in Trade Practices: Multinational Corporations and Global Governments

Sirpa Salenius: Rose Elizabeth Cleveland: First Lady and Literary Scholar

StenVikner and Eva Engels: Scandinavian Object Shift and Optimality Theory

Chris Rumford: Cosmopolitan Borders

Majid Yar: The Cultural Imaginary of the Internet: Virtual Utopias and Dystopias

Vanita Sundaram: Preventing Youth Violence: Rethinking the Role of Gender and Schools

Giampaolo Viglia: Pricing, Online Marketing Behavior, and Analytics

Nicos Christodoulakis: Germany's War Debt to Greece: A Burden Unsettled

Volker H. Schmidt: Global Modernity. A Conceptual Sketch

Mayesha Alam: Women and Transitional Justice: Progress and Persistent Challenges in Retributive and Restorative Processes

Rosemary Gaby: Open-Air Shakespeare: Under Australian Skies

Todd J. Coulter: Transcultural Aesthetics in the Plays of Gao Xingjian

Joanne Garde-Hansen and Hannah Grist: Remembering Dennis Potter through Fans, Extras and Archives

Ellis Cashmore and Jamie Cleland: Football's Dark Side: Corruption, Homophobia, Violence and Racism in the Beautiful Game

Orrette D. Clennon: Alternative Education and Community Engagement: Making Education a Priority

Scott L. Crabill and Dan Butin (editors): Community Engagement 2.0? Dialogues on the Future of the Civic in the Disrupted University

Martin Tunley: Mandating the Measurement of Fraud: Legislating against Loss

Colin McInnes, Adam Kamradt-Scott, Kelley Lee, Anne Roemer-Mahler, Owain David Williams and Simon Rushton: The Transformation of Global Health Governance

Tom Watson (editor): Asian Perspectives on the Development of Public Relations: Other Voices

DOI: 10.1057/9781137446466.0001

palgrave▶pivot

Personal Media and Everyday Life: A Networked Lifeworld

▶

Terje Rasmussen
University of Oslo, Norway

DOI: 10.1057/9781137446466.0001

First published 2014 by
PALGRAVE MACMILLAN

Palgrave Macmillan in the UK is an imprint of Macmillan Publishers Limited, registered in England, company number 785998, of Houndmills, Basingstoke, Hampshire RG21 6XS.

Palgrave Macmillan in the US is a division of St Martin's Press LLC, 175 Fifth Avenue, New York, NY 10010.

Palgrave Macmillan is the global academic imprint of the above companies and has companies and representatives throughout the world.

Palgrave® and Macmillan® are registered trademarks in the United States, the United Kingdom, Europe and other countries

ISBN: 978-1-137-44647-3 EPUB
ISBN: 978-1-137-44646-6 PDF
ISBN: 978-1-137-44645-9 Hardback

This book is printed on paper suitable for recycling and made from fully managed and sustained forest sources. Logging, pulping and manufacturing processes are expected to conform to the environmental regulations of the country of origin.

A catalogue record for this book is available from the British Library.

A catalog record for this book is available from the Library of Congress.

www.palgrave.com/pivot

DOI: 10.1057/9781137446466

Contents

1   Introduction: Personal Media   1
Writing, talking, watching   8
Modes of personal media   9
Autonomy and Ambivalence   11

2   Encircling the Person   16
Writing/reading   18
Writing with software   23
It's only about communication now   24
Tertiary orality   26
Talking/listening   28
Watching   32
Individualisation   32
Media of Self   34
Media of self-presentation   37
Extended familiarity   39

3   A Networked Lifeworld   42
Everyday life   43
Lifeworld in modernity   46
The Lifeworld Today   51
Domestication as personalisation   53
Everyday tactics   56
Relative distance   60

4   Communication in Personal Media   67
The interpersonal in the media   69
The 'communicative turn'   71
Luhmann on communication   74
Plurality of communication forms   83

5   Personal Media Theory   85
    McLuhan   88
    Modes of mediation   92
    Undermining representation?   96
    Situated simulation   97
    Convenient media   101

6   Personal Media and Social Capital   104
    Elements of social capital   107
    Capital in personal media   109
    Investing in the mobile as 'Link-up'   112
    Skills   114
    Capital dynamics in social media   115
    The problem of trust   122
    Resource distribution   125

Bibliography   127

Index   140

DOI: 10.1057/9781137446466.0001

1

Introduction: Personal Media

Abstract: *This chapter introduces the central argument of this book and its key terms like 'personal media', 'personalisation' and the 'lifeworld'. It exemplifies the unwritten history of personal media by focusing on media of writing, talking and watching, and also between their primary functional modes that are called* orientation, interaction, presentation and archiving.

Keywords: communication theory; digital media; everyday life; lifeworld; media theory; personal media; social capital; sociology

Rasmussen, Terje. *Personal Media and Everyday Life: A Networked Lifeworld.* Basingstoke: Palgrave Macmillan, 2014. DOI: 10.1057/9781137446466.0002.

This little book addresses the convergence of the mediated and the (inter) personal in personal media of everyday life. From the convergence of new multifunctional personal media and the lifeworld, a series of new questions arises that this book only begins to address, concerning sociability and social integration as well as power and control.

The book introduces three main underlying arguments: First, that what I call personal media has its own history and its own sociology, distinct from the mass media. Second, that the concept of the lifeworld helps to understand meaning and power in contemporary everyday life in western societies, and, yet, that it needs revision according to the new reality of personal and mobile media. And third, that the overarching values of society give way to more or less mediated social networks as generators for social cohesion and integration.

Unlike the mass media, personal media favour interpersonal contact with family members, friends, colleagues and others we know. Our 'face time', as Rich Ling notes, is being extended and embroidered by mediated interaction. The notion of an everyday life refers to something we all experience, but is far from established as an analytical concept in social theory. Concepts like 'everyday life', 'the private sphere', the 'lifeworld' and 'domestic' tend to overlap, while they are also tied to different theoretical traditions. From a Marxist perspective, the private sphere is the space of reproduction and consumption. From a Weberian perspective, everyday life in the modern world remains the sphere of non-instrumental action. As everyday values and practices constitute a foundation of the understanding of technology presented here, we should develop a conception of the hermeneutics of everyday reality. We can derive such a conception by beginning with Husserl's lifeworld concept as it is developed by Gadamer, Schutz and Habermas, and continuing to sociological interpretations by Heller, Lefebvre, Goffman and Gullestad. A concept of 'everyday life' should keep the basic hermeneutic epistemology intact, while leaving out a too rigid and descriptive understanding of the term. Methodically, it should be able to guide empirical investigations and to make sense of specific day-to-day practices in a larger context of social integration.

Everyday life is a mixture of the unnoticed and inconspicuous on the one hand, and the partly strange and abstract arsenal of goods and services for consumption on the other. In his essay on the urban way of life, Simmel famously discussed this confrontation between the ordinary and modern life. The familiar world of daily life is continuously dealing with standardised and mass-produced objects and structurally planned

DOI: 10.1057/9781137446466.0002

environments. The media explosion of course is one particularly noticeable aspect of the last two decades. How does this disruption take place when the computer and the mobile are placed in the terrain vague between the trivial and the unfamiliar? Is it really a question of disruption or confrontation, or a smooth assimilation? In subtle ways, everyday processes adjust and absorb new technologies and media, as they must with regard to news and information. This has interested ethnographers and sociologists for a long time, as they stress the appropriation of domestic consumption (Gershuny), objects (Miller), TV (Morley, Lull, Silverstone), mobile (Ling, Prøitz) and other media. Sociologists and theorists like Henri Lefebvre, de Certeau, Bourdieu and others have attended to studies of the ordinary with various motives, most importantly because that is where life is lived, this is where the world presents itself, conditioned by class, gender, ethnicity and the brutal randomness of life.

The mobile and the laptop are being massively incorporated into people's lives, which cannot remain unchanged. The integration of digital media in expressive and instrumental operations in everyday life matters and practices is considerable. It is difficult to say how radical the implications of personal media are on our lives precisely because communication and its devices are fundamentally ingrained in nearly everything we do. But common sense signals to all of us that the changes are dramatic – not because they disrupt the humdrum of daily life, but because they change the way we do ordinary things. Just like people in Europe did one hundred years ago, we read, play, talk, shop, cook, write, enjoy, listen and travel every day, but the ways in which we do it change because new technologies invite us into more convenient avenues of practice. We are surrounded by voices, music and other sounds, texts, images and textures, but from very different sources than those of our parents' generation. For the last decades or so, everyday communication in particular is affected fundamentally deeper than when the telephone, the radio and TV were introduced. Web, webmail, Youtube, Facebook, Google and a variety of app-based services are now basic ingredients in our lives that reorganise our experiences and practices in time and space; they enable new social networks in new forms and genres.

Much of the changes are about the transfusion of power from social institutions like the school, the workplace, the church and the university, to markets, media, the home and the individual. Synchronisation is made more flexible by social institutions, which make the individual and the family much more the centre of the world. Individual movements and

DOI: 10.1057/9781137446466.0002

interactions in everyday life are now more in the hands of the individual. This rearrangement of power, giving private life a new dimension of flexibility that was unknown to ordinary families in the post-war era, has been a central nerve of modernisation since the 1970s. It implies more freedom of choice for individuals, within structural delimitations. It changes the lifeworld. The rigid regularity of Weber's 'iron cage' is turned into something softer and more flexible, or with Bauman, more 'liquid', however also more integrated into techno-social structures than ever in the history of modern society.

This is the contextual background for this book in conjunction with technological change. In the following, I address changes of everyday life in theoretical terms, and argue that we need a different conception of the lifeworld to contextualise social interaction with personal media. The lifeworld concept helps to make sense of daily life if it can account for actual changes in everyday life as related to individualisation of identity formation and personalisation of media. An understanding of the particular values, practices, habits and rituals of domestic life is vital to the understanding and use of new media practices. In this regard, I think we need a quite different notion of lifeworld than Habermas' version.

Once we acknowledge that personal media technologically and analytically belong to another world than the mass media, another media history and media sociology appears. This history does not start with Gutenberg's mass production of holy texts, followed by newspapers, film and broadcasting. Rather, the history of personal media probably begins with private notebooks in Greek and Roman antiquity, followed by letter correspondence through couriers and postal systems. It continues with electro-magnetic telegrams followed by telecommunications and a variety of innovations on the Internet and the Web. This history is not about audiences but about social relations in an extended space: on how individuals and groups interact with absent, and yet specific, others, and by necessity – with oneself.

The emergence of a national and international media industry from the 17th to the 21st century (printed books, the press, magazines, broadcasting etc.) was based on various forms of technological means that served as media, from the production (supply) side to the consumption (demand) side of the audiences. These technical media served as dissemination media, and constituted in their very structure a rupture between production and consumption, which prevented responses and input from the members of the audience. This paradox, the bridging

DOI: 10.1057/9781137446466.0002

and fencing, the dissemination and separation, which constructed and addressed audiences precisely, enabled, from Gutenberg on, an enormous international media industry. Because this industry created audiences who were impossible to actually observe, the industry had to rely on implied audiences.

However, since 1995 or so, and based on more than 150 years of telecommunications and 40 years of Internet communication, media forms have emerged in daily life that deviate radically from the paradoxes of the mass media. A remarkable wave of innovation in the area of personal communication, largely connected to the laptop, the web and the mobile, constantly offers their services to the modern individual. This is mostly evident with regard to the Internet. Due to the distributed end-to-end architecture of the net, new innovations constantly emerge in its periphery that increasingly rely on user-produced content in one way or another. In the 1990s, the Internet and hypertext converged in the web. Around 1998, a new generation of the web began (outside the news sites) with a wave of innovations, which much more actively integrate user-produced content. In the telecom sector, large-scale investments have allowed for a wave of innovations based on the upgraded mobile as terminal. Involved in what Weber called rationalisation has personalisation as one of its most evident trends characterising contemporary complex society.

In social research, the term 'personalisation' has been used primarily by Japanese researchers to describe the trajectory of telecom-based media from the business market to the household and the individual, and the transformation of the media during this process (see Kohiyama 2006, Okada 2006, Matsuda 2005). In Britain, 'domestication' caught on in the 1980s as a concept describing the introduction of various media into the household. Also in the 1980s, diffusion theorist Everett Rogers applied the term 'demassification' to account for the range of new computer-based media like electronic bulletin boards and email. By personalisation I mean the reorganisation of technology according to the expectations of persons. Kohiyama (2006, 71) argues that personalisation involves enabling access to the broadest possible range of Who, What, When, Where and How, as well as enabling people to specify and restrict access based upon their individual needs. Personalisation refers to devices and their design, such as smartphones, handsets and laptops, to personalised connectivity through passwords, credit cards, and other security and authenticity functions, and finally to personalised services,

DOI: 10.1057/9781137446466.0002

like shopping and downloading. While laptop-based communication was ahead of mobile-based communication, this gap is closed. Phones, tablets and laptops are rearranging their places in everyday practices continuously.

A central distinction thus needs to be made between personalisation of information and personalisation of media. While the first is a transformation that concerns all media, the latter is a distinct trajectory in media history. Personalisation of information relates to selection and specialisation of services and features in the mass media along with linking to other media to establish feedback channels. Most of this kind of personalisation relates to strategies in the press and broadcasting to appear 'closer' to the audience through a number of techniques, ranging from informal talk, studio audiences, call-ins, SMS-TV and so on. This is largely an effect of the endemic structural paradox of the broadcasting industry and the press, the separation from the audience that the industries want to reduce. From the 1980s, the 'audience' has been a concept in crisis, as much more complex models of individualised and segmented audiences have emerged that use broadcasting as well as digital media to create new hybrids of communication and consumption. For instance, in the beginning of the 1990s, the TV-companies started to implement measures to gain individual TV ratings, rather than household ratings.

This book addresses implications of the personalisation of media, which refers to the neglected history and sociology of mediated interaction in private life, from the private letter to the telephone, the personal homepage, email, instant messaging, photo-blogs, the mobile and social networking sites. The sender acts as an autonomous being, as in taking holiday snapshots, making phone calls or running a personal blog. And for the last decade or so, the personal aspect has been even more intensified since personal media now make us each personally addressable and more or less perpetually accessible (Ling 2008, 3).

Of course, the processes of personalisation of media and the explosive adoption of personal media cannot be explained by technological change alone, but also by changes in society, particularly increasing personal wealth, urbanisation, changing consumption and lifestyle patterns, including for instance that young people spend more time away from home.

Typically, the history of personalised media is the story of the transition of communication media from military, organisational, domestic and then to personal contexts. In contrast to the mass media, the distinction between sender and receiver is often not of prime analytical

DOI: 10.1057/9781137446466.0002

relevance, as in letter correspondence and telephone conversations. Even the distinction between the initiator and the responder may not be necessary in order to understand social relationships. Personalising of media relates to transportation infrastructure and telecommunications, rather than to the history of mass media from Gutenberg to Fox. Rather than entertainment, journalism and adverts, this kind of information is about personal notes, practicalities, downloading useful information, chat for no particular purpose, making appointments, and airing of personal opinions in blogs and Twitter and so on. Thus, what is here called personal media does not produce mass communication and is non-mass media. They rather make up lines or threads of social networks.

As noted, the extraordinary about our new personal media is that they have entered the entire realm of the ordinary in less than two decades. They have become part of our conventions and habits, which in return have made the media ordinary and indispensable. The ordinary refers to what we do in everyday life and particularly the ways we conduct everyday practices like shopping, reading the paper, chatting with the bus driver and friends and family, listening to music, watching TV, wearing clothes, spending holidays and cooking dinner. Although many of these practices are signals of lifestyles and self-expression, they are also the low-key life itself, what we do while making plans and producing memories. The ordinary is a topic for reality shows, which is frequently discussed (see Bell and Hollows 2005). Here, ordinariness particularly denotes the mundane practices of keeping in touch, fulfilling one's obligations, relaxing, searching for a recipe, enjoying something and socialising in the ongoing business of everyday life. The indispensable emerges for exactly the same reasons. In brief, what seems to take place in everyday life is a series of expansions or transfusions which will be addressed in the following:

- ▸ from reception to production
- ▸ from interpersonal context to interpersonal communication
- ▸ from messages to communication
- ▸ from audiences to networks
- ▸ from domestication to personalisation
- ▸ from audiences to Self and other
- ▸ from the history of mass media to the history of personal media.
- ▸ from the history of media to the history of mediated communication

DOI: 10.1057/9781137446466.0002

Writing, talking, watching

Personal media are not new and have always been connected to meaning-constituting sensorial practices, particularly writing, talking and watching. While we normally use our senses in subtle combinations, media tend to specialise or combine more rigidly. The manuscript is for writing or reading, and occasionally we admire its beauty. Monocles and telescopes are media for watching. They tend to condition one another: writing follows reading, and talking on the phone is combined with hearing. The history of personal media is partly a history of combining sensorial practices linked to time and space in new combinations. Often, one of the sensorial practices is prioritised, with other sensorial practices accompanying. For the sake of ordering personal media in a social history, I believe it makes sense to study the history of personal media according to the leading sensorial practices that they manipulate. There is a history of writing (reading), a history of talking (hearing) and a history of watching (talking, hearing). I return in more detail to this point in the following chapter.

Personal media cannot meet the general expectations that media research traditionally formulates about the mass media. Rather, they ought to be conceptualised as media for personal production and reception of information, usually generating communication. The major sociological significance regarding the smart mobile for instance, is not that it is mobile as such (mobility is an effect of wireless protocols, its main technical feature), but that the mobility makes the phone personal, more so than the personal computer ever was. It enables constant personal contributions to verbal or textual conversations. And the number of web-based features and apps for the mobile that have emerged since around 2008 stem from new software and transmission capacity that make the web into a personal medium for presentation, interaction and archiving.

User-produced content is the substantial part of the genres and communication of personal media. We speak of personal media (today, mostly based upon the laptop, the 'pad' and the smartphone as hardware platforms) as something distinct from mass media. Personal media are designed for private individuals and are used for communication with one or many others in public, private and semi-public settings, and in institutional as well as non-institutional contexts. They are not only individualised (as are many mass media) but also personalised, as

DOI: 10.1057/9781137446466.0002

evidenced by user-identities and password-protections. In this, they go further than what Raymond Williams called 'mobile privatisation', and what Roger Silverstone and associates called 'domestication'. Another defining feature of personal media is that they enable user-initiated co-production of media content. Information and utterances become integrated as in phone conversations, SMS-interactions or networking sites. User-production affords presentation of self-reflective meaning, and thus a state of being in the world. It enables ongoing contact with distant and distinct others, and helps to coordinate everyday life.

Modes of personal media

Proposals on what distinguish new media from the mass media have put forward a series of analytical distinctions (digital media vs. analogue media, passive vs. active, interactive vs. non-interactive, monological vs. conversational, symmetrical vs. asymmetrical and so on), which quite often remain on the level of specific technological variants. But the convergence much debated in the 1990s also includes convergence between the digital and the analogue, between the digital media and the mass media. This obfuscates a clear-cut distinction between groups of media on technical grounds. And even if we were able to distinguish new media technically from the traditional mass media, our business is rather to understand the interplay between, or integration of, media and social life. Of interest are the social configurations that the various media provide.

In personal media, I distinguish between four ordering modes (or functions), which I call orientation, presentation, interaction and archiving. Up until the 1990s, they were connected to distinct technological platforms, such as post- and phone-based media of interaction and web-based media of presentation (personal websites and web-diaries, blogs), and computer-based archives and databases. The orientation function made a giant step with GPS and could be combined with the three other platforms.

With digitalisation and network convergence, technical distinctions blurred. The term 'convergence' referred to the fact that several networks, corporations and devices serve multiple functions, particularly the mobile and the laptop, and increasingly the TV set. Writing letters may afford presentation, interaction and archiving. Services may be used for

DOI: 10.1057/9781137446466.0002

other tasks and purposes than they were designed for. The platforms are increasingly used interchangeably for all functions, even if we still live in a world where archetype media like the wristwatch, wall calendar, camera and the plain old telephone co-exist with digital converged media. The smartphone is used for web services, which is an inroad to mobile TV and online news. Also, a number of websites and blogs draw upon presentation, interaction and archiving functions. A number of networking sites, such as Facebook and LinkedIn as well as blogs, apply both presentation and interaction functions in the construction and reproduction of relevant social networks for various purposes.

Thus the four functions in personal media – orientation, presentation, interaction and archiving – could refer to four types of media were it not for the facts of convergence and divergence as effects of social change and media digitalisation. Although it becomes less and less relevant to distinguish between personal media of orientation, presentation, interaction and archiving, they remain as modes in networks and platforms, which indicate the leanings and biases of distinct media architectures. Moreover, they indicate the existence of historical and theoretical inroads, which help us to understand these new developments more in depth. The distinctions between orientation, interaction, presentation and archiving are important to maintain for both historical and analytical reasons.

Orientation functions refer to meaningful location and mobility in time and space, such as is evident with the camera, the diary, the clock, the planner and the wristwatch. The perception mode refers to information about where and when, one's own or other's location in time and space. Perception refers to the body of the agent. In this case, the person acquires information from media like the map, the compass, the microscope and the telescope, the watch, glasses, the hearing aid, the calendar and GPS.

The presentational mode refers to what, to directing and attracting other's attention to one's publication of ideas, thoughts, opinions and information, as for instance in letters, SMS and on personal homepages on the web, blogs and twitter. Presentation functions are to be found in media as letters, business cards, books, homepages and blogs, where the individual (or group) presents itself to the world.

Interaction functions are for interacting with oneself and other individuals and groups such as with the personal letter, telephony, email and social media. The interaction mode refers to who, to media for social

DOI: 10.1057/9781137446466.0002

interaction between two or more persons, as with letter correspondence, the electro-magnetic telegraph, the phone, email, and social media. These media are often referred to as dialogical or two-way oriented, as opposed to one-way mass communication.

Archiving functions refer to the ability to store/save documents in a retrievable way, such as notebooks, letters, photo albums and databases. The archiving mode also refers to when, to material memory, to storage media used to preserve meaning for the future, to retrieve past information, as on tape, answering machines, laptop hard discs and other personal archives such as photo albums, Filofax and other personal filing systems. It also, as I will address in a later chapter, constitutes a method of forgetting, and thus a method of directing culture.

Autonomy and ambivalence

Features of communication technologies indicate that they enhance greater personal freedom and independence. They enable communication with friends, work-relations, information providers and so on, at the time and place decided by the individual agent. It seems possible to tailor information and communication to habits and routines of personal life. We can have our cake and eat it too: work, play, go fishing and skiing, drive a car or live in rural areas while still flexibly communicating and transmitting information with others. From this, one cannot but conclude that the individual is more in control of her own life than before. At least for the well-off western individual, the world consists of an abundance of social and technological systems of expertise and technology, with all kinds of needs and interests at our service.

This autonomy is of course an illusion. The only way to live a normal life is to make use of system-produced services in a stable and efficient fashion. The process may present itself as an option, but it also implies social control. Systems providing services and comfort necessary in modern life can rarely be ignored. In exchange, we renounce the knowledge and power to question, understand and evaluate decisions concerning our lives. Everyday life is to 'go on' in a practical and reflexive manner, by the use of system-produced support. Modern life is lived in the grey zones of what Weber called value-spheres (private life, politics, science, economy) with their corresponding roles. Individual pseudo-autonomy is reached through mobility in space and flexibility in time (Rasmussen 1996).

DOI: 10.1057/9781137446466.0002

Personal media play a decisive role in this, since they modify and stabilise everyday networks. Related to this is the argument that personal media are not technologies in a usual sense, as analysed by social philosophers from Karl Marx via Herbert Marcuse to Neil Postman. They are not simply standardised means and rules under the rationality of instrumentality and calculation. They may be media of power but whose power is not immediately clear. Their communicative dimension seems to make them evade the definition of technology as instrumental, which explains why personal media and everyday life easily adapt to one another. Their rationality is as much a reflexive and communicative kind, as a purposive or strategic. With the growing autonomy that follows the modern world of communication technologies, parallel forms of freedom and dependence emerge. To live a modern convenient life implies that identification as well as socialisation increasingly draws on media connected to large-scale systems. This implies freedom as well as vulnerability and risk, as when the credit card is not accepted, when the suitcase never appears on the baggage belt and when the computer ignores our commands. The paradoxical development of autonomy and dependence poses new challenges for the modern individual.

It is through the many good things that online personal media offer, most of all enhancing love, friendship and family relationships, that they also occupy our time, present mindless adverts and harvest and aggregate our data for their customers. As Edward Snowden explained to a world audience in the summer of 2013, the National Security Agency in the United States taps and processes our private communication. There are many things to worry about concerning some of the personal media. However, Sherry Turkle's worry is not among mine: 'On social networks, people are reduced to their profiles [...] We are increasingly connected to each other but oddly more alone: in intimacy, new solitudes' (Turkle 2011, 18–19). As long as online relations are mixed with offline relationships, this worry is exaggerated. The ones we text and talk and email with through our mobile or laptop tend to be people we often meet face to face. Yes, they are time-consuming, distracting and trivial, and yet also social and occasionally vital in the struggle for democracy. They may be used for harassment and in campaigns for social justice. It is a natural part of our rationality to seek out the most convenient ways for achieving our goals. Sometimes, the most convenient is what serves us in a long-term perspective, but sometimes it is not.

*   *   *

DOI: 10.1057/9781137446466.0002

In Chapter 2, I go into more detail concerning the history and evolution of personal media along the three sensorial categories presented in the introduction. One of the purposes is to demonstrate the diversity of personal media excluded from media history. Another purpose is to connect this history to the sociological perspective of individualisation. Important aspects of the media evolution took part in the definition of the person as a self-conscious and autonomous being. This is the 'mediatisation' of the human being as an individual and as a person that took place alongside other rationalisation processes examined in sociology, from Weber to Luhmann, Beck and Giddens, that created the self-reflective individual and (high)modern society. I address aspects of the media of writing, talking and of watching and illustrate their development historically. I argue with theorists like Giddens, Goffman, Bauman, de Certeau and particularly Foucault ('Technologies of the Self') that this development has formative power on the formation of identity and self-reflexivity of the individual. I address social relationships in everyday life as the application of a mode of 'extended familiarity' between intimacy and formality.

In Chapter 3, I introduce 'everyday life' as a sociological category and examine more specifically and critically the concept of the lifeworld. I follow the concept from phenomenological philosophy to sociology, and offer critical remarks on Jürgen Habermas' version of the concept, which points towards a revised notion of the lifeworld more compatible with a modern, mediated everyday life. I then link the concept of the lifeworld to more recent theoretical and empirical trends, particularly concepts of 'domestication' (Silverstone), another concept that needs to be updated according to recent social and technological change. I address domestication more specifically as 'personalisation'. I also connect to de Certeau's theory of strategy and tactics in everyday life in order to reach at a critical but bore network-like, 'thinner' (more individual-oriented) understanding of the lifeworld. With this chapter, the basics of the setting for sociological research on the uses of personal media have been set in an analytical sense.

Chapter 4 addresses media and communication research. It begins with assessing the role of interpersonal communication in mass communication research and concludes that mass communication models will not do in examining the use of personal media in current, everyday life. If communication at all, mass communication is a special type of communication that deviates from intuitive understandings of communication

DOI: 10.1057/9781137446466.0002

as some form of interaction or dialogue. Most types of personal media are true communication media. Therefore, we need to take a step back to the basic models on direct, unmediated communication. I briefly address the 'communicative turn' from Husserl to contemporary philosophy and sociological theory. Some communication-theoretical proposals are discussed that might position media studies and sociology of everyday life to make sense of communication in personal media as everyday communication. I particularly discuss N. Luhmann's communication theory in some detail in relation to actual media use. I argue that it serves examination of personal media well at the same time as it connects such use to more general sociological insights.

Chapter 5 takes the step from communication and genres to media technologies. It presents some reflections on the relevance of what has been called 'medium theory' in order to approach an understanding of personal media. I particularly revisit M. McLuhan's ideas, including his less known or understood 'Laws of media'. I then address some other medium theories inspired by McLuhan (Bolter & Grusin, Langer, Watzlavic, Meyrowitz and others) Medium theory, I argue, through its theoretical balance of technology and message, grasp the power of the technology and to what extent it can be 'tamed' or domesticated. I address both the discomforting aspects of dealing with virtual (simulated) realities and the convenience they offer in our sociality. I address the ongoing discussion both in research and daily life itself, about the relationship between the online and offline in everyday life. I illustrate with the very recent development of augmented media/situated simulations.

Chapter 6 examines the accumulation and dislocation of social capital in everyday life and the intermediary role of personal media, particularly social media. The concept of social capital I argue is sociology's main gift to the personal media researcher; it helps to get an a priori balanced view on mediated social relationships in everyday life, with an eye on power. I address various approaches on social capital (Bourdieu, Coleman, Putnam, Granovetter and Burt), and from this I define the main elements of social capital. Individuals (and groups) are embedded in social relations, but are not necessarily exercising pure purposive rationality. A balance between a conception of the 'undersocialised' and 'oversocialised' individual can be found, using the concepts of skills, social capital and social network. This is done in order to emphasise the structural and relational character of resources in everyday life, without ignoring individual abilities and the uniqueness of social situations.

DOI: 10.1057/9781137446466.0002

Thus the concept fills an analytical gap between individual practices and everyday social networks, whether face-to-face or mediated. I refer to research that illustrates the relevance of the concept in various situations and for various kinds of media, and towards the end I particularly address the problem of trust.

DOI: 10.1057/9781137446466.0002

2
Encircling the Person

Abstract: *This chapter goes into more detail concerning the history and evolution of personal media along the three sensorial categories presented in the introduction. It addresses aspects of the media of* writing, talking and watching *and argues with theorists like Giddens, Goffman, Bauman, de Certeau and Foucault that this development has formative power on the dynamics of identity and self-reflexivity of the individual. It presents social relationships in everyday life as the application of a mode of 'extended familiarity' between intimacy and formality.*

Keywords: communication theory; digital media; everyday life; lifeworld; media theory; personal media; social capital; sociology

Rasmussen, Terje. *Personal Media and Everyday Life: A Networked Lifeworld*. Basingstoke: Palgrave Macmillan, 2014. DOI: 10.1057/9781137446466.0003.

DOI: 10.1057/9781137446466.0003

It is certainly correct that mass media took part in the encircling of the modern mass society of electoral democracy, mass consumption and mass education. The story is normally reconceptualised in sociology as modernisation, rationalisation, differentiation and similar terms. In the shadows of this evolution of mass society, another trend also implicated the media. A glance at the history of personal media indicates that the nature of these media in mundane, everyday contexts up through the centuries and decades has told an underlying story connected to the theme of rationalisation as well, about how a long history of material means of communication has gradually 'staged' the human being as an autonomous individual. This chapter offers a few retrospective snapshots of the history of personal media to illustrate the evolutionary trend towards personalisation.

Unlike most histories of digital technologies, a personal media history stresses everyday unique communication rather than standardised production, and private and personal involvement rather than professional use. Here, I simply want to state the point that the long history of such media has been overshadowed by the relatively short history of mass media and mass communication on the one side, and the even shorter history of computers and telecommunications on the other side. While the first analytically excluded such media as the letter and the telephone, the latter focused on professional use. The hitherto unwritten history of personal media may lead to a richer understanding of past and present social life where such media play an increasingly prominent role. The history of personal interaction over distances adds to the understanding of long-term trends.

Media and their physical elements (quills, brushes, pencil, pen, paper, typewriter, keyboard, joystick etc.) are material things that culture use for the production of meaning. Whether manuscripts, printed documents, radio programmes or websites, they are dead things that can talk to us and for us through the invention of code and genre. They are therefore both dead and material, and human-related and social. We study the material aspect in order to see how different media, through their internal dynamics, have influenced different cultures and epochs, and we study the social aspects in order to see how genres and styles have endured across epochs and media shifts. They are neither neutral information vehicles, nor are they only the productive and seductive forces of history over which we have little influence.

DOI: 10.1057/9781137446466.0003

Certainly, a key aspect of many personal media is that they transcend local, place-bound contexts of practice. The mobile is used for private matters, often in public contexts, occasionally to the irritation for others. Typically, personal media tend to define new social contexts in and through their use, but increasingly the use of personal media is omni-present and close to context-independent. Most personal media used for communication undermine established boundaries for social interac-tion. And new ones are created, such as coffee-places now often serving as office landscapes. To understand the media-daily life dynamic, it is therefore important not to define media contexts rigidly. The range of information and communication from the intimate to the very public appears as a continuum where even the involved parts are often not in accord with their status. The main point here is to highlight the diversity of mediated communication that is not produced by mass media organi-sations, and to suggest perspectives on how they influence everyday life.

To present a comprehensive history of personal media lies beyond the scope of this book. Here I can only indicate, with some elements as examples, the range and span of such a history. As indicated in the intro-ductory chapter, we may observe the history of personal media according to the leading sensorial practices that they manipulate as sub-histories of writing (reading), talking (hearing) and watching (talking, hearing).

Writing/reading

While talking is the synthesis of social action and communication, writ-ing is the synthesis of social action, communication and the media. It probably began with the papyrus, the grass-like plant that has grown in the Nile river delta for thousands of years. With papyrus, nature was transformed into materiality. The plant was sliced lengthwise into long strips and laid in rows dried in the sun. It was, however, paper that made writing into a social practice. Paper was invented in China in the second-century CE and was carried to Europe in the 12th century by Arab traders (Levy 2001, 9). In European medieval monasteries, paper production was based on the mashing of plant fibre, spread out in thin layers and dried. The sheets could then be written on with a quill or a brush. Even if paper was more fragile than parchment from skins, it was cheaper to produce. But because of the quality of skins, paper did not supplant skins completely until the end of the medieval ages. When

DOI: 10.1057/9781137446466.0003

animal skin was used, the hair was removed, then stretched and sanded. The surface was thin and extremely durable. Unlike papyrus, parchment could be marked on both sides (Levy 2001).

Of course, the printing press created great demand for paper. Paper was then made out of rags from old clothing made of cotton, linen or hemp. As late as the mid-19th century, with the invention of the steam engine, techniques for making paper out of wood became commercially viable, and laid the foundation for a society that relied more and more on documents of all forms. Already by the end of the 13th century, a written document could serve as a witness and statements of facts. With the invention of carbon paper (in the 1820s), paper came to work well with the general need for speed and type-written documents in the late 19th century. This again gave way to new filing methods, such as the Dewey Decimal System (Levy 2001, 68).

By that time, the private sphere needed written and typed communication such as receipts, prescriptions, travel guides, tickets, maps, memos, job announcements and passports. Collections of such everyday media are historical documents telling stories about prices, appearances and travels. Private life needed documentation. Collections of tickets inform about moments of travels and events. And greeting cards, business cards, and postcards are all examples of everyday genres that do not seem to disappear with digitalisation, simply because they provide convenient forms of interaction. Most of these forms of notes and cards, including the Christmas cards, came into use in the 18th century. These are modern phenomena that indicate a growing complexity of social settings, with the corresponding need for social rules.

In Japan, textual communication (writing) has been more preferred than mediated talk. The most popular internet service on the mobile is email, and text messages are used more than voice calls among young people (Okada 2006, 49), beginning with the display on the pager in the early 1990s, where the caller typed in the number he or she wanted the receiver to call. This initiated a learning curve applying small mobile means for textual communication. Other reasons for this are that voice was more expensive than text, and that, in most countries and more in Japan than elsewhere, norms reduce speaking on the phone on collective means of transport and in other crowded public places.

With News-groups and email, the Internet was a text-only medium up until the early 1990s, and still text is dominating, however in junction with other medium forms. With the web and the *blog*, new writing

DOI: 10.1057/9781137446466.0003

media appeared that could quickly reach a limited group of readers who are familiar with the author or share the author's interests. Features known from the personal homepage were combined with elements from the discussion forum and online news sites into a flexible personal medium for both presentation (individual control) and social interaction (Hodkinson 2007, 626). Whether the emergence of the blog and other personal media like the mobile is likely to encourage more individualistic developments of identity cannot be positively confirmed. And yet we may safely assume that individualism and personal media generally coincide in time and are interrelated and mutually reinforcing in complex ways. No doubt the individualistic zeitgeist in our times encourages innovation in the areas of personal media and of personalisation of mass media, which provide means for developing identity. There are clear signs that parts of the audiences of radio and TV, as well as users of collective digital media like user-groups and large-scale discussion forums, expand or migrate to a wide range of media that underline individuality and identity. For instance, Hodkinson (2007) found that, when interaction moved to blogs, communication became more distinctly individual both in the form of diversity of content, format of conversation and networks of 'friends'. Personal media 'expect' and 'encourage' personal style and content at the expense of group or mass cohesiveness. Blogs (through their link features and comment facilities) and the mobile (through their conversations and messages) encourage sociability in the shape of networks, a more flexible and less norm-influenced form of sociability.

We used to think about intimate relationships as *close,* but that was before chatlines, partylines and datelines emerged in the late 1980s. In such services, a dial up chat may lead to conversations with another individual, without revealing identities, which may lead to a face-to-face meeting. In many countries, this service began as a low-status activity, partly associated with prostitution. In contrast, the chat rooms on the Internet that were introduced in the late 1980s and reached high popularity when appearing as web-services in the early 1990s were often seen as valuable and serious alternatives for singles. Today the diversity of discussion forums is vast, covering most segments, interests and tastes. The seriousness was also higher for Instant Messaging Systems that appeared in the mid-1990s (ICQ, AOL, MSN, YIM) and provided chat rooms as well. Anonymity is a feature that in most face-to-face and mass media settings is unacceptable. With the Internet, anonymity and pseudonymity was turned into a force to boost new services, making anonymity and intimacy not adversaries but companions. Technological

DOI: 10.1057/9781137446466.0003

innovation along with the human taste for carnivals and masquerades allowed this. In modern 'single' society, such forums provided new sites for romance and intimacy.

Beginning around 2005, the mobile entered this laptop-dominated landscape of 'lonely anonymous hearts'. In many countries following Japan and South Korea, major Internet portals offered chat rooms and conversation possibilities for strangers on mobiles, such as Dodgeball, Playtxt and Livedating. Already in 1998, devices enabling teenagers to find each other when out were introduced in Japan. Lovegety, Coofy, ImaHima and Navigety were simple devices for locating friends and sending small messages (Tomita in Ito et al. 2006). Online and mobile communities dedicated to various interests appeared, similar to the ones already established on the laptop. The smaller screen and keyboard proved no serious drawback, at least not compared to the advantage of extended mobility. Also, when linked to GPS, the location of services and people were included in digital personal communication. This digital managing of physical place implied that offline and online worlds merged even more.

In 1996, the now ended service ICQ ('I seek you') was introduced that made the service freely available for anyone with Internet access. A number of Internet messaging (IM) services were introduced by AOL, Microsoft, Yahoo and others. IM grew out of the use of electronic bulletin boards and online services built on dedicated software from providers such as Prodigy and AOL, and also from the Internet activity in the 1990s in chat rooms implemented in web communities. IM had a number of characteristics that made it suitable for youth communication. IM was a medium for quick asynchronous interaction, usually between two persons, in contrast to Internet Relay Chat, which was normally group-oriented. IM enabled private 'rooms', and one could have several dialogues going simultaneously. But IM also contained possibilities for chat, file-sharing, talk, streaming content and so on. And contrary to email, it assumed constant presence, similar to text messaging, its successor. Contrary to texting, it provided information on whether the other is online, and so provided an additional element of social control. When entering IM, one immediately could see who among one's friends were logged on. The buddy-list was a document of nodes in one's personal networks. The IM could enable individual relationships and at the same time underline one's membership in a peer group. It is precisely this duality that made it suitable for children from around the age of ten.

DOI: 10.1057/9781137446466.0003

Particularly for the youngest, the importance of having a long buddy-list was an ongoing confirmation of popularity, as is the case with the phone list and the friends-list on Facebook.

With IM, one could have a sense of control with several persons in one's peer group. It could be used as a secondary (background) medium, while doing primary activities. In this medium, it was not the group but the me–you relationship in the context of a larger peer group that proved attractive. Also, the group had a sense of being together even if the members of the group were not actually communicating. A message saying one has to 'leave' for dinner with the parents confirmed togetherness. The privacy of the channels made them trusted and suitable for intimate talk. Still, research indicates that youths did not find IM particularly enjoyable (Kraut et al. 2002, 215). This however could simply be a sign of integration in everyday life. As with the phone, it seemed to be the mundane convenience offered by IM that made it into a very frequently used medium for a distinct cohort. Following ICQ, MSN Messenger and Yahoo! Instant Messenger appeared, but did not apply any open protocol. The proprietary nature of these services prevented interoperability and undermined their robustness. The results of the work of Internet Engineering Task Force Group on this (the IMPP-working group) came too late. After around ten years of existence, IM lost its attraction, due to the popularity (and universality) of text messaging and chat-functions at web-based social networking sites.

The first text message (SMS) was sent by NOKIA engineering student Riku Pihkonen in 1993 (Agar 2003, 177). Expectations are generally high that messages are responded quickly to keep the network sufficiently dense in order to keep the awareness of a chat alive. Not contributing would create speculations and disappointments. Studies of SMS use report on the pressure to interact and the worries that emerge if messages are not returned. SMS thus represents an immediate mode of communication, and works on the assumption that the others are already 'here' even if the connection is not kept open (Ito and Okabe in Kraut 241). What emerged was a social network of binary interaction that fostered a temporary social space of 'us'. The network created an impression of togetherness in a stripped or 'thin' way. Particularly for young people, this medium appeared as a 'place' for socialisation among peers. Text message sequences are media for direct or pure interaction in the sense that openings, greetings and conventions of politeness are considered redundant.

DOI: 10.1057/9781137446466.0003

Particularly notable about everyday text messaging ('texting') was that the meaningful unit of analysis was not the singular message but the ongoing sequence of exchanged messages between close friends during the day. The singular message is often only a line or queue in an ongoing chat. In communication terms, the SMS channel does not open and close for each message but is already open and accessible as in face-to-face talk. That is why delayed SMS-replies are considered rude or exceptional. They generate a private space that is filled with everyday half-baked utterances or expressions and signs, each with little significance, but important as constitutive elements in talk. No other medium comes closer to being assimilated in everyday talk in this way.

Writing with software

A sociological remark is apt here. To apply technologies of writing to talk in email, on blogs and on Facebook is not an altogether trivial matter. Today, power is to a large extent what the sociologist Talcott Parsons called *influence,* or even *ideological* power, and ideologies are mediated through writing. That is why so much energy is invested in the design and rhetoric of modern texts, in all media, in all genres. Writing is a careful practice receiving its social significance from its rhetoric as much as from its substance.

Ideological power lies with those who possess this technique of producing rhetorically efficient writing, in the shape of novels, political propositions, scientific publications, schoolbooks and web pages. It is a form of power, which changes the social hierarchy of society by lending social status to the scientist, the bureaucrat and the author of books, web pages and documents. The power is exercised on behalf of all of us when we act out our roles as family members and consumers who only read and talk.

The web page does not alter this constellation between readers and writers by changing the imbalance between written power and oral-reading powerlessness. It is, however, quite clear that the web already has triggered new ideas of participation and new updated forms of democratic activity. The questions are: how are these structures to be handled? Can the human character, the person's integrity be identified on Facebook walls? Can we disclose the ethos, the common sense of the competent individual behind the blog?

DOI: 10.1057/9781137446466.0003

The resources at play here are of two types: (1) the medium of writing that records experiences and tells the stories and (2) the hardware and software as instruments of writing that cut across whatever is reported through them. *Inscription,* in actor–network theory, belongs to the latter type. Inscription means the way artefacts embody patterns of use. The term describes how anticipations and restrictions are involved in the development and use of a technology.

Media technology puts its mark on social expressions by leaving certain distinct traces of such action. Methodologically, we need to go beyond what is written as a road to the writing itself, and further, to the changes in self-presentation as a consequence of technological structures. The mark of the technology is seen in the design. The use of communication technology is constituted by semantic and normative rules, power and skills, along with material resources applied by the actor in interaction processes.

Anthony Giddens (1991) defined *structure* as sets of rules and resources that both empower and constrain social action, and that tend to be reproduced by that action. Structure is the medium and outcome of action. Applying software like Dot.mac Homepage, Yahoo's homepage program, Powerpoint or Blogger implies that one adjusts one's practices to certain flexible, but also already existing, structures. We are involved with the 'acquisition of technology and its dispositions' as Pierre Bourdieu could have formulated it.

It's only about communication now

Among the first modern philosophers of the modern and autonomous Self, Rousseau pointed out that to become a subject both in terms of reason and in terms of emotions, one must stand out from society. A distinction is made between me and not-me. The text appears as an object and it works upon the subject because the subject articulates itself through the text. As Jay Bolter (1991, 210) noted, the reflexive character of writing gives the writer a new awareness of self. The writer observes her objectified or externalised other on the page or on the screen. The words stand out as if delivered by someone else to the writer, as if the writer was the addressee. Over time, it influences memory and gives continuity to meanings and attitudes. Writing creates a text and affects the author. It becomes an instrument for self-change.

DOI: 10.1057/9781137446466.0003

The paradox of the recurrent objectified text describes a modern fact of writing as a medium of identity-formation in modern societies and itself a hallmark of these societies. The truth is no longer out there, in old tales or from the reading of the Holy Book. Even the Bible now is more than anything else simply *a book*. For most people, Christians as well as non-Christians, the Bible must be read critically, interpreted, worked on, invested in and so on. This requires dedication and will. Basically, this is the case with all relations we have with those that George Herbert Mead called the Generalised Other, that are involved in our personal development. To be or not to be is a question of hard work. And this lends authority to the texts that we draw upon in our lives, authority not as the voice of tradition, or the voice of God, but as *produced* authority, authority as a written text.

Therefore, as any other Self, this Self has no final form. Unfinished selves that appear on the screen indicate the Self as something dynamic and unfulfilled. New life experiences are added, and old events are described with new words, with new programmes and revised design. In this way, this Alter ego Identity can be easily updated (and therefore also *outdated*). Still, a norm or a line of continuity must be followed, as it is the same individual who is presented in this running autobiography. What does the updating of the screen-based self imply for the subject? What kind of discourse is narrated? The blogger operates selectively. Cutting and pasting, writing, showing, linking, documenting, narrating, playing with words and images is the nature of autobiography, as it probably is for all sorts of self-documentation practices. For the reader, the personal homepage is not a miniaturised, textualised version of the author. It is *not* a projection, *not* an extension of the Self, it is a mask in front of someone, with a complex relationship to what is behind. The blog or web page as a writing tool for autobiography is designed for this shaping and structuring of a presented self. History and the past are easily wiped out, the mistakes and the disappointments of life disappear. The pure Self remains on the scene in an almost parodic position. It is a subject that acts upon the world, that makes achievements, that explores his world, that makes statements and that is conscious about his ability to change his living conditions. The blog therefore became a performative symbol, a writing act that gives the author a name in public or semi-public space in the universe of the web, and which places him or her in the world of meanings and people. Keeping a web page or a blog is to make space for oneself in a world of stories, citations and recitations. It is an act of

DOI: 10.1057/9781137446466.0003

identification, like showing a driving licence or a passport, only far more detailed and informal, and apparently digging much deeper in the Self.

In sociology, this paradox of freedom and dependence of social integration is theorised in terms of differentiation, system colonisation, trust and risk. Giddens conceived of trust as a medium of interaction with the abstract systems that both empty day-to-day life of its traditional content and set up globalising influences (Giddens 1991, 3). And what Habermas called 'colonisation' is a displacement of action from the hermeneutical processes of understanding embedded in lifeworld contexts which produces an instrumental and objectivating attitude, rather than an understanding of engagement with other subjects. In a system-theoretical approach, the development of a Self marks the manifestation of a personal autonomy from society, and at the same time the individual's increasing dependence on society. Society is characterised by individualisation and system-formation. Ulrich Beck and Zygmunt Bauman formulate this point similarly to Luhmann: society applies individualisation as a form, in which society can reproduce itself as society. Society cannot any longer integrate its members entirely through encompassing values and tradition – it has to find other ways, relying on communication networks. The credo is mobility and reflexivity under the condition of social contact!

Tertiary orality

The blog is produced by individuals (or families/private groups) in the mixed capacities of private persons, clients, citizens or consumers. The blog's relationship to its author is not one of truth, objectivity or accuracy. It constitutes itself as a relative autonomous space where the author invites himself/herself to a social space. The asynchronous nature of blog presentations makes them more comparable to personal and private textual forms like the notebook, the diary and the letter than to speech interaction. But the potential mass audience of blogs and personal web pages makes them into quite a different type of presentational medium. They are not only writing media, they are media for personal publishing, often composed as a multi-modal collection of texts and other media – and genres. As text, it is dynamic and flexible, some would say more 'alive'. It is far more synchronous than printed books. To some extent, it can be compared to a newspaper, which contains several media forms,

DOI: 10.1057/9781137446466.0003

and which is updated daily, within the same format and style. Both homepages and blogs are referred to as *personal journalism, self-publishing* and even *self-advertising.*

Speaking involves appropriation of language; it establishes a social bond with the other in a network of places and relations. These characteristics are also valid for practices like 'using' in day-to-day life, and create room for innovative practices about system preferences laid down in products. To indicate the boundaries of everyday life, Michel de Certeau (1984) made a distinction between *literacy/writing* and *orality*. *Writing* represented the formal power of documents, isolated from the context where it originated. This imposed an impersonal character on messages. In the scriptural economy, writing mediated strategic relations, whether scientific, bureaucratic or economic. It represented the modern way of defining lifestyle, morality and truth, and thus a way of codifying and controlling life. On the other hand, the *oral* exists for the speaking and the hearing, and is informal, emotional and intuitive in its nature.

de Certeau is probably right in that typed text is still the primary medium of modernity – TV and film never changed that fact. When the spoken word seeks authority, it needs the dis-enchanting verbal reflection in writing. This is the case in education, politics, economy and science. The word must distanciate itself from the simple and universal magic of the voice without any backup. As de Certeau writes: '... one can read above the portals of modernity such inscriptions as: Here, to work is to write, or: Here, only what is written is understood. Such is the internal law of that which has constituted itself as Western' (de Certeau 1984, 134). Orality became subject to a scriptural intervention and containment, as in TV and radio. This is Walter Ong's 'Secondary orality' (1982/1991). Even poetry had to give in to the typed book.

Today, we have entered another stage of orality. Now orality relies on rewriting, downloading, recording, transmission and networking. Oral voices are heard everywhere, but given authority through a number of presentation and storing media, from the blog to pod-cast. This is the 'third orality'. This new orality possesses some sort of autonomy, which gives it freedom to present itself in many different shapes. It is manipulated text in a much more subtle and complex way than the word. It is often involved in a strategic game. The page on the screen is a place involving not just utterances – it has become a more lasting product in time and space, which gives the text an objective and also personal touch, and therefore more responsibility. It not only *derives* from the external

DOI: 10.1057/9781137446466.0003

world, it turns *towards* the world from the outside and wants the world to conform to it. Unlike the spoken comment, the web page wants to be a social fact, if not in a big way, and regardless of the content as such. In this sense too, it is not only a statement, but also a perlocutionary speech act, an appeal or a demand.

The text consists of verbal text and photo and establishes a detailed and explicit system of elements, a complex and ordered composition or *bricolage*, such as the newspaper or a birthday invitation or a homepage on the web. The text may include several genres or media forms. Still, it is the verbal text that gives the other media elements a place in the hermeneutic patchwork and therefore the text as a whole is the shape of an ordered totality. Writing (verbal and pictorial) has primacy.

In this multimodal process of rhetorical convergence, both writing and images seem to receive new functions: As Bolter and Grusin (1999) argued, technology has the effect of making text image-like by representing its verbal structure graphically. On the web, the emphasis on design is radicalised. Java applets, icons, touch screens and clickable links give the writing a visual, symbolic style. This writing is more informal, inventive, less rule-bound and more rule-playing, more talk-like. Email and the blog seem to be another way to 'write the voice', as perhaps is the case with typed poetry. It seems like this hybridity gives this kind of writing a more oral style, and so opens the way to undermine the regime of the written. Maybe it gives the oral a new chance through these new forms of writing. Maybe this is a new way in which everyday talk makes use of writing to reach beyond then-and-there situations.

Nevertheless, to repeat, the semiotic difference between writing and orality prevails. They remain distinct systems of meaning-combating as well as supporting one another from without. Furthermore, the written document still has priority because systemic rationalities in science, politics, law, markets and education depend on it.

Talking/listening

While the telephone revolutionised talk as a collective medium for the working place and the family, the mobile telephone brought in the personal dimension. Technically it all started in the beginning of the 20th century, and socially, at the end of it. In 1910, the Swedish engineer Lars Magnus Erichsson built a telephone into his wife's automobile. In order

DOI: 10.1057/9781137446466.0003

to use the telephone, one had to stop the car and wire the telephone to the telephone wires on poles alongside the road. Power was generated by cranking a handle. This was the first Erichsson phone and a playful beginning of the substantial role of mobile telephony in Scandinavia (Agar 2003, 10). However, what made the mobile an 'impossible' medium up until the 1970s was not the idea of connecting telephones to one another through radio, but that the limited radio spectrum was already reserved for military and commercial interests. The requirement of one unique frequency for each phone call made radiotelephony a dream. Of course, the dream came closer to a reality when D. H. Ring developed the idea of cells that divided up the spectrum, which allowed for several callers to use the same frequency at the same time as long as they did not occupy the same cell. The idea was constructed in such a way that the system could identify all users, and the driver did not have to be concerned with passing from one cell to another. Still, even if Bell Labs invented the transistor that allowed for smaller and lightweight handsets in 1947, switching technology was too slow to handle the cell method. Unlike today, the technological development was almost completely the responsibility of large-scale national and quite hierarchical monopolies that did not rush to change the direction of a very successful ride.

Later, in the early 1990s, the US radio spectrums were auctioned or handed out through lottery in each city or district, which created a system of local monopolies and modest competition. Also, the receiver of a mobile phone call was partly charged for the call. This made it into an issue of money to keep one's number limited to some few callers. It was a kind of reversed network effect that served to keep the growth lower than in Europe. Also portable phones were not an immediate success because the car radio took care of much of the need in the car-culture of the United States (Agar 2003, 43). In contrast, in Scandinavia, the Nordic Mobile telephone system (NMT) and then the European GSM mobile system were products of long-term research hosted by the national telecoms. The radio spectrum used was considered a national resource that was dedicated to the new kind of phone. Similarly the new digital standard GSM in the 1980s and 1990s was made into one of the pillars of the European project; it was to provide a material basis for increasing cooperation in science and industry, and in the next instance allow stronger political and cultural integration. And in GSM, some small and hidden possibilities were waiting to be discovered, first of all SMS. The success was undisputed; the GSM phones were smaller, lighter and

DOI: 10.1057/9781137446466.0003

better designed. The first truly portable and personal phone had reached the market of personal communication.

In Japan, NTT first developed the first 'Shoulder phone', a car phone, in 1985 that could be carried around in a shoulder strap. In 1987, the first handheld cellular phone was offered by NTT, primarily for professional and organisational purposes (Okada 2006, 41). It was typically an organisation and not an individual that was listed as the rental subject, which indicated its collective and not yet personal status. Around 1996, the adoption rate for mobiles was 25 percent in Japan. But Personal Handyphones (PHSs) (see later) were still the preferred mobile device for teenagers. Partly due to the competition from the PHS, the telecom dropped its rental model on mobile phones and introduced discounts.

When the privatisation wave hit the telecoms in the 1980s (England) and 1990s, (Scandinavia) the infrastructure was all in place. In Japan, NTT DoCoMo launched a new digital standard in 1989, which created a fast growth of subscribers. DoCoMo's I-mode service took off around 2000. Like the WAP in Europe, the content providers of I-mode had to be approved by DoCoMo, but this meant quality as much as censorship. With the I-mode service, one could reserve tickets, check bank balances, transfer money, subscribe to a number of information services, and send and receive email. It became immensely popular among teenagers and young people in particular.

In the beginning of the1990s, *the pager* developed into a personal medium through a number of changes in Japan. In the late 1980s, and after deregulation of the Japanese telecom market, NTT marketed the 'Pocket Bell' pager, which showed digits and letters on a small display (Okada 2006, 43). The sender could type in a call-back number, subsequently independent of organisational limits. In conjunction with the phone, this made the pager into a useful device for private and personal use, particularly among teenagers and students. Students quickly relayed messages in their own codes, which we more famously know from SMS texting. This was largely a Japanese phenomenon. From around 1993, the clear majority of the subscribers were private subscribers. Typically the peak hour of use changed from early afternoon to 10 pm (Okada 2006, 44). In 1996, pager subscriptions hit around 15 percent nationwide in Japan. Among high school students, the adoption was close to 50 percent (Okada 45).

Soon, of course, the mobile took over. However, in Japan, a substantial part of younger users took a detour via Telepoint. London's Telepoint System was introduced in 1989, but was mainly in use in Japan, China

DOI: 10.1057/9781137446466.0003

and Thailand, and to a lesser extent in India, Indonesia, Vietnam, The Philippines, the United Arab Emirates, and Ethiopia (Kohiyama 2005, 65). Telepoint is a system that can either be seen as a digital element of the (analogue) home cordless extension of the regular telephone system, or as mobile telephony 'light'. Technically, it was a system of cordless phones connected to the fixed telephony system, and was generally conceived of as a mobile system. It consisted of several small antennas in an urban area to be used by small wireless terminals. In Japan, PHSs were launched in 1995 for Telepoint, and were far cheaper than the mobile phone, and the terminal was lighter, smaller and with a longer battery life. Telepoint could not be used within homes, but it was possible to call from some urban point and it could be maintained up to walking speed. However, already in the mid-1990s, it was clear that the operator could not make profits, partly due to network charges paid to the NTT. Terminal manufacturers lost interest, since the terminals were given away by the PHS providers. At the same time, the Japanese *keitai* (the Japanese mobile) approached the size, weight and battery life of the PHS (Kohiyama et al. 2006, 65).

As Okada (2006, 45) points out, the pager and the *keitai* began their career in professional spaces, and extended their territory as the flexibility of the media increased and users' demand and experimentation transformed them into private and personal devices. That personalisation involves de-professionalisation as the typical process of the telephone, pager, the mobile, the computer, email and the web. However, the process is even more fine-grained than the step from the office corridor to the living room and the pocket. First, most communication technologies emerge not in the business sector, but as military technologies, which subsequently get 'civilised'. This is the case for a wide range of media from the electro-magnetic telegraph to GPS. Second, as Japanese studies show (Yoshimi in Okada 2006, 45), the phone moved from the office, to the hall, then to the living room, then cordless and extension phones were set up in bedrooms, before eventually being further extended and transformed into the pocket phone.

To be sure, this transfusion from defence to business to the household and then to the individual is not without variations and exceptions. More importantly the journey will not stop with the personal terminal. We see a continuing personalisation of products and services on the Internet. Personalisation moves further – from individuals to things, from houses and cars to fridges, bikes and suitcases.

DOI: 10.1057/9781137446466.0003

Watching

Finally, a brief note on long-distance seeing. Around the turn of the century, mobiles quite rapidly became camera-phones, and less than a decade later, almost everyone carried cameras in their pocket. This phenomenon took advantage of another tradition, that of family snap-shots. Amateur photography reached a new personal and at the same time more public level with George Eastman's Kodak camera in the 1880s (Kitzmann 2004). It documented domestic events such as birthdays, holidays and weddings (Jacobs 1981/1986, Levine and Snyder 2006). The web camera wave probably got its boost from the Kodak, and later the one-time use camera was introduced in the 1990s, which made the family camera into an individual and more mobile device, and was very popular among Asian teenagers.

In Japan, Photo Club was another very popular service that preceded the camera-phone (Okada 2006, 58). Photo Club was photo-booths on arcades in the cities to take photos and make them into stickers. The 'cam-phone' quickly generated a variety of services on the Internet like iPhoto and other programs on computers, and sites like Flickr, Photo.no on the Internet. More importantly, during the first decade, third-generation mobile telephony was adopted considerably slower in the United States and Europe than expected by terminal and service providers. In Japan and South Korea, Internet on the mobile quickly became a success from the beginning of the century, and is primarily used for email to mobiles and laptops. This was a step forward, as SMS messages could only be sent to other subscribers of the same service provider. Other services currently provided to the mobile besides the Internet are location-based services (GPS) and TV. The introduction of Skype and competing services trans-formed it further into an even more universal machine for communica-tion. The mobile more and more resembles the internet-connected laptop functionally in that it is used for a variety of weak-tie purposes: checking one's business -mail, watching the news, trying to get in touch with the plumber, planning the week or ordering a haircut.

Individualisation

I have sketched some aspects of the transformation towards mediated personal communication, emphasising Asian developments in order to

DOI: 10.1057/9781137446466.0003

highlight cultural variation. My argument is that this development is deeply implicated in what sociology terms individualisation. Forms of individualisation or 'cultural privatisation' take place when institutional rituals in local communities, trade unions and churches have their influence and authority reduced as the private sphere becomes even more important, and when traditions and rituals take place in the home rather in the local institutions. This is interconnected with a growing emphasis on the individual as a meaningful unit for rights and responsibilities and leisure, with less confidence in politics and the news media, and with other local social changes such as immigration. Sources for social identification move from work and church to family, friends and the media. This trend of transmitting responsibilities from institutions to domestic space leaves the family with pressures that it does not have the capital (human, social, cultural) to handle, and therefore must delegate decisions to the individual. The individual must more than ever reflect and act on her own course of life as an individual in a social environment of strong and weak social ties. Individuals with the help of social resources, rather than groups, make decisions concerning the individual. This is also of course a question of social capital. Individualisation is thus often a side effect of de-collectivisation, which again is a consequence of higher standards of living, expansive capitalism, and deregulation and privatisation of public affairs. This does not indicate that social groups and neighbourhoods are devoid of social significance for the individual. Individualisation and cultural privatisation should not be exaggerated and taken for granted in social analysis. Communities of various forms tend to be important background-resources for the well-being of the individual. We are talking about a general trend, first addressed by classical sociology, and currently in, for example, lifestyle and consumption studies (Blokland 2003, Bell and Hollows 2005).

Personal identifications do not necessarily mean a sense of belonging and direct dependence, only familiarity and recognition, indirect interdependence and therefore sufficient trust. The lifeworld provides background-resources that enable the individual to make coherent interpretations of his/her social reality. Rather than only being members born into social groups like the family, they are, to a larger degree than some decades ago, also 'associate members' that gives them the freedom to select and make priorities among social contacts. Identification, as Blokland (2003, 210) notes, is a less straightforward affair, however still a social matter.

DOI: 10.1057/9781137446466.0003

Institutions are to a lesser degree 'social facts'. Communities unite, but they may also divide. Ties are of many kinds, involving the whole sociological repertoire of rationalities and group constellations. They create bonds and bridges. None of these possibilities should be *a priori* excluded in studies of everyday life. In the analytical landscape between rational action, personality theory and theory of morally integrated communities lie the pragmatic and critical observations of this book on person and his/her media.

Media of Self

In the early 1980s, Michel Foucault became interested in how individuals work to make themselves into subjects. There was a certain change in his interest from the discourses that objectify the Self, to the question of how the individual constitutes *himself* as subject. This became clear in the third volume of *History of Sexuality*, and in a number of his late, 'ethical' texts. Foucault addresses this as a question of how the individual forms himself/herself into an autonomous subject. The question for the individual, and more so in modernity than before, was: 'Who are we in our actuality? Who am I today – in the world I am living in?' The answer has increasingly indicated an autonomous subject. This reflection and the freedom and ability to act upon it puts the individual into a position where it can, with more or less success, influence itself by certain means that it has at its disposal. Today, we may say that a more independent image of a Self gradually appears as a model for self-development. Current ideas seem to indicate the process as follows: I am not just like others, I am something different from what the expectations say I am, I can be different according to situations, I can perform in different ways, *I can change myself!*

To understand oneself as a subject, the individual draws upon certain techniques, what Foucault called *Technologies of the Self*: 'Technologies of the Self [...] permit individuals to effect by their own means or with the help of others a certain number of operations on their own bodies and souls, thought, conduct, and way of being, so as to transform themselves in order to attain a certain state of happiness, purity, wisdom, perfection, or immortality' (Foucault, in *Technologies of the Self*). Foucault notes that the question of writing and the self must be posed in terms of the technical and material framework in which the Self exists. He traces such

DOI: 10.1057/9781137446466.0003

writing back to Seneca and Greek and Roman antiquity, where the ethos became to take care of oneself, and to know oneself. One had to occupy oneself with oneself. The primary technology of the self, of course, was writing. From Plato onwards, taking care of oneself became differentiated from concerns about political life. To be concerned with oneself became related to ongoing writing activity. The individual became a subject for writing.

The Notebook: first, the notebook or copybook (the hupomnemata) was used in Plato's time. It was used for accounting, public registers and as a personal notebook serving as an aid to memory. One wrote down quotes, extracts, examples, things that one had seen and experienced, and reflections. The notebook served as an objectified, materialised record of things of significance for the individual. This new technology, says Foucault in the early 1980s, was as disrupting to the ancient Greeks as the introduction of the computer is today. The notebook served as an object to be written into, to be constantly read and to be an object for conversation. It was always at hand in everyday life, and was important in the subjectivation of the discourse. The purpose was to capture what had happened, to collect the past, as a resource for the shaping of the Self. It was meant to counter distraction and sudden changes of mind, by directing one's attention to this gathering of thoughts and reflections. It involves a selection of different elements, and of omitting and adding. It was a personal exercise for oneself. The point is to constitute a sort of unity of all these fragments of experiences and thoughts.

The letter: the other early Technology of the Self is the letter. Writing letters involved that one read what one wrote and in this way also addressed oneself, as well as the one who received it. The letter did, unlike the notebook, constitute a way to present oneself to another. The writer becomes present to the one who receives it – both through the telling of the facts of his life, and through the assurances that the other is in one's thoughts, that they are together, in spite of the physical distance. In a sense, Foucault writes, the letter sets up a face-to-face meeting. And the letter sets up a gaze outside the writer. The letter looks back on the writer, and shows the writer for himself.

Later on, writing as a means for self-examination, and for the cure of souls, was and is important in Catholicism and later in the Protestant movement. In Christianity, this was developed further as question of morality and conscience. In this cultural context, to know yourself was, rather paradoxically, to renounce one's needs as in ascetism, as a

DOI: 10.1057/9781137446466.0003

condition for salvation. The confessional, purification and sexual abstinence are other self-forming techniques that belong to this tradition.

The 18th century was, as Habermas notes in his book on *The Public Sphere*, the century of the letter because of the more developed public postal systems in Europe, and literacy among the growing working class. The postal system enabled quicker circulation and more meaningful exchanges of information. The letter is a genre, involving a sub-genre such as the love letter. It unites the privacy of the diary with the confession. But it is also a medium, and the genre is coloured by the technical features of the letter (its private character, its storing and objectivation of the written word, its circulation in time and space, its rhetorical way of reconstituting the dialogue in spite of absence). In the 18th and 19th centuries, it developed into a medium for the family and private life, more distant from religious reflection than the diary. By the end of the 18th century, the literate population felt at ease with the new subjectivity it mediated.

In the 20th century, a number of other modern techniques of self-expression are late contributions to this long development of personal media, which serve as media of the Self. Current cases of personal media of self-presentation like the personal website and the blog, as well as a number of network-oriented sites, can be interpreted in this historical context, and so indicate what is new and not so new in this recent development. Drawing on and extending Foucault's work, we may bring historic light to some aspects of this technology that appears to be so fresh and new, but really falls into a long tradition of self-mastering and self-caring. To construct a personal web page is to equip oneself with a dynamic mirror where social relations and contacts, personal experiences, what one has read, seen and understood can be seen, not so different from Seneca's notebook.

Interestingly, Foucault discusses this in terms of ethics. The Care for one self is an ethical practice, because it is supposed to constitute the individual as a moral subject, a subject that is responsible for his own actions. For what is ethics, says Foucault, if not the conscious practice of freedom? Freedom is the ontological condition of ethics. Ethics is the considered form that freedom takes when it is informed by reflection (Foucault 1994, 284). To become a subject is ethical work. It is a self-generating ethics. Then the question is: what are the means by which we can change ourselves in order to become ethical subjects? In recent times, it has been viewed as an aspect of *Bildung* (education) in a broad sense. What are the instruments of ethics that enhance reflexivity?

DOI: 10.1057/9781137446466.0003

Media of self-presentation

Perhaps, Foucault exaggerated the self-caring argument. There is also another aspect, here, which Foucault and others could not consider in full: what is truly new with the web is the element of self-mastering through *self-publishing*. Now, not only The Other, or a few Others, enables the resonance for self-caring, but conceivably *the whole Internet world*. Even if the actual number of Others remains relatively few in most cases, this potential public recognition changes. Thus, we need to consider the vital technological differences that exist between the media that Foucault addressed and the web. It is quite interesting that this writing in public, this 'Tertiary Orality', is available for all, not only for intellectuals. Is it not the first time in history that the individual as a private person has the possibility to write whatever he wants to a public? Is it not the first time in history that an ordinary person can present himself in writing to an audience? The personal web page and related genres are the voice of the people, in a form that makes it visible and recordable; that is, *another* voice outside the edited reality of the mass media. This technology of the Self has become a publishing medium for the Self, a medium for public presentation of Self.

The web presents itself as a new medium of self-presentation and self-reproduction, along with a number of other more symbolic resources, if more general in their articulations. In other words, since this form of self-writing, this form of Technology of the Self, takes the shape of *Media of the Self*, the practice is not only turned inwards, and not only towards a distinct individual, as in letter correspondence. It is a form of self-orientation that takes a loop outwards to a larger audience. It lies in the technical nature of the medium. It is a presentational mode. In order to present oneself to others, one presents oneself to oneself. To write publicly is to write to oneself, in a different way than in the case with writing letters to another individual. It is to observe many others' observation of oneself, because one has to read what one writes. It is to place oneself in the centre of the public eye, even if the eye is usually more local than global.

This presentational mode leads to practices as *performances*. To understand such everyday performances, we must realise that everyday life is a drama. Dramaturgical action is one of the main forms of action models analysed in sociology. More than anyone else, this model is associated with, and elaborated by, Erving Goffman. Here, social action is

DOI: 10.1057/9781137446466.0003

understood as an encounter where participants appear as the audience for one another and not only act, but perform for each other. The performance makes it necessary for the individual to act in specific ways, in order to present himself positively, to get positive attention and to avoid conflicts and disappointments. The projection of a certain impression is done in accordance with principles of dramatic performance. Every social act has a performative dimension, a stylistic dimension, which is a confirmation of the social aspect of the act. We play, and play out different roles in a reflective way that may conform to the definition of the situation.

This is about how we all behave performatively towards the external world. This cuts across norms, instrumental aims, feelings and desires. It consists of this adopting an attitude towards the world and oneself in order to go on in everyday life, to keep what Goffman calls the 'Interaction order' in place. This is a dramaturgical model of interaction as a medium of self-presentation in social encounters.

A useful conception for understanding the difference between performance and preparation are Goffman's well-known terms 'front region' and 'back region', which refer to different motivations and conventions of conduct (Goffman 1959, Meyrowitz 1986). Goffman labels as 'front region' that part of the individual's performance which regularly functions in a general and fixed fashion to define the situation for those who observe the performance. 'Front region' is the facade; it is expressive equipment of a standard kind intentionally employed by the individual during the performance (Goffman 1959, 32). The front region is the place where the performance is given. On the other hand, the 'back region' is defined by Goffman as a place, relative to a given performance, with aspects of the activity, but consciously suppressed in the front region. In front regions, performers are in the presence of their 'audience'. In back regions, on the other hand, performers are sheltered from their audience and so behave differently, apparently more real or natural or relaxed, although back-region behaviour can be regarded as playing roles as well (Goffman 1959, Meyrowitz 1986, 30).

Goffman's metaphors aptly illustrate how individuals change behaviour according to context and how both kinds complement and support each other in reproducing personal and social life. Everyday life consists of a wide range of stages of all shapes, serving as back and front stages for each other in a mosaic of contexts, varying in size, temporality, explicitness, level of activity and hierarchy and so on. The web page is another very clear case of this, where the web presence is very carefully

DOI: 10.1057/9781137446466.0003

put together in a sheltered space, later to be observed on the front region of the screen. Goffman's work is about the nature of face-to-face encounters, and is a very suitable place to start in order to get a clear picture of differences and similarities between face-to-face interaction, and electronically mediated interaction.

Extended familiarity

After the depression in the 1930s, the conditions for mass consumption improved because of a stable increase in standards of living and public intervention in social security. Taylorism had already introduced principles for rational and efficient mass production. Fordist production of consumer goods accelerated after the Second World War focussing on the family as primarily a consumption unit. An emphasis was put on design, fashion, taste and improved ways of distribution and retailing. Middle-class norms achieved hegemony in consumption modes (Bell and Hollows 2005, 3). Through design and marketing, consumption goods achieved more explicit symbolic power and entered the expanding world of lifestyles more directly. A further differentiation of style and trends followed in the 1960s and 1970s led to deeper symbolic boundaries between generations. Production and marketing for the exploding consumer market headed a post-Fordist trend of the exploring segments and niches. The consumer was increasingly someone who made frequent aesthetic choices, to affirm cultural memberships and reproduce distinctions. These distinctions are connected to relationships to the labour market, as it is related to ethnicity, gender, generations and so on. However, increasingly consumption appeared as a series of personal and family decisions in a project of the Self. Lifestyle consumption is today investment in modes of sociability, with the individual as chief investor.

The path highlighted here can be addressed by a wide range of terms that characterise communication as consumption, with aspects of civility, friendship, intimacy and contact enrolled in commercial services and products. They involve relative trust and familiarity, referring to social relations where the communicating parts have sufficient information about the others to establish stable social relations. Talja Blokland (2003) argues that *the familiar* lies between anonymity, where information is minimal, and intimacy, which denotes relationships where the ratio of exchanged personal information is very high. Blokland

DOI: 10.1057/9781137446466.0003

(2003, 91) distinguishes between three forms of familiarity: private familiarity between people in private spaces, institutional familiarity between people who generally feel affinity to the same values and usually belong to the same category (a peer group, a school class, a football supporter club) and public familiarity between people who are anonymous to each other (as in a neighbourhood and in a virtual chat forum). Taken together, the familiar characterises the bulk of ordinary relationships in and outside personal media.

While communication based on the mobile and the computer is seen to serve loose social networks, it could be argued that it also serves to keep subcultures together. This is particularly the case for the mobile. While it clearly integrates youth culture and business cultures, it is also a channel for the individual who switches between cultures, from family to business, or from schoolmates to the soccer team. When people act as bridges between networks, the mobile increasingly is a prime medium. International data also suggest that the prime use of the mobile measured in frequency of calls is to call home, which could be as much a sign of family integration as of individualisation. Whether the increasing sensation of necessity to communicate among family members is furthered by, or a consequence of the mundane mobile, the fact is that it is a tie to children and spouse. Another frequent form of use is to call friends and relatives, which similarly could be interpreted as practices leading to community and integration. What Habuchi (2006 in Ito et al. 2006) calls telecocoons are zones of intimacy where individuals can maintain their closest relationships even if they do not see each other much directly. This fact of course has much to do with establishing exclusive trust. Prøitz (2007) has studied such telecocoons through ongoing text-message conversations between close friends. The smartphone along with longer battery life, flexible pay-models and ubiquitous connectivity underline and facilitate loose couplings between individuals and their social groups and communities. Social integration slowly modifies itself; it gradually takes the form – not so much of networked individualism, but of *networked personalisation* (Wellman 1999, Wellman and Haythorntwaite 2002). We are dealing with 'media of mass destruction'.

Although the owner of a mobile gets a rather 'personal' feeling about the device, it is not more of a body part than the wallet (see Habuchi 2006 in Ito et al. 2006). Certainly, particularly in its first years, the mobile was personalised through ring tones, background image and stickers. After the possession of one or two mobiles, the most significant

DOI: 10.1057/9781137446466.0003

personalisation steps are the implementation of the contact list and the selection of 'apps'. However, the mobile is included in a small number of objects that individuals constantly need to be aware of and bring, like keys, wallet, wristwatch, handbag and so on. Rather than embodied, these objects are personalised; they are made into natural and yet significant objects that are taken into consideration, especially before some form of mobility. Our relationship to the mobile is rather that of awareness. They are elements in the small-scale plans we produce and revise during the day. They are certainly personalised in several ways, but only to the extent that we are able to have a reflexive relationship to them whenever necessary. Precisely because our lives consist of plans and decisions, these objects also need to be kept at a certain mental distance, and thus be reached reflectively.

In these ways too, the person came into being as a modern subject; his/her senses were mediated and at the same time ensnared by convenience and progress. Identity and sociality benefitted from and grew dependent on media that not only explained the large world, but helped us reach the Other, and simultaneously the Self. Our lifeworld became rebuilt, not only in its human and social dimension, but in its very structure.

DOI: 10.1057/9781137446466.0003

3

A Networked Lifeworld

Abstract: *This chapter introduces 'everyday life' as a sociological category and examines more specifically and critically the concept of the lifeworld. It examines the significance of the concept from phenomenology to sociology, and points towards a revised notion of the lifeworld more compatible with a modern mediated everyday life. It links the concept of the lifeworld to the more recent Anglo-American concept of 'domestication', addressed more specifically as 'personalisation'. It connects everyday personal media use to Michel de Certeau's theory of strategy and tactics in everyday life.*

Keywords: communication theory; digital media; everyday life; lifeworld; media theory; personal media; social capital; sociology

Rasmussen, Terje. *Personal Media and Everyday Life: A Networked Lifeworld.* Basingstoke: Palgrave Macmillan, 2014. DOI: 10.1057/9781137446466.0004.

DOI: 10.1057/9781137446466.0004

The classical sociologist Georg Simmel once wrote: 'On every day at every hour, such threads are spun, dropped, picked up again, replaced by others or woven together with them. Herein lie the interactions between atoms of society, accessible only to psychological microscopy, which support the entire tenacity and elasticity, the entire variety and uniformity of this so evident and yet so puzzling life of society' (Simmel 1997, 109). Here, Simmel comes close to describing what more than a hundred years later appeared as a networked lifeworld. In the following pages, I would like to examine the concept of the lifeworld as a portal to the meaning of personal media in their current use. In order to be useful for such empirical research, however, the concept needs to be revised on several points in light of tendencies in advanced societies in general, and recent media change in particular.

Everyday life

An a priori distinction between face-to-face contact and personal media use in everyday communication has little explanatory value and is increasingly misleading in the understanding of young people's everyday life. The distinction between face-to-face versus mediated 'virtual' contact is not of prime interest. Rather, the question is how individuals use their skills to maintain their everyday life with the networks and means they have at hand, along with the skills and reflections involved in reproducing their social ties. This would indicate how various media and social practices are interwoven, and may inform changes in everyday life, particularly among young people. Thus, the guiding distinction here is not direct versus mediated contact, but rather how sentiments of intimacy, trust and social capital are socially differentiated according to different social practices and spheres, with or without media. Rather than organising research according to a distinction left behind by most people, the question is simply how people handle their repertoire of media according to their needs, aspirations and actual possibilities. This is a *pragmatic* perspective on media use: people tend to choose among, and use media in ways that are practically (instrumentally) useful and convenient for them. Questions of media use are brought a step closer to a familiar sociological theme: how people get on in everyday life, related to socialisation, advancement, friendship, love and so on in a media-saturated network society.

DOI: 10.1057/9781137446466.0004

Social research has long since stated that materiality and technology are embedded in particular contexts and social structures that make up everyday life. We can only make analytical distinction like the ones by Venkatesh, Chen and Gonzales (in Kraut et al. 2006, 110). They distinguish between three main elements of domestic space: social space, technological space and physical space. Social space consists of members and activities, time spent on them and interactions in the home. The technological space refers to technologies and artefacts that are embedded in the physical space and used by the members in the social space. The physical space consists of the physical materiality and layout of the home. In real life, the three forms of space are interwoven.

Therefore personal media are always, if only partly, socially shaped in and through contexts of use and society. This is quite obvious for us now, but it surely makes it more complicated to establish general statements about social use of media in daily life. Additionally, with personal media, the materially based reaching out of the user, and the motivations and purposes, may vary even more than with the radio and TV. The structures that create regularities in the use of personal media probably belong more to general social structures of everyday life, its mechanisms of privatisation and intimacy, than to the technological features of the media.

What has been termed the 'transformation of intimacy' includes transformation towards mediated intimacy as a central component. The 'pure' relationship endures only through romantic love and cannot rely on underlying, sustaining support like paternalism and tradition and negative sanctions against divorce. As traditional expectations have weakened, it lives more on its internal communication in various forms. As such, it is a vulnerable and a risky journey. As we know, the dissolution rate is high. Communication, and therapy when it fails, is expected to carry the burden of integration of a relationship or a family for a long time period. This has, as has personalisation and individualisation, been interpreted as one strand of rationalisation or modernisation among many (Jamieson 1999, Giddens 1992). The transformation involved is intimate communication and mediated communication. Contemporary intimacy is, to a large extent, flows of words to which feelings and understandings are attached – in the text messages, the blog, the emails, the Skype and the dating website. This does not mean, as Gross (2005) notes, that traditions have lost their grip; what he calls 'meaning-constitutive traditions' continue to shape new intimate relationships. However, these

DOI: 10.1057/9781137446466.0004

are more to be located in communication itself and less in the values of society. This too puts personal media into a more strategic spot. Social identities are deeply enmeshed with individual identities – we build self-representations by linking to others (Baym 2010, 111). Online connections embed us into collective pools of information and social networks that invoke shared conception of insiders and outsiders. Social networks may confirm and intensify sociological variables like social status, social class and gender.

Everyday life is a mixture of the unnoticed and inconspicuous on the one hand and the partly strange and abstract arsenal of mass-produced goods and services for consumption on the other hand. Georg Simmel famously discusses this confrontation between the ordinary and the new urban life more than one hundred years ago. The familiar world of daily life is continuously in process, dealing with standardised and mass-produced objects and structurally planned environments. The media explosion of course is one particularly noticeable aspect of the last two decades. How does this disruption take place with the computer and the mobile placed in the terrain produced by the trivial *and* the abstract? Is it really a question of disruption or confrontation? In subtle ways, everyday processes adjust and absorb the news of objects and media, as they must with regard to news and information. This has interested researchers in ethnography and sociology for a long time, as they stress the appropriation of domestic consumption (Gershuny), objects (Miller), TV (Morley, Lull, Silverstone), mobile (Ling, Prøitz) and other media. Sociologists and theorists like Henri Lefebvre, de Certeau, Bourdieu and others have attended to studies of the ordinary with various motives, most importantly because life is lived right there – in the ordinary everyday life in fasions conditioned by class, gender, ethnicity and the brutal randomness of life.

The idea of the lifeworld is helpful here because it provides a foundation for a hermeneutic view on everyday media use as meaningful activities. Personal media use is fairly coherent and rational. Also, it may indicate how personal media transform everyday life, through the new forms of social interaction in time and space that media technologies provide. The question is how media technologies mediate and reproduce the lifeworld in different ways. The lifeworld concept, I argue, can potentially greatly help us to make sense of daily life changes if it can account for individualisation of identity formation and personalisation of media. An understanding of the particular values, practices, habits and rituals

DOI: 10.1057/9781137446466.0004

of domestic life is vital to the understanding and use of new media practices. As will become clear however, I think we need a quite different notion of lifeworld than what has become known through Habermas' theory of communicative action. In the following, I address the changes of everyday life in theoretical terms, and argue that we need another conception of the lifeworld to contextualise social interaction, with and without personal media.

Lifeworld in modernity

Generally, the idea of the 'lifeworld' is a key to the phenomenological critique of the philosophy of consciousness. While the philosophy of consciousness conceives of the individual as an independent subject vis-à-vis the world of objects, the lifeworld designates individual experience as produced by immediate interaction with the world. The unconscious, ongoing constitution of the lifeworld precedes ordinary interaction with the objective world.

Alfred Schutz (1967) converted central ideas from Husserl's phenomenological thought into sociology. He also derived his concept of action from Weber and viewed it as subjectively meaningful behaviour oriented towards the practices of other individuals. He did not, however, accept Weber's emphasis on purposive rationality, as he considered it a too narrow perspective on human life. For Schutz, the lifeworld is constructed through non-reflective practices, the natural, non-theoretical, taken-for-granted imperative of action in everyday life. The lifeworld is the world always within reach, consisting of significant projects within a definite time–space. The lifeworld is the *Umwelt*, the 'vivid presence' populated by fellow individuals, between past experiences (*Vorwelt*) and future projects (*Folgewelt*) (Schutz 1978, 136; Rasmussen 2000).

> It is central that first, Schutz understands the lifeworld to be an *a priori* dimension of reality recognised by common sense. Within this province of meaning, experiences are designated as unquestionable. Second, the lifeworld is an intersubjective, shared world. As the reality is self-evident to the subject, it also incorporates awareness about the experience of others. The subject takes for granted that this knowledge is accessible to others. Third, the lifeworld is precisely defined by the taken-for-grantedness. It forms settings where situational horizons shift, though it constitutes a totality of what is taken for granted. It is placed in the flow of experience as a given and familiar province.

DOI: 10.1057/9781137446466.0004

As we move outside the given setting, into the *Mitwelt*, new complexes of meaning open for us as lifeworlds. Schutz also distinguished between different zones of operation. The primary zone is the lifeworld in its real sense; a primary world within reach, with the ones with whom one has a sense of shared time. In contrast, a secondary zone is populated by contemporaries within a greater, and normally mediated whole, which may always potentially be included in the *Umwelt*. (Schutz 1978, 258; Rasmussen 2000)

For Schutz, the lifeworld stands in contrast to the increasingly anonymous and bureaucratic relations of modernity. He argued that the pressure on the everyday lifeworld from societal structures is a key problem of modernity. According to Habermas, however, the differentiation of structures in modernity and the less penetrating taken-for-grantedness in modernity cannot easily be accounted for. Since the lifeworld concept in Schutz is an *a priori* fact, it is unsuitable for investigation as to how it has changed historically, and how its social condition could be otherwise. According to Habermas, the problem with phenomenological sociology is that it constitutes a basis for not much more than descriptions of the internal occurrences in the lifeworld from the perspective of the members. Habermas thinks that the social phenomenology from Husserl and Schutz is unsatisfactorily connected to the philosophy of consciousness. It is too trapped in the internal self-interpretation of the members in the lifeworld, and is thereby inhibited in pinpointing structural problems.

Habermas thinks that the sociological turn in Schutz' contribution to phenomenological sociology is therefore incomplete and seeks to repair it through two important revisions. *First*, he adds a system perspective so that the lifeworld can be seen from without and from a developmental perspective. *Second*, from the lifeworld, communicative action develops as a *complement* to the lifeworld. These two moves make it possible for Habermas to demonstrate how the rationalisation of society creates structural gaps and conflicts, and opens up a potential for rational development – a fulfilment of the project of modernity.

However, in Habermas' theory of modern rationalisation, the concept of the lifeworld appears in different shapes and for different theoretical purposes. First of all, it is: 'a reservoir of taken-for-granted, unshaken convictions that participants in communication draw upon in cooperation processes of interpretation' (Habermas 1987, 124). The lifeworld is a source of situation-definitions that are presupposed by participants as unproblematic. It is an intersubjective world hermeneutically demarcated

DOI: 10.1057/9781137446466.0004

from the common objective world as well as from the individual subjective world and it is present as long as it constitutes a background for an actual context of action. (Habermas 1984, 70) As soon as the context itself is brought into the scene, it becomes a part of the situation and loses its triviality. It is then no longer taken for granted as an unproblematic background. The lifeworld '...supplies members with unproblematic, common, background convictions that are assumed to be guaranteed; it is from these that contexts for processes of reaching understanding get shaped, processes in which those involved use tried and true situation definitions or negotiate new ones... Every new situation appears in a lifeworld composed of a cultural stock of knowledge that is 'always already' familiar' (Habermas 1987, 125; Rasmussen 2000).

Practices are embedded in the unproblematised realm of the lifeworld: 'Communicative actors are always moving *within* the horizon of their lifeworld; they cannot step outside of it. As interpreters, they themselves belong to the lifeworld along with their speech acts, but they cannot refer to "something in the lifeworld" in the same way as they can to facts, norms or experiences' (Habermas 1987, 126). The lifeworld is, drawing on Parsons', differentiated into the structural components of *culture, society and personality*, each of which produces resources for maintenance of the lifeworld, which Habermas accordingly labels cultural reproduction, social integration and socialisation. The lifeworld reproduces itself through cultural tradition (culture) which supplies meaning, social integration through norms (society) which supplies solidarity and community, and through socialisation of the young (personality) which supplies 'I-strength', the competence needed to stand forward in relation to others. The structural components of culture, society and personality are realised linguistically in the lifeworld. They produce cultural understanding through symbols, regulation of action and personal identity. The lifeworld reproduces itself through all three levels when contexts are interpreted in relation to the social order culturally, socially and subjectively. If the reproduction of *meaning, solidarity or identity* fails, the lifeworld ends up in a pathological shape.

Linguistic interaction takes place against the horizon of the lifeworld, against an unproblematic background of convictions, derived from the interpretative work of preceding generations. The lifeworld, as a conservative counterweight, constitutes a complement to rational argumentation. The less a cultural stock of traditional knowledge is present, the more dependent the communicative situation is on rational

DOI: 10.1057/9781137446466.0004

agreement. The modern dilemma of the lifeworld is that it is located in the dynamic between the normatively ascribed agreement (e.g. tradition) on the one hand and rational, communicatively achieved understanding on the other hand.

However, Habermas' perspective poses problems (see McCarthy 1978, Bernstein 1985, Honneth and Joas 1991, Rasmussen 2000). Habermas initially introduced the concept of the lifeworld from the participant's perspective, but transformed it to an observer's perspective, as a concept for critical analysis. The concept then focuses on the sociologist as an observing participant, and becomes transformed into 'everyday life' (Schnädelbach 1991, 18). An unfortunate dualism appeared with this: 'The action-theoretic approach inserts at least two actors at the microstructural level of groups and leaves the macrostructural level to be modelled in terms of systems theory'. Habermas does not intend system and lifeworld to operate towards one another as macro- and microlevel (Habermas 1991, 262). Still, due to the connection of lifeworld to everyday life, and of systems to formal organisations and markets, this dualism not only appears as a methodological abstraction, but as a dualism that runs substantively throughout the theory (Krüger 1991, 153). What systems theory refers to in modern society, Habermas (1991, 256) argues, is more than analytical. Modern capitalism has created economic systems that operate as self-steering, functional sub-systems (Habermas 1991, 257).

This dualism in Habermas' theory is doubled with the dualistic notion of steering media (communication vis-à-vis money and formal power) as coordinating the lifeworld or social systems. The system-originating media (in contrast to communication) appear structurally as independent of or only strategically connected to action, containing a 'deworlding" effect, rather than *as media and outcome* of different action orientations. Habermas therefore has no satisfying solution to the vital problem of how coordinating symbolic media *transform* while they fulfil their mediating functions. A rupture appears between the individual action and the functional rationality of social systems. System and lifeworld tend to refer to different societal spheres (e.g. formal organisations vs. family life, the public sphere and social movements; see Habermas 1987, 309). This, I argue, prevents us from viewing lifeworld and system as *analytic* dimensions of society irrespective of domains, and makes it difficult to see digitalised processes of communication (within, as well as between systems and lifeworlds) as 'political', that is, as contested processes that reproduce both system and lifeworld aspects in distinct ways.

DOI: 10.1057/9781137446466.0004

Habermas distinction raises questions about the ontological status of the two categories: are we talking about social areas, action types or impersonal mechanisms? Are we dealing with a concept that can possibly be filled with empirical content in sociological research? Habermas distinguishes between lifeworld and system according to the following: *principles of co-ordination* (social vs. system integration through the media communication vs. money/power), *rationalities* (communicative vs. strategic and instrumental action orientations) and *spheres* (everyday life vs. economy, and public bureaucracy).

The status of the lifeworld as both a social–philosophical concept (differentiating between hermeneutics and systems theory) and a substantive sociological concept (differentiating between 'the world within reach' and formal systems) is confusing. The second notion leads to a sociological concept of everyday life, with which a practical understanding of mediated social interaction can be addressed. It differentiates between cultural zones on the grounds of the logic of day-to-day practices. However, if this second conception of the lifeworld seems most applicable empirically, it is problematic to call this perspective a lifeworld, since it tends to obscure the necessary distinction between phenomenological and sociological investigation. The first 'phenomenological' understanding of the lifeworld cannot be omitted, and it should not be mixed with sociological conceptions of social groups.

The agent cannot relate to the world without somehow being situated in the common world of fellow agents. The lifeworld is the subjective and experiental dimension of individual agency, constructed by inter-subjectivity. In pragmatism, action is not the pursuit of ends that the agent establishes *a priori* and then resolves to accomplish (Honneth and Joas 1991). Communication technology is not mere material means at the disposal of human intentionality. Rather, there is interplay between intentions and impulses of the agent, and the possibilities of a given situation; we find our ends in the world, as they become reproduced and changed in the connection between possibilities and intentions. Only in this sense is action, whether it involves personal media or not, teleological and purposive.

The conflating of the lifeworld and everyday life, which seems to appear in Habermas' theory, leads to the reduction of the phenomenological argument, in favour of everyday life as leisure time, reproduction time, consumption and so on. This institutionalising of the lifeworld tends to ignore the fact that individual experience takes place wherever

DOI: 10.1057/9781137446466.0004

human beings act, regardless of institution. It confuses phenomeno-logical sociology with institutional sociology, transforming institutional boundaries into experiential horizons. The unhappy consequence is that the lifeworld is seen as something outside systems rather than as a pragmatic and experiential dimension of society in general.

The Lifeworld Today

Consequently, an idea of how such media may, through subtle herme-neutic processes, become transformed into *individual* lifeworld resources is necessary. The lifeworld-system model must be balanced with an understanding of the reversal process where lifeworld norms (traditional values, participation, compassion, morality) penetrate system media to the extent that they do not only serve system-integration. Examples of this may be social experimentation, political participation and coopera-tives on the market, hacker-cultures, social uses of TV and other mass media, and a number of practical, invisible processes in daily life. This reversal process is neglected in Habermas' theory. In an interview, for example, Habermas admitted: 'But this way of approaching systemically induced disturbances in communicatively rationalised lifeworlds was one-sided: it failed to utilise the whole range of potential contribution of the theory. The question as to which side imposes limitations has to be treated as an empirical question that cannot beforehand be decided on the analytical level in favour of the systems. ... colonisation of the lifeworld and the democratic control of dynamics of systems unrespon-sive to the "externalities" they produce represent two equally justified analytical perspectives. The one-sidedness of a view captured by a certain diagnosis of the time is certainly not inherent in the structure of the theory' (Habermas 1990b, 109).

The problems, routines and concerns of everyday life always revolve around generalising systems media in both constructive and destructive ways. Media of social systems are drawn upon as devices for manoeuvres within the modern existence of social systems. Everyday life takes place not only *against* the steering media of mass consumption, science and bureau-cratic power, but *through* them. They do, however, enhance individualised ways of handling problems and personal outlooks on the world.

A specification of the relationship between everyday life in the household and society with regard to media technologies is suggested by

DOI: 10.1057/9781137446466.0004

Roger Silverstone and associates. Silverstone characterises the household as a 'moral economy' (Silverstone et al. 1992). It is part of a transactional system of economic and social relations with the rest of society. The *domestic* communication environment consists of media with increasingly differentiated technical characteristics related to time, space and modes of mediating and presenting meaning. In order to understand the communication environment that participates in the mediation of the links between everyday life and society, their differences as well as their similarities should be elucidated: 'The technological culture of the household provides a framework for domestic, social and indeed political relations, mediating between members of the households and offering objectifications of their identities and competencies as well as mediating between them and the outside world. The domestic socio-technical system consists of a bundle of skills, tastes and competencies, expressed in styles and practices that construct and mark the cleavages of gender and age-based relations within and beyond the household' (Silverstone 1991, 141).

We should consider agency and its subjective and experiential dimension, the lifeworld, in relation to modern social systems. Then, the concept of the lifeworld does not belong to the sociology of institutions, but to the methodology of phenomenological sociology. The lifeworld is then understood as meaning-production, for the intersubjective, and yet individual, experiences and interpretation, the world and self-understanding in the different life phases of the agent. Further, the lifeworld is then connected both to the bodily *and* communicational spheres. When everyday experiences are mediated increasingly via personal media supplementing face-to-face encounters, transformation and extension of meaning from place-based to network-based lifeworlds occurs.

The 'lifeworld' is personal, tacit and reflexive considerations of personal life and integrity in the 're-embedding' of agency in the world of social systems. With the rise of digitally mastered social systems, the former lifeworld of unmediated social integration needs to be seen as differentiated, personalised and extended. The lifeworld appears individualised as the modern risk enhances a strong I-strength and ego-identity of creativity and competitiveness. Also erosion of the traditional community is compensated by modern support systems that provide security and safety (insurance, hospitals, police etc.), competence and information (education, the mass media etc.), spiritual support, work, culture (theatre, concerts etc.), capital (banks), food, clothes, housing and so on.

DOI: 10.1057/9781137446466.0004

The individual lifeworld refers to the personal politics of moral considerations of integrity, life plans and self-reflexivity as opposed to, and in confrontation with, systemic boundaries.

The individual status can be characterised as both autonomy and dependence. Individual autonomy is reached through mobility in space and flexibility in time. Security is transferred to human-made, flexible and adaptive 'trust mechanisms'. Individual dependence is expressed through ignorance of the functionality of systems, lack of pre-modern trust mechanisms like religion and kinship, lack of contingency and as a general sensation of risk and insecurity. This is not to say that there is no life outside the social systems for the individual. Day-to-day life, in shorter spans of time, consists of unpredictable and coincidental encounters and interaction and so on. And yet, in the long run, the individual 'project' depends increasingly on social systems.

Domestication as personalisation

The concept of domestication is a good place to continue the tracking of what is going on, given that it too undergoes revisions on a number of accounts. In addition to media-related elements comes the complex social dynamics outside the media themselves that in various ways and for various groups domesticate technologies into particular contexts and culture. A way to start is simply to read the theory of domestication as a theory of personalisation. If we exchange the domestic for the personal, we may have a conceptual framework with which we may approach the personal 'taming' of various media, from the app-filled mobile to social media. Silverstone et al. (1992) distinguish between four elements or phases in the dynamics of media relations:

> *Appropriation* refers to the process where an object leaves the world of the commodity and is taken into possession by an individual. It becomes owned or possessed as cultural object and participates in a cultural totality. Acts of appropriation become a symbol of personal positioning and self-creation. Appropriation refers to both hardware and software, to the TV set and programmes, and to mobiles and apps.

> *Objectification* reveals itself in the display of objects, as they signal the person's place in the social world. It reveals itself in the usage and in the location of objects around the individual, how they are carried, ordered and arranged, with varying coherence and consistency, into the functional aesthetic of the person.

DOI: 10.1057/9781137446466.0004

Incorporation refers to the idea that media technologies are used in various ways, which sustain or change personal practices. Technologies in particular may be used for different purposes than intended by the market or in different ways than the usual due to specific personal needs and interests. They influence the usage of time, routines and rituals and so on. In this way, they may become taken-for-granted, or 'invisible'.

Conversion, together with appropriation, refers to the relationship between the individual and the world around him/her. Through the use of texts and technologies, the individual claims status in reference groups outside the home. The use of mobile on Facebook becomes a medium for achieving status and sociality, and a way to draw upon social and cultural norms of style, taste and morality as resources. This is the way fashion, TV programmes, computers and their software work, particularly for youth in relation to their peer groups. Conversion implies condensed private statements about the public culture and vice versa; they indicate membership into specific cultures by signalling judgement and competence of taste and style. Material objects both enable conversion and they are objects of conversion.

These are the ways that the boundary of the personal lifeworld is extended and blended into the public economy. The concepts are intended to provide a framework for the supply of meaning to objects by describing acquisition and use, in both private and public relations. As we see, they describe plausibly personalisation as much as the intended process of domestication. Although these four processes seem to refer to communication technologies as commodities and artefacts, and less as media for communication between the private and the public, they illustrate the process of appropriation noted above. The individual learns to apply principles of practice towards cultural products in new areas. The individual acquires the competence to reproduce certain cultural principles and to apply them pragmatically in new contexts. Habitus also inspires subjective probabilities that give aspirations and prospects towards social hierarchies. For instance, habitus provides the individual with classificatory schemes towards art and cultural artefacts. To a variable degree, artefacts have symbolic value. Habitus mediates differentiated appropriation of external facts. Accordingly, it provides systematically different interpretations of cultural artefacts (Rasmussen 2000).

The framework is clearly phenomenologically informed, and addresses technology use as interpretation and experience in the lifeworld. The non-instrumental aspects of the technologies, for example, their symbolic and cultural aspects, were emphasised as much as what they could do. This appears in the phases of domestication – and personalisation. While

DOI: 10.1057/9781137446466.0004

appropriation and conversion refer to particularly the symbolic aspects, objectification and incorporation refer more to the material expression. Briefly put, appropriation refers to the initial imaginations and projections of technologies as something that can fill a space or a need in one's life. The term objectification refers to the process of giving the artefact a concrete position. During incorporation, the technology finds its function or role in personal or embodied space. In the conversion phase, personal expectations place the images of technology in social space. This is a process of consumption as integration, of commodification of personal practices. It is about making things familiar and ordinary, and finding a place in a formal economy.

One important feature with several personal media is that one can be sure to reach a particular person, not only a family (home phone) or a group of chatting people. With media such as email and SMS, one can target particular persons, a fact that lowers the threshold for contact. Other people are not needed as intermediaries, and the significance of the medium as a trusted peer medium increases. A central theme in the following is that the marking of boundaries for communication is a fundamental aspect of human interaction, in spite of studies on the 'blurring of boundaries' or 'no sense of place'. Personal media are a modern marker for communication, often replacing the private/public boundary of the household. As Fahey (1995) argues, the public/private boundary in relation to the family may be simplifying a much more complex system of boundaries and zones of intimacy and privacy. Domestic space is undermined by personal (mediated) space. Livingstone (in Kraut et al. 2006, 128) argues that children, and even more teenagers, seek privacy and use online media to get it. The telephone provided ways to transcend the boundaries of domestic space for teenagers. With the text and voice functions of the mobile, the possibility to be in touch with friends late at night, when with parents on holidays and so on became more feasible. Studies indicate that most young people tend to use their mobile to call friends rather than using the home phone, despite higher personal cost (see, e.g., Ito and Okabe in Kraut 239).

Young people use personal media on the Internet to create boundaries around themselves and others, to communicate about embarrassing matters (sexual health), love and intimacy, and to experiment with identity and peer culture. What takes place is flexibilisation of the private conversation in the bedroom (with the sign Keep Out! Private! on the door). Now the possibility is larger in time and space to have such

DOI: 10.1057/9781137446466.0004

conversations through Facebook, however in a more rigid medium of communication than face-to-face talk. Personal media are actively used for privacy, for purposes of communicating in controlled circumstances. There are however boundaries that need to be marked and reproduced through frequent social interaction.

Everyday tactics

From Simmel, we are reminded that we must deal mentally with the dramatic changes involved in urbanity: noise, lights and speed of transportation systems, housing, schooling and shopping. From Walter Benjamin, we might bring with us the insight of the everyday objects that are not new and filled with the future, but the outdated ones, like the deep TV, the telephone in the hall, the stationary PC in the study. They are witnesses to how transitory norms about the convenient seem to be, particularly in an urban way of life. From Henri Lefebvre, we should keep in mind the point that everyday life is repetitious and habitual within constrained time and space', in contrast to the linear logic of markets and bureaucracies. We can pick up even more from Michel de Certeau (1984).

Michel de Certeau's perspective is more successful than many others in showing this linking of structural preferences of the political economy with the agency and construction of meaning, so that they are seen as a duality, that is, as both oppositional and conditioning. de Certeau (1984) examined the obscurity of everyday practices and its ways of operating things and articulated them into a sociology of everyday life. He suggested to: 'make explicit the systems of operational combination (les combinatoires d'opérations) which also compose a "culture", and to bring to light the models of action characteristic of users whose status as the dominated element in society (a status that does not mean that they are either passive or docile) is concealed by the euphemistic term "consumers"'. Everyday life invents itself by poaching in countless ways on the property of others' (de Certeau 1984, xii).

De Certeau focused on people's use of the media, on consumption of goods and services, on daily life in urban space and so on. People reproduce their everyday reality in 'hidden' ways, in different and scattered social areas that are defined and occupied by systems of production (TV, urban planning, telecoms, commerce etc.). These systems undertake a

DOI: 10.1057/9781137446466.0004

centralised and spectacular production that leaves no place for discourse on what people make or do with the products of the systems. People's consumption of products is on the contrary dispersed, everywhere, in a sense silent and 'invisible' because it does not draw on its own production, but on *ways of using* system products.

All these ways of using contribute to a cultural field that is 'unsigned, unreadable, unsymbolised' because of the pressure of the productivist economy, but which nevertheless is *there* in various degrees and patterns. Certainly, the practices are differentiated along socio-cultural lines. Similar strategic signals produce different effects. 'Hence the necessity of differentiating both the "actions" or "engagements" (in the military sense) that the system of products effects within the consumer grid, and the various kinds of room to manoeuvre left for consumers by the situations in which they exercise their "art"' (de Certeau 1984, xvii). This cultural field articulates temporary conflicts and tensions, approximately culturally administered through symbolic compromises, balances and legitimacy. The forces of systems are met with the tactics of everyday consumption.

Technologies of power open a space, an interiority from which those elites may act on society (Feenberg 1991, 85). To act out its domination, systems require some space for operations. This space, however, cannot be reserved exclusively for the dominating part. Spaces are neutral only in that they offer themselves as sites for alternative manoeuvres as well. Consequently, the tactical operational autonomy of subjects corresponds to strategies. As opposed to strategies of power, *tactics* are the response of dominated subjects, their operating within the processes of the dominating system. Tactics are subversive rather than oppositional in that they operate on the terrain of the dominating, combine its elements into tactical 'tricks'. Tactic relates to strategies as speech (or rather, talk) relates to language. Tactics are the playing out within the game of other powers. They redefine and modify established values and practices and social forms. Andrew Feenberg calls this autonomy of alternative practices a 'margin of manoeuvre' (Feenberg 1991, 86). In everyday life, these manoeuvres take the form of informal communication, improvisations, unauthorised simplification of procedures, 'ignoring' and 'forgetting' orders, and numerous innovative modifications of established routines. Practices on the margin of manoeuvre may produce change (and thus be incorporated into dominating strategies) or they may contribute to the social order (like informal communication in formal bureaucracies).

DOI: 10.1057/9781137446466.0004

The concept of tactic suggests that deterministic perspectives on the technologising of the private sphere are unfortunate. From a 'macro' perspective, de Certeau's perspective negotiates between Habermas' reformulated critical theory of modernity and specific everyday practices. From a 'micro' perspective, it draws upon theories of tacit knowledge (practical consciousness, implicit knowledge etc.) and everyday practices in a world of social systems. Tactic is a form of practice that relates to the Other and the Other's space without taking it over, it plays itself out in sequences of time where opportunities are 'gently' seized. Tactics combine events and turn them into resources and opportunities. Most everyday practices are tactical in character, involving imagination, innovation, cunning manoeuvres, simulations, playing and discoveries.

De Certeau operates with a dichotomy that in some respects seems similar to Habermas' distinction between lifeworld and system. Everyday tactics of consumers in their lifeworlds stand against (although in a subtle fashion) strategic systems of production. In this symbolic battlefield, practices that can be empirically studied take place, which may refer to and further inform about the systems. In Habermas terms, de Certeau advocates empirical investigations of lifeworld practices, and their autonomy or interdependence with societal systems, whether political, technocratic, commercial, educational and so on. But in a much clearer way, de Certeau articulates the innovative and creative manoeuvres in daily life, playing upon structures whose system-oriented origin is alien to them. De Certeau explores incorporation and *appropriation*, the day-to-day operations that reproduce the meaning of everyday life in a productivist society. Because people, in their daily lives, are 'unrecognised producers, poets of their own acts, silent discoverers of their own paths in the jungle of functionalist rationality' (de Certeau 1984, xviii).

De Certeau's perspective helps us gain a better understanding of cultural activities as products of both systemic mechanisms and of the web of everyday life experiences. The transformation of systemic products by and through everyday interpretations becomes clearer. To disentangle this process, one cannot narrow the understanding of such practices to communication processes alone. One then leaves out the dialectic between the symbolic and the material, which is constitutive of daily life experiences as theme and context. The material and tech-

DOI: 10.1057/9781137446466.0004

nological reality provides a manifest fact to which people ascribe meaning and so incorporate it as rules and resources to their constitution of common sense. De Certeau emphasises that system media, as they are materialised as information, technology or goods, not only colonise everyday life, but also *become* colonised or appropriated by the dynamics and diversity of everyday life. Everyday life is a battle zone where rationalised and centralised system production is confronted with the quiet, differentiated and creative art of use in the trivial and invisible contexts of everyday life.

Roger Silverstone saw the relevance of de Certeau's perspective on the study of TV use. TV audiences do not read TV passively as a mass: 'We consume television not just in our relationship to the content of its transmissions, but also in our relationship to it as technology, as an object to be placed in our domestic environment and articulated into our private and public culture. Both sets of consumption practices involve us in a type of creative work. Our individual and social identities are defined through them. The paths we trace through television culture (the ways we talk about television, incorporate it into our gossip, or the ways in which we integrate television as technology into the pattern of our family life) are our own paths. We need to enquire into the specificities of those paths, their uniqueness and their universality, if we are to understand the dynamics of television's integration into everyday life' (Silverstone 1989, 81). The distinction goes between strategy and tactics, between agency and system. To Silverstone, de Certeau's perspective allowed for critical thinking about TV (or other media) in the mediation between everyday life and systems. It offers a framework for thinking constructively about media use as consumption, mediation and action. However, de Certeau exaggerates the ability in everyday contexts to converse and transform system output, which means that he is close to undermining his own critical perspective on strategies. Still, he presents an important approach to everyday consumption and uses of communication technology in several ways, which serves as an appropriate modification of Habermas' theory. Common-sense notions and practices in everyday life are not only a confrontation of the dominant strategies of systems. Everyday practices involve the linking of tradition, identity and system output. The meaning of everyday life is not constituted exclusively in opposition to strategies of systems; these strategies also provide the raw material for such construction of meaning.

DOI: 10.1057/9781137446466.0004

Relative distance

The main sociological connection between research on the use of personal media and general features of modernity goes through the notion of 'individualisation'. Individualisation is the way modernity has construed human identification since Kant and Rousseau. We teach our children how to make their own choices and take responsibility for their own actions. The child is to be given full opportunities to express its personality and individual difference, relatively independent of the historical and cultural past of family and relatives, which are now often seen as constraints for personal freedom. When our marriage does not work out as expected, we divorce. When we dislike the neighbourhood, we move elsewhere. After three years in a job, many look for new challenges. References to values of family and nation are not a priority in upbringing or in current pedagogical thinking. To be oneself is the true virtue, meaning that identity now is what is unique in one's personality. These virtues of difference and excellence in a democratic society open a space that needs to be filled by an emphasis on authenticity and self-construction of knowledge and norms. It is hardly necessary to enter the long debate from Kant to post-modernism on the nature of freedom to see that freedom is neither about complete independence, nor about cultural embeddedness.

On the one hand, freedom only rarely implies detachment from family and friends. On the other hand, the freedom we claim is a product of social interaction with others and with the past. As the later Foucault and many others point out, there seem to be two kinds of Self, the one that recognises its social foundations and another that suffers under the narcissistic delusion that freedom is private property, which one does not have to give, but only take. Diachronically, no one is the origin of one's self – we are all successors. Synchronically, we are all embedded in social contexts that are constitutive of our life and well-being. And for this reason, we do not have the power over our own life that we tend to imagine or are forced to imagine. Our life is conditioned by society, and the realisation of Self is a social construction. The Marxist-structuralist term 'relative autonomy' (referring to the State) could be used to describe the status of the modern individual vis-à-vis society. Another term is the late Roger Silverstone's 'proper distance', which in his conception refers to a balanced ethical approach between indifference and absorbtion.

DOI: 10.1057/9781137446466.0004

Let me illustrate by a brief note on Rich Ling's interesting study on the uses of mobile telephony in everyday life as forms of ritual interaction. Ling (2008) addresses mobile telephony in the light of the classic sociological theme from Emile Durkheim on social integration and social cohesion, or our sense of social solidarity. How is social solidarity generated in a modern and mobile society? Does the mobile telephone contribute to our sense of cohesion? Unlike Durkheim and Randall Collins, Ling argues that mediated interpersonal communication reproduces and develops relationships among those who are close. Ling argues that what he calls ritual interaction – in co-presence or mediated – is the glue that holds society together. The idea of classic sociology of religion is that rituals tend to enhance social solidarity. This may explain the universal and timelessness of rituals in functional terms. It is not difficult to see this in the mass media and broadcasting, but what then with mobile telephony?

The mobile is used for a wide variety of practical and social purposes: to make dates and appointments, to stay in touch and to coordinate everyday life. They may consist of very brief messages, jokes, gossip, shopping lists for the groceries and so on. Some of these conversations or text sequences may have ritual character, other may not. But they all expand and extend everyday interaction, Ling argues, and support the development of cohesion in this way. An important sociological point here is that social capital and social networks are forms of social interaction made extremely more efficient and flexible through modern personal media. The inter- and multi-personal in mediated social networks have become widespread precisely because of the multitude of innovations leading to the current forms of personal media. While Ling eminently demonstrates the role of the mobile phone for ritual interaction, the dramatic changes that this form of interaction enhances are somewhat underplayed. Ling rightly notes that such communication tends to be lightweight, simple, brief and often as a secondary engagement. It most often complements unmediated interaction among family members and friends. This points towards the observation that 'ritual interaction' through the mobile phone enhances a more flexible, loose and less constraining form of social solidarity. Social cohesion is probably not the adequate term for what the mobile phone generates sociologically in everyday life. Constant contact and interaction enhance elastic interaction and communication with less binding force. This does certainly not imply that the mobile phone makes personal or intimate

DOI: 10.1057/9781137446466.0004

relationships of less importance for the individual. It makes them more flexible. They encourage connections and networks rather than communities. To understand modern relationships and the role of mediated interaction to maintain them, we should look less on their normative or binding forces and more on how they make use of time in constructing patterns of contact.

In the *terrain vague* of everyday life, individualisation and digital personal media is a social realm of civility and solidarity, however usually without strong constraining values. The relationships are certainly moral, if rarely passionate. Intimacy, familiarity and friendliness may not only characterise atmospheres but also the proper distance that is needed. The point is nicely addressed by Goffman: our priority is to make everyday life work, and adjust the temperature of our social relations thereafter. What Goffman (1983) called *interaction orders* are reproduced – a substantive domain in its own right with its own structures and patterns. Interactions and conversation have an autonomous status insofar as they keep their own boundaries. Following Goffman (1967, 113), a conversation has a life of its own with its own heroes and villains. The features involved in a conversation between at least two persons create their own norms and ways, which make the conversation into the basic unit of a society. Interaction itself, not the involved individuals or their values and norms, is the unit of analysis, which everything else sociological is built upon. In fact, Goffman describes a social system similar to what Niklas Luhmann called interaction systems. Unlike Goffman, Luhmann considered communication as the basic unit, creating various forms of social systems (interaction systems, organisations, function systems and social movements). Goffman for his part describes conversations as a systemic element from which everything else social is built. Of course conversations take different shapes and forms, not only according to participants and immediate purposes, but also according to changing structural conditions. Personal media as new tools for personal networks influence Goffman's conversation in ways unimaginable for him and everyone else a few decades ago. A central task for a sociology of everyday life today is to enquire into how media create new and modify 'conversations' in daily life, and in the next instance the sociability of society, or to put it more in the line of both Goffman and Luhmann, how conversations reorganise themselves in order to make the new tools productive.

We may use the term *relative distance* to designate what I think is an apt sociological way of seeing the relationship between individuals,

DOI: 10.1057/9781137446466.0004

acknowledging of course that both isolation and embedding occur in different stages of life and in different cultures. *Relative distance* is both a descriptive and prescriptive term in that it somehow describes the current state of affairs in many aspects of daily life, *and* that it prescribes itself as a norm guiding the modern individual.

Personal media have become essential in 'identity politics' where relative distance plays an important part. Gerard Delanty (2003, 128) refers to 'personalism', to put emphasis not only on contemporary demands on self-fulfilment, but also on commitment, solidarity and collective responsibility. The self is seen as shaped through social participation and is sustained by a normative belief in collective goods. This, however, changes the perception of the social from a traditional lifeworld-approach to a looser network-oriented lifeworld. Rather than being integrated through given and strong values and norms, this kind of lifeworld is constructed by overlapping social relations. As Delanty (2003, 130) argues, they are products of practices rather than of structures. Or in structuration-theoretical terms, they are medium and outcome of practices. They are wilfully constitutions of both needs for belonging and independence.

In response to dark diagnosis of American civic life and claims about the decline of social capital in western societies, it is argued that the sociability of individuals simply takes new forms, less detectable by the community-oriented sociologist. If normatively integrated communities are losing ground in favour of looser social networks, a modified perspective is needed, which focuses on networks of association rather than on shared values and norms. If people are finding new ways to relate to one another, if they replace authoritative norms with communication and tasks, the focus should be on the associations, relationships and contacts, rather than on taken-for-granted values. 'Network integration' is a term that indicates these trends, which may help the sociologist to explore and explain the question of social order in the current society. That concept leads to a modified understanding of community as something deriving from social relations more than values, and that may be less stable.

Taken together, a 'thinner' or 'liquid' version of the lifeworld emphasises cognitive experience and information and weak-tie sociality, at the expense of immediate values of belonging, whether in spatial or cultural versions. A network conception of lifeworld is more flexible, more complex and more open than the traditional value conception. A lifeworld is today more reflexive in that its members are tacitly aware

DOI: 10.1057/9781137446466.0004

that it is embedded in an increasingly present and visual globality of overlapping communities and networks. To a large degree, communities are created through negotiated practices in order to enjoy a sense of belonging, and to avoid insecurity and loneliness.

A network conception of lifeworld may draw on network theory. That social communities can be seen as social networks is an insight greatly developed by Barry Wellman and his associates, based on the sociology of Mark Granowetter and others (Wellman et al. 1996, 1999; Granowetter 1973, 1983; Rasmussen 2007). Social network analysis does not take the normatively integrated community as a given, but is able to approach the question of lifeworld more subtly. It has led to the observations of non-local ties, adding other social variables for social organisation in urban settings, thus putting the often geographically defined community in a more nuanced picture. The emphasis on normative integration has been balanced by a perspective of social relations as complex, often non-local and not necessarily embedded in a community of values and norms. In much of Wellman's analysis, community is viewed as personal networks of a wide variety of tie types, and constitutes a valuable corrective to the lifeworld perspective. Generally, social network analysis has developed and refined an analytical distinction between sociology and geography, and thus helped sociology to avoid 'geographical determinism'.

However, analysis of social networks based on quantitative data tends to give the impression that personal networks are established instrumentally for accessing resources (Blokland 2003, 50). Community is often understood as simply interlocking personal networks. This leaves a lot unexplained, related to the stability and also the changes in social networks, which can only be explored by bringing in the wider social and historical context. Furthermore, a proper theoretical understanding of how people reproduce networks needs to be developed that matches findings of network analysis. Social network analysis tends to leave out too much of what social life is about, related to intersubjectivity and pragmatic, meaningful action. In a sense, the term 'networked individualism' is unfortunate because what we observe in contemporary urban settings is far from individualism, networked or not. To de Tocqueville, individualism meant love of family and near ones, but indifference to everyone else. Social relations are important but social and material and mediated contexts matter. If the community perspective overlooks sociability without normative integration, the personal network perspective may overlook memories and norms as well as traditions (Blokland 2003,

DOI: 10.1057/9781137446466.0004

60). The term leaves out too many sources of the social, and tends to ignore the fact that the individual is as social today as one hundred or five hundred years ago.

Individualisation implies some individual capacity for critical judgement and reflection, if social conditions allow it. As we know, observations indicate that much individualisation follows a pathological track for a substantial portion of the population in western societies, seen in the statistics of meaningless crime, depression and nervous illnesses, suicides, stress and borderline illnesses. Research on the social conditions of childhood in western countries reports on high degrees of harassment, lack of trust of parents, childhood pregnancy, school drop-out, discipline problems and so on. The obvious sociological diagnosis of this sorry state is that too many individuals are left alone with their self-development, or influenced in destructive ways by individuals and popular culture. Civil social networks are in decline in parts of society (Putnam 1995), which leaves a great burden on the shoulders of individuals who do not have the resources and support to manage 'self-realisation'.

Autonomy can only be reached if one is given the chance to acknowledge one's social peers and origin. Freedom can only be reached if interacting meaningfully with others. This diagnosis should not be confused with value-conservative complaints about the withering of traditional authorities and values. The point is simply sociological and political: the challenge is to help individualisation back on the constructive social track, leading to a democratic society capable of creating meaningful and relatively happy lives for most individuals and with public communication processes able to legitimate politics. The members of this kind of society must re-establish its bonds to ancestors and their achievements (not only their mistakes), as well as to future generations.

Analytically, a task for social research is to find a balanced way between individualism and exaggerated sentiments of social belonging, while leaving open possibilities for traces of both. Egocentrism and instrumental action are elements of everyday life, as is imagined and real communities. Individuals identify with other individuals, as well as with groups, and they constitute loose collectives. Research on personal media use in everyday life needs to be sensitive to a variety of sources for action on micro and meso levels. Our solidarities are based on both mechanic and organic constellations, leading to both Gemeinshaft- and Gesellshaft-like social forms. But mostly, everyday networks are hybrids of these, or to be found between them. The interest in sociology for

DOI: 10.1057/9781137446466.0004

analytical dichotomies has left a large, grey and seemingly insignificant territory unexplored between them, so far better addressed by literature and other kinds of fiction than social analysis.

The question here is not simply how people should be empowered through resources from society. Rather it is: do people themselves *already* have the means for re-establishing social ties and access resources they would need for a good life and a more just society? Could we trace such means in the very process of individualisation itself, not only in the established arsenal of welfare resources that are on the weakening front? Polemically asked: to sustain social networks, should we put our bets on the daily press or the mobile telephone? My point is neither that political nor cultural programmes to remedy social integration are mistaken, nor that they should be enforced. Rather, we should continue to look at the other end, by examining the social energies in the rapidly proliferating, digital personal media, media that are embedded in the wave of individualisation itself.

DOI: 10.1057/9781137446466.0004

4
Communication in Personal Media

Abstract: *This chapter introduces 'everyday life' as a sociological category and examines more specifically and critically the concept of the lifeworld. It examines the significance of the concept from phenomenology to sociology, and points towards a revised notion of the lifeworld more compatible with a modern mediated everyday life. It links the concept of the lifeworld to the more recent Anglo-American concept of 'domestication', addressed more specifically as 'personalisation'. It connects everyday personal media use to Michel de Certeau's theory of strategy and tactics in everyday life.*

Keywords: communication theory; digital media; everyday life; lifeworld; media theory; personal media; social capital; sociology

Rasmussen, Terje. *Personal Media and Everyday Life: A Networked Lifeworld.* Basingstoke: Palgrave Macmillan, 2014. DOI: 10.1057/9781137446466.0005.

In the 1980s and 1990s, research on the use of digital media was influenced by a North American fascination for virtual communities and digital identities. The emphasis was put on role-playing and experimenting identities as well as on electronic communities as new, democratic spaces on electronic bulletin board systems (BBS), MUDs and chatrooms (IRC). The theorising by early observers like Howard Rheingold (1993), Sherry Turkle (1997) and Steven Jones (1997) tended to stress the virtual as a separate existence, cut off from people's social status in actual life and everyday life circumstances in general. The unwarranted optimism probably derived from the novelty of electronic networks that were open and decentralised and emerged as a part of counter-cultures. It was also inspired by the writings of McLuhan and other media visionaries. A third source for this enthusiasm was post-modern speculations on the fundamental undermining of modern truth and certainty by popular culture (Poster, Jamieson, Lyotard).

In the late 1990s, this wave of irrealism waned as an effect of sociologically informed research on the relationship between online and offline practices. A number of studies on identity formation in MUDs found connections between online and offline existence, and that electronic social interaction was embedded in people's unmediated social life (Cherny 1999, Kendall 2002, Markham 1998). Generally, studies pointed out the connections between life online and offline. The reorientation came not only as an effect of sober analysis, but also as a consequence of actual media change. From the mid-1990s home pages appeared on the Internet as a channel of self-performance and self-presentation. From 1998 blogger-tools appeared on the net and from 1999, new blog and network sites like LiveJournal (1999), Blogger (1999), Wordpress (2003), MySpace (2003), Flickr and Facebook (2004) MSN LiveSpaces (2004), YouTube (2005), Twitter (2007). The sites are all dedicated to participation and user-generated content, which in systematic and accumulated form become added value for each user and create an exponential growth. The key is management of personal information and social relationships. Users present themselves in distinct and purposive ways that in accumulated form appear as social databases. Interaction of different sorts among users is stimulated and organised. There was no need for specialised computer or network competence on the part of the user.

In the 1990s, the main forms of online activity tended to be chatting, through emailing, chatrooms, the mobile and SMS and messaging services. Increasingly, software allowed young people to create content

DOI: 10.1057/9781137446466.0005

for web-based sites. The change was quick. Network development, improved user interfaces along with further individualisation, brought media change to the current stage of digital personal media. What were peak phenomena at the beginning of the millennium soon became mainstream. The affordability and improved user interfaces of multi-functional mobiles, laptops and mini-computers increased the competence and consciousness of both technologies and services on the net.

As digital personal media proliferated, pioneer users (the bases of early research) became the majority and young people with digital media experience brought their everyday life into new mediated forms. The new media were not simply alternative channels for interaction and expression, but media for the very social life they lived among friends, family and associates. For instance, Prøitz demonstrated how young people used mobile text messages and camera-phone images in their performance of sexuality and gender relations (Prøitz 2005, 2007). The use of mobile telephony that exploded from the mid-1990s was predominantly associated with maintaining existing social relationships. From the turn of the century, we have been observing a growing interdependency and infiltration between the online and the offline to the extent that the distinction has less explanatory value than in the 1990s.

In this and the following chapters I develop some suggestions for what communication and media theory we may bring to the workings of personal media in society. The topic here is communication theory for personal media. We cannot rely on theories of mass communications that were constructed to serve research on broadcasting and the press. I begin by briefly addressing the role of interpersonal in existing mass communication research to demonstrate this. But there is no need to start from scratch. Since personal media have inherited features from both interpersonal interaction and mediated communication, the trick is to carefully pick and develop insights from the existing reservoir of human research. In this chapter I therefore pay a visit to some insights from sociology and communication research to clarify personal mediated communication.

The interpersonal in the media

Interpersonal communication involves two persons or a small number of participants who exchange messages designed for those involved. The

DOI: 10.1057/9781137446466.0005

motivations, purposes are often shaped by the actual context, and it may have both instrumental and expressive aims. Broadly two lines of research on interpersonal communication are related to the mass media. First, there is the research on interpersonal communication in *audiences*. The interpersonal aspect has been present in mass communication research since the Second World War. It has been growing and can now be seen as an ever more significant aspect of the total communication context. An emergent mass media sector without direct contact with its audiences was the premise for the emerging research on mass communications and the mass media, and subsequently of theories of human beings as audiences and publics. The theories positioned people not as individuals, citizens, patients, students or clients, but as abstract members of uniform audiences. For instance, Lazarsfeld and his associates discovered (in *The People's Choice*) that mass-communicated political information was processed further, sociologically one might say, through interpersonal communication, managed by a particular communication role, the famous *opinion leader*. The receiving end was thus divided into two levels: 'leaders' and 'followers'. (They also applied the terms 'advisors' and 'advisees'.)

We also see this emphasis on the interpersonal in other macro studies of communication processes, like the agenda setting approach in diffusion studies, the spiral of silence thesis in reception studies and so on. In Katz and Lazarsfeld's study *Personal Influence*, the terms 'leaders' and 'followers' were applied as well, finding that leaders used the media more intensively than followers, and thus were more influenced by the media. In diffusion studies, notably in Everett Rogers's *Diffusion of Innovations*, six new communication roles, from innovators to lag-behinds, were conceived and tested on large-scale empirical material. Taken together, these studies, through the years, signified a more differentiated set of communication roles in mass communication, which not only transferred information, but also played a more normative role of influence and co-orientation (norm-building). The relationships between people, which applied the media as a reservoir of references and topics for face-to-face conversation, gradually received more attention in communication research.

Second, there are the studies of interpersonal communication, or simulations of such, in media *production* (such as studies of journalism and other genres in the press and in broadcasting). A number of mechanisms have been identified that serve as functional equivalents for a true and present communication partner. Phenomena such as liveness, authenticity, informality, proxemics and studio design all serve as simulations of

DOI: 10.1057/9781137446466.0005

communication, arising from the absence of interpersonal communication through the medium itself. Such media trends remind us that the interpersonal element has been present in mass media research since the 1940s, several decades before digital personal media appeared on the scene of private life. It has also constituted an increasingly important branch in studies of mass communication production.

Both in studies of consumption and production, the interpersonal element constitutes an added, contextual element, outside the actual transmission of the mass media. Interpersonal communication served as something mass media research imported in order to make sense of the contextual character of mass communication. Yet, whereas theories of effects gratification, influence, diffusion or reception lead to better understanding of the increased significance of the interpersonal in mediated communication, they cannot, since they are explicitly developed for mass communication, overcome its focus on interpersonal communication as something *external* to the actual work of the media.

Personal media then constitute a *third* connection – a synthesis – 'between' or beyond – the interpersonal and the mass media in that interpersonal communication is located right in the *medium itself.* This fact changes the communication situation dramatically, and in paradoxical ways. It provides its own (virtual) context, at the same time as the personalisation and mobility of personal media reduces the significance of the common material context as a reservoir of topics for communication. This suggests, among other things, that we need to study the media-internal context, as it appears as interface, genres, multi-modal composition, design and so on. Since the common social context for these kinds of interpersonal communication breaks down due to the fact that the communicating parties are distant from each other in space and time, the mediated communication itself provides some sort of virtual social context. The micro-oriented sociologist, let's say equipped with some of the insights from Erving Goffman's works, must look for contextual elements, or meta-elements in the mediated communication itself, which is coloured substantially by the nature of the medium.

The 'communicative turn'

It seems appropriate here to address the growing interest in communication as a compensation for overarching values and norms. The argument

DOI: 10.1057/9781137446466.0005

here is that this turn – called the 'communicative' turn – indicates the growing importance of mass media and personal media as generative for social integration. To throw some light on this, we may turn to some insights in sociology and social theory for the last 25 years or so. Along with the changes in media development I have sketched briefly earlier, new understandings of society have also emerged that underline the communication aspect of society. That is an expected effect of what the late Richard Rorty coined the linguistic turn in philosophy, with Ludwig Wittgenstein as a key reference. This turn implied that philosophical problems related to truth and knowledge as well as justice should be rephrased in terms of linguistics and language use. In all of the social sciences the linguistic turn has, along with technological change, left traces of a *communicative* turn, which emphasises the practical use of language in the construction of identity as well as in social inequalities and conflicts. Social action and organisations are seen as communication systems reproduced by observations and decisions. Society is seen as constituted in and through communication, which constantly reproduces and reorganises itself in order to cope.

This suggests that we need to address the process of communication and its media forms and genres, rather than (only) specific considerations of specific subjects. Let me explain this by briefly recapitulating some points in the process (the communicative turn) from subject philosophy to communication theory.

As part of his philosophical method, Descartes 'doubted' all existence, and through this could demonstrate that all wrong thoughts about the world were still thoughts about the world, which had to come from something other than the world. This was his way of proving the existence of God, which forced him to reconsider his doubt on everything. Husserl exchanged the Cartesian doubt with the phenomenological reduction, which begins with the fact that the world is as we experience it. We can become conscious about our consciousness about the world by suspending parts of it, bracketing it, to let consciousness affirm the existence of it. What then about the consciousness of fellow human beings? How do we meet the objection of solipsism?

To Husserl, intersubjectivity is the ability of subjects to overcome themselves, to communalise, where 'I' or the subject becomes a world for all. Unlike Descartes, this common world is not constituted through the relationship between consciousness and object, but between consciousness and phenomenon. The subject becomes integrated in a world, which

DOI: 10.1057/9781137446466.0005

is for others. The subject relates itself and understands itself through the interpretation of others who interpret the world from other points of view than its own. Objectivity was seen as intersubjectivity (Crossley 1996, 3). Through this interpretation and meaning-production, the subject becomes an intersubject. This process comes before the objective (scientific) perception of the object. From this one may say that Husserl was the last subjectivist and the first intersubjectivist.

However, Husserl did not take fully account of the role of language in the production of the social world. Husserl's ideas were elaborated in the social sciences by Alfred Schütz and the American pragmatists, the symbolic interactionists G. H. Mead and later Herbert Blumer, and in speech act theory. Jürgen Habermas was the one who brought the notion of intersubjectivity a step further by building on the linguistic turn as well as on Schütz, pragmatism and Goffman. As we have seen, Habermas projected the lifeworld as a mutually constituted taken-for-granted background context reproduced through socialisation, solidarity and culture. From the lifeworld, communicative action receives its competence to reason and criticise. Communicative rationality is considered precisely to be the grounded motivation to enter into rational interaction on issues of general interest. As reflexivity, it complements the lifeworld horizon, and still merges from it. The intersubjectively shared lifeworld becomes a sociological (empirical) reality, and communicative action a specifically modern effect of rationalisation (of systems, mediatisation and colonisation). Communicative action involves the automatic ability to produce some specific expectations of others through idealisations, that is, criticisable validity claims about the subjective, the objective and the intersubjective worlds as subtext of their arguments. Thus, reflexive communication grounded in cultural integration (the intersubjectivity of the lifeworld) generates rational intersubjectivity and mutual understanding – and possibly, consensus.

Habermas's concept of the lifeworld, as we have seen, rests on two empirical observations: First, it is an empirical fact closely associated with the concept of everyday life, although *how* the concept of the lifeworld is to be understood sociologically is not perfectly clear. Second, the concept of communicative action and communicative rationality pose the possibility of handling disagreements and conflict rationally. Conflict and disagreement are unavoidable in all societies, but only modern societies have the linguistic resources to transform them into arguments and mutual understanding.

DOI: 10.1057/9781137446466.0005

In contrast, Niklas Luhmann's theory of society has reserved a peculiar place for acting subjects. In complex societies, the individual has reached an independent and reflexive position vis-à-vis the norms of society, and is now considered to be outside communication and thus outside society. Autonomous individuals enable communication, and communication is normally *attributed* to individuals so as to make sense of it. The out-differentiated, self-referential communication systems (function systems and organisations and face-to-face interaction systems) operate as subjects. Communication is differentiated through semantic codes and various types of media.

Let me sum up the distinction between what we might call the norm-oriented perspective and the communication-theoretical perspective as follows: First, Goffman and Luhmann (unlike Husserl and Habermas) see meaning and norms (as the quintessential *social*) as *arising from communication*, rather than *producing* communication. Communication generates illusions of intersubjectivity, and it produces simulations of a common world. Second, to Luhmann and Goffman (again unlike Habermas and Husserl), the phenomenon of communication (neither the human subject, nor the text or work itself) is the crux of the social. This is the *Interaction Order* that Goffman quite famously proposed as a research theme of itself, or Foucault's discourse, or Luhmann's communication. Third, unlike the focus on community and values, this indicates that personal mediated communication increasingly presents itself as an interdisciplinary field of research, spanning the new and post-hermeneutic aesthetics of Martin Seel, Hans Ulrich Gumbrecht and Friedrich Kittler, to the non-normative, communication-oriented micro and macro sociologies of Goffman and Luhmann. In spite of the emphasis of much sociology on individualisation and the focus on particular texts, such as films, advertising and computer games, both the human subject and the singular text have less explanatory value compared to mediated communication as the generator of sociality. Correspondingly, a readjustment (or widening) of focus in media research is needed (and underway).

Luhmann on communication

Interpersonal communication in personal media changes the significance of media in communication models. Consequently, other

DOI: 10.1057/9781137446466.0005

communication theories and modes appear more relevant. One such relevant theory is Niklas Luhmann's 'subject-less' communication theory already mentioned, constructed in connection with his sociological systems theory. Luhmann's theory accounts for construction rather than transmission, since the sender does not give up anything that the receiver acquires. Furthermore, communication is not about the ability of the sender to get his message across, but about the understanding of the receiver, and what he or she does with it. The identity of a message lies in the *reception* of the message. For Luhmann, communication is a result of three selections: *information*, *message* (Mitteilung) and *understanding* (Verstehen). Communication only constitutes itself as a fact if all three selections are made. Information is the selection of something in the world that can be uttered in some way. It is the meaning-construction of something that potentially can serve as a message. It actualises something from the infinite latency of human existence.

Next, a message must be selected from the information and formed as a message. This refers to the expression of the information in some distinct fashion, through some language or image, through the telephone or TV and so on. Information must be given comprehensible form. An utterance is interpretable as a selection. Only when a message is produced does the third selection – understanding – come into play. Understanding refers to the change of the state of the one who receives the utterance. Understanding is a selection based upon a distinction between information and message. However, for more communication to follow, the receiver must confirm or manifest him or herself through some reaction to the information or message of the sender. Therefore, there is often something in communication that works to enable new communication (through questions, friendliness, counter-arguments, provocations, appeals, etc.). Social systems can only reproduce themselves if communication follows communication. This is, I may add, precisely the constant challenge for communication in modern societies. It cannot rely fully on moral values, as was more the case in traditional society.

A dimension of the success of personal media lies in the combination of their motivational and pragmatic character, in that they carry a systemic rationality as both aims and means. The pragmatic aspect lies in their practicality and convenience, as a resource at hand to reach others, retrieve information, be entertained and so on. Personal media are resources that we use to act upon information and meaning from

DOI: 10.1057/9781137446466.0005

others, because such action usually appears easy and pleasurable. The threshold is lower than the gratification. This also entails that they are successful in narrowing our latent aims of action by presenting a distinct set of possible ways to act. As practical and useful means, they influence our motives and goals for action. They are thus not only resources but also motivators in that they quickly and conveniently present the other person or persons the useful information in and through the medium itself. To be sure, when we order a book at Amazon, the book arrives in the post some days or weeks later. Online ordering is a convenient instrumental action only. The postal system and the book medium must take care of the rest. In most cases however, as when we call someone, or respond to someone's posting on Facebook, the social contact, the social purpose, the meeting, is immediately established. The laptop and the mobile now present a fairly broad repertoire of output and input channels to persons, organisations, data bases and so on, which give us access to both, and actually present, people and information, in one and the same operation. We do not really think of the cultural and social possibilities as narrowed at all. On the contrary, we are all amazed about the new digital possibilities. Precisely this invisible selection of communication possibilities is at the heart of their success.

Karl Bühler's communication theory, on which Luhmann builds, was published in the 1930s and inspired the theory of speech acts by Austin and Searle where distinctions were made according to what is emphasised in the speech act. In Bühler and later Luhmann, speech acts and their intentions are not really relevant, only the possibilities inherent in language to fix information in an information universe, to utter messages and to allow for understanding. The three selections are not separate elements but components of a unity of communication. Communication happens when information, utterance and understanding are achieved (Luhmann 2012, 216).

Information is always a part of communication and always operates within a system. A sentence, a document, a statement, a lecture and a TV program are all chosen from a set of potential sentences and so on that could have been presented. What is actually presented depends on what has been presented beforehand in a conversation, in a research discipline, in TV schedules and so on. This background of information constitutes a context for the one who receives the message, which allows for such messages to occur. To follow a lecture or see a TV talk show, it is necessary to know something about previous lectures or talk shows in

DOI: 10.1057/9781137446466.0005

order to make sense of such utterances. Information is information about the selection of possible understandings, and assists the understanding as such. Thus, receiving the message or utterance in a mere technical or perceptive sense is not enough; the risk of not understanding or misunderstanding would be extremely high. The utterance is a coupling to or a selection from information, which is observed by someone who has the task of understanding. The lecturer or the TV program presents specific messages against the background of the information it has selected itself from.

One could certainly discuss what is actually the utterance in a phone chat, a lecture or a TV program, but it is not necessary here. The point is that it helps to carry communication further by producing a distinction between itself and information, making it possible for someone to observe, understand and possibly respond to with another distinction between information and utterance. The understanding concludes the communication and possibly begins another communication sequence. If understanding does not occur, the student leaves the auditorium or chooses to quit the course; if the TV watcher changes the channel and so on, the communication ends. Still, group or mass communication may proceed as long as there are others who enjoy the utterances. In personal communication with or without personal media however, the communication ends. Note that misunderstanding and non-understanding may serve as communication. The student may ask questions to the lecturer who is then given the chance to specify her explanations. The receiver of an invoice may complain to the sender. The TV station may, when ratings decrease, take a show off the schedule.

Information, utterance and understanding constitute a unity, but among the three understanding is the truly critical component that sees the distinction between information and utterance in order to continue with more communication (Luhmann 2012, 220). Understanding must relate to the utterance-in-context. Unity happens in understanding, including misunderstanding and disagreement. Such responses also often tend to provoke response (what did you mean? I disagree!). However often this does not happen in part because it may not be technically possible, as when watching a TV program or when the student is too shy to ask questions.

The speaker will attempt to anticipate his or her audience or conversation partner, to estimate what is needed to entertain, engage, or perhaps to provoke in order to establish a conversation, an intimate relationship,

DOI: 10.1057/9781137446466.0005

to attract an audience or in short to create a circularity of communication. Rhetoric and conventions of genres are helpful here, and so are disciplinary concepts, humoristic clichés and other language-immanent resources. If however understanding does not occur, what happens next is entirely open.

The information concerns what we are talking about; the utterance concerns how a specific selection of this is communicated (written, shouted, broadcasted, etc.) and understanding concerns the registering of the utterance qua utterance. A unity appears from the three selections or components that may have feedback effects on those who make communication possible and who may continue the communication.

Luhmann's communication theory begins with the face-to-face communication where simultaneity and mutual physical context and immediate perception tend to reduce contingency; that is narrow down the range of possible utterances and understandings. In mass communication, strong and stable genre conventions, familiar personalities and external emotive means like music and studio applause help the communicating sequence to go on. In analogue writing (script, letters, books, etc.) the writer is alone and can only anticipate or imagine his or her receiver or audience. From this fact, a history of linguistic, semantic and literary innovation – most of all rhetoric – has arisen. The aim is seduction: to make communication continue by creating understanding among the absent in time and space.

In written communication through electromagnetic telegraph, email, blogs, text messages and social media, there is normally no common context in space or time even if the possible audience is narrowed down considerably. One has to rely on imaginary, motivational aspects in language, perhaps supported with images and design. In mobile telephony, the time frame and the oratory context enabled through a familiar voice is mutual. The geographies are however uncertain and often changing during the conversation, and provide little help for creating unity of information, utterance and understanding. How is communication possible under these new conditions? As we know, misunderstandings are frequent in social media and ignorance is as well. All the same communication continues. Blogs and Facebook and other similar platforms for communication have developed yet another set of technological features in addition to the ones inherent in language, such as specialisation and motivational aspects. These I will return to in another chapter.

DOI: 10.1057/9781137446466.0005

To Luhmann, the anticipation in utterances to seek understanding on the one hand, and the contingency present in all communication on the other, can be grasped with what he calls the theory of bifurcation (Luhmann 2012, 228). For communication to go on, for communication to be *anslußfähig*, responses with the principal 'yes' and 'no' ought to occur with equal frequency in the long run. As mentioned, misunderstandings and non-understandings are often occurring, but cannot occur all the time. The bifurcation – the choice between yes and no – takes place in every communication, and often the no enables communication to continue. Disagreement leads to justifications and new disagreement and so on, perhaps to the point where everyone involved agrees on their disagreements.

The observer who is to understand the utterance must understand what is uttered in relation to the world it is selected from. Or: the observer must ask: What distinction is operating here? Then the complexity remains reduced – the world of possible communication is contingent and rests on the distinction in use. This is second-order observation that dispenses with ontological truths, and as a European specialty, seeks what lies behind. We are more and more aware of the fact that things may not be the way they seem and that they may be different to another person. What is it that the other does not see? And does the other see that he cannot see? None of us have the complete picture. As Luhmann formulates it: We may be dealing with a circulation of a blind spot (Luhmann 2012, 115).

Luhmann has suggested (from C. J. Friedrich) that authority may be understood as 'the capacity for reason elaboration' as the ability to give reasons (Luhmann 2012, 224–225). Authority is in the one who always asks what reasons one has and finds further reasons for these justifications; this functions as an absorption of uncertainty, which since Herbert Simon's work in the 1950s has been considered as a critical function in organisations. Unlike Habermas, Luhmann sees this ability not as practical reason, but as a form of power capable of reducing complexity and defining topics on the ground of reasons. This authority is in fact necessary for communication to go on: 'It serves as the precondition of continued autopoiesis [self steering] and the precondition of connecting operations' (Luhmann 2012, 225).

Communication happens when a piece of communication is passed on as an utterance or message for someone to understand. The operation of uttering simultaneously creates a distinction between hetero-reference

DOI: 10.1057/9781137446466.0005

(information) and self-reference (utterance). Re-entry takes place through the copying of something into itself by itself. Communication creates or reproduces a social system and is an internal operation.

In personal media, one does select not only understandings, but also information and messages. In a Luhmann's frame of reference, one may argue that mass media require reception, which entails selection of understanding, whereas personal media require selection of information (hence co-production), messages and understanding. In contrast to mass media (and intermediary forms of interactive media) personal media are involved in all three selections involved in communication sequences: selections of information, messages and understandings. In other words, communication in and through personal media draws upon selections involved in both mass media and personal communication. This also gives a communication-theoretical account for why personal media are not well suited for particular sectors, or in Luhmann: function systems. Unlike mass media, which have out-differentiated their own function system, personal media do not mediate any specific set of communication codes. Personal media are as such suited for *all* social fields and systems and organisations in society, including private, interpersonal communication.

Luhmann (1996) argues that in the modern society of functional sub-systems, one particular system has been given the task of selecting information for societal interaction among social systems and individuals The media system produces communication about communication produced by other social systems, including the media system itself. Information and debates about unemployment, financial crisis, elections, the world cup, scandals, the incompetence of teachers and so on are all second-order communication, produced by the self-reference of the media system.

But media forms riding on the Internet do *not* fit within the demarcation criteria of the mass media system. True, email, web and social media certainly diffuse information across time and space to millions of people. Furthermore, news, advertising and entertainment are to be found on the net. Still, the web was transformed through protocols of interactivity and co-creation (Web 2.0) into a communication medium. The Internet cannot be considered as any other kind of dissemination media in the mass media system or any other particular social system. On the contrary, the rapid diffusion of the Internet in the 1990s should partly be explained with its *complementarity* vis-à-vis the electronic mass media, as

DOI: 10.1057/9781137446466.0005

an infrastructure for personal media and interpersonal and networked communication. Communication on the Internet is not restricted to the mass-mediated information codes, which shape the principles of news, advertising and entertainment. The openness of the Internet makes itself useful for all sectors of society. As the mass media present their messages through the code of information/not information, this fact restricts the mass media from participating in *other* function systems and their internal information requirements. Although people in the financial business read the yellow press, they cannot rely on the press for internal, detailed, restricted and personal information. Scientists cannot publish in popular science magazines only, and the political system cannot use the mass media for their internal exchange of information.

In contrast to mass media, personal media normally produce groups and networks rather than *audiences*. An audience is the receiving environment for mass media content. It has no concrete status and does not consist of any particular number of individuals. In mass media, audiences are rarely spatially located. This abstract character of the audience means that it cannot be identified as such. It can only be observed indirectly. 'The audience' represents a range of *implied* or assumed ways to receive mass media output, an image or construction from the side of media organisations. It signifies a host of anticipated and assumed schemes or codified practices, enabled by the joint products of mass media output and intelligible individual media habits. Therefore, the mass media can only gradually improve and adjust their media output according to attention responses and indirect feedback with the help of the ratings industry and through reviews and debate in the public sphere. In other words, audiences do not consist of individuals but of measurable aggregations of typifications, images or models of media-use behaviour. Only in this way can the audience be transformed into a political community – or a commodity.

In personal media, including Twitter and Facebook, audiences are not invisible, they do not exist. In their absence, a number of individuals are performing communication in groups and *social networks*. There is no operative separation between production and consumption, and consequently readers are always potential producers of messages. Furthermore, personal media are available in and for *all* social systems, not only for what Luhmann calls the mass media function system. The rapid diffusion of the Internet in the last decades is little different from the dissemination of analogue telecommunication from the latter part

DOI: 10.1057/9781137446466.0005

of the nineteenth century. Its flexibility makes it applicable for military, governmental, economic, private and probably all other communication processes in society. It encourages rather than prohibits interaction. The information is produced by the communicating parts (as in email) or by small-scale publishers (as on the web) rather than by a gigantic media industry only. The Internet refuses to be restricted to a singular social system, it rejects the favouring of one particular code, because it is to be allied neither with a symbolic medium like money or power, nor is it a dissemination media of the non-interactive profession-based sort.

A simple sociological distinction throwing light on the difference between the genuine features of the Internet and traditional mass media is between category and network, stated by Harrison White (1965/2008, see Calhoun 1995, 220). *Category* distinguishes a group of people by their common features. It refers to boundaries, which the individuals in a group have in common in contrast to the external world, whether geographic, cultural or otherwise. Category defines the basic conditions for membership in a certain group or movement. It characterises the similarities of the members in a group which distinguish it from other groups. Cases, on the one hand, are members of a local or national community, subcultures with some common characteristics and so on. *Networks*, on the other hand, refer to a particular group of individuals among a social whole delimited by the social relations *between* the individuals. The network aspect refers to the density, durability and multiplicity of social ties irrespective of common features, geography and place.

We can connect this simple distinction to media technologies in order to see the features of different mediation processes and mediated integration. Television and radio establish cultural communities by exposing their common features to others. Mass media enhance social change by visualising living conditions for certain social groups who then become defined as a *category*, like the poor, students, immigrants, Roma people, gays, members of a particular community and so on. Television, in particular, visualises common characteristics of certain individuals and as such defines them or confirms the definition of them as a social group. The reach of TV is global, irrespective of age, gender, class or nationality. It has largely transcended class distinctions, even if what people actually watch differs. For technological and other reasons, television has, in the post-war era, become the all-inclusive medium that reaches everyone, occasionally with the same programme at the same time.

DOI: 10.1057/9781137446466.0005

Somewhat crudely, we may say that while the mass media meditate contexts as *categories*, personal media forms mediate contexts as *networks*. Compared to the category making of the mass media, personal media based on the Internet and telephony enhance *networks*. A set of email sessions does not expose or demonstrate in public common features or similar characteristics that would construct them socially as a group. Rather, they define groups through their actual mediating of social relationships. The characteristics of the group would appear through the variability, durability, regularity and density of the interaction. However, personal media like social networking sites and blogs construct hybrid forms. Boyd refers to networked publics as reconfigured publics with network technologies. What Chambers (2013, 57–59) calls personalised networked publics, particularly in social media, highlight personal control, 'yet also the problem or challenge of the nature of the interaction'. In the context of social media, 'listed "Friends" become personal "publics"'.

Plurality of communication forms

On the one hand, unmediated face-to-face interaction is probably considered to have a prominent, ideal-typical status among most people. On the other hand, there is no reason to consider the unmediated as a pure or ideal form, isolated from the diversity of media use. Mediated interactions are as real as unmediated communication – both in terms of interacting persons and topics for communication and for friendship and relationship to develop (Tanis and Postmes 2003, Brandtzæg and Stav 2004). The mediated and the unmediated are not different ontologies, nor are they different social spheres. Various media influence communication and interaction in different ways, but they all support the individual in his and her everyday interaction and meaning-production.

Social motivation is the main reason for participation in social network sites (Brandtzæg and Heim 2007). Blogs, for instance, appear as individual and even intimate forms of self-expression through text, photos and videos, but are also a way of maintaining social interaction with others. Users create profiles dedicated to online and offline friends and visualising networks of relationships, which all have real social effects.

As we are well into the second decade of the new millennium, new technologies for perception, interaction, publication and archiving are

DOI: 10.1057/9781137446466.0005

constantly thrown at the consumers. Many of them have quickly been absorbed by, and embedded in everyday practices. To most people in countries far beyond the developed part of the world, the 'mobile' and the 'laptop' have become near-universal machines. Both are devices for a multitude of trivial and advanced tasks in daily life. In this, personal media enhance social change in that they accelerate certain changes and compensate for roads not taken. This has always been the case with media technologies – what is new is that these forms of social regulation have reached the private realms of the individual in a much more fundamental way. Social interaction to a greater extent than before rests on the responsibility and the possibility of the individual, and is shaped by the time–space features of media.

Rather than focusing on distinct media with their distinct functions and purposes, a media-pragmatic approach addresses communicational selectivity and practicability in the constant social–technological interplay which establishes routine preferences and choices by skilled social actors. Personal media belong to the social lives of people who are much more than 'users'. The person and their personal media knit a complicated web of meaning, where face-to-face contact plays the most prominent role. Along with face-to-face interaction, personal media are entangled and continue to approach one another and our various social ties in our individual lifeworld. From a media-pragmatic perspective, this range of media alternatives and supplements are channels not only to a wider world, but also in the personal world of meaning-making, and of things present and absent, practical and impractical, convenient and inconvenient, impulsive and calculating. They are, as language itself, non-human, but still very human-made tools for constructing and maintaining reality.

DOI: 10.1057/9781137446466.0005

5
Personal Media Theory

Abstract: *This chapter takes the step from communication to media technologies. It briefly revisits Marshall McLuhan's ideas and some other proposals in the medium theoretical tradition in order to grasp the power of media technology and to what extent it can be 'tamed' or domesticated. I address both the discomforting aspects of dealing with virtual (simulated) realities and on the other hand, the convenience they offer to our sociality. It also charts the debate on the relationship between the online and offline in everyday life, and illustrates with the very recent development of augmented media/situated simulations.*

Rasmussen, Terje. *Personal Media and Everyday Life: A Networked Lifeworld*. Basingstoke: Palgrave Macmillan, 2014. DOI: 10.1057/9781137446466.0006.

Apparently, personal media require a higher degree of involvement from the users in interactive and immediate dialogical processes. The difference from the mass media is often conceived of as one of the different levels of commitment on the part of the user. As the *sender – medium – receiver* model becomes obsolete, personal media require more determination about the intentions of the process than the more habitual media reception. However, this intuitive 'observation' masks deeper and more significant social and cultural differences between action orientations and kinds of media. Personal media use should be approached hermeneutically, both from a typology of everyday genres and from a rough typology of technologies.

Nancy Baym (2010, 7–12) suggests that media as well as face-to-face communication can be compared along seven features: interactivity, temporal structure, social cues, storage, replicability, reach and mobility. The mobile is primarily an extension of hearing and voice capacities. The relations in space (and with answering services: time) are fundamentally altered since I may not even know where the person on the other end (the object) may be located geographically (or in time), and this gives me the reason to ask: 'Where are you?' The object may be reduced to a voice (even with unsatisfactory technical quality), that is both 'here' and 'there'; it operates in a partly irreal near-distance (Ihde 1990, 78) – in a self-generated *virtual context*. The mobile phone seemingly narrows the distance between the subjects, by 'magnifying' the other. A spatial, contextual change takes place in that the other comes closer to one's bodily context. The telephone *itself* 'withdraws' to clear way for the enlarged view of the other who becomes more 'present'. Through this kind of use, it is a tool for a moment of intersubjectivity. The phone is no longer an object, but refers to a human *co-subject* that must be reached in a process of meaning-in-constitution (Rasmussen 1996).

As such, the smartphones are taken-for-granted, 'naturalised' facts of daily life. This demonstrates the necessity to view media technology hermeneutically, to notice its contextual relationship to the subject, how it is constituted through its use. New means always imply modified uses and perceptions. Despite their transparency or even triviality, the mobile and other personal media transform perception by isolating, framing, amplifying and revealing (new aspects of) the object, and also through the relativisation of distance. They enable production of meaning dialogically. In the case of the telephone it is important that one hears (however

DOI: 10.1057/9781137446466.0006

modified) an *actual* voice in time and space. The pseudo-transparency of the mobile implies that *one hears through it, not at it*. The medium is 'close' to the subject, that is, it is a tool for the subject in his/her contact with the world. The technology is 'here', compared to the other out 'there'. Also, in a telephonic conversation, the other becomes a 'co-subject', because of the converging of utterances into one communicative process.

These facts about telephony stand in contrast to the relation between the human subject and mass media like television (TV, or the radio). The TV becomes an object of perception *in itself* while it also refers to something else in the world. What is immediately interpreted is the technology of sound and images – not the world through it. We watch 'TV news', rather than 'world news'. With the TV, the focus of the subject is directed much more towards the terminal than in the case of the telephone. Similarly, while the telephone is predominantly a channel for interaction, the TV and radio *themselves* constitute objects of mediation. Although the technology is located in the same locale as the viewer, its significance is 'out there', merged with the world of events and people, which it mediates into the locale. TV presents dynamic, audio-visual representations of the world rather than verbal interaction with co-subjects in a discursive mode. By contrast, if the telephone presents the object in a distorted way (supplying the object with a false voice, etc.), it is due to changes of the other agent herself or to error committed by the subject, and not caused by the interpretative use of the media technology itself. In the case of the telephone, one perceives the other subject *through* the technology, and thus gives the technology relatively few opportunities to present cultural versions of the world.

The point here is not that all media behave as either the mobile or as the TV. The web is the most important example of a medium that transcends the distinction by importing and integrating communicative and hermeneutic features. Various media entail different weights of the communicative mobile aspect and the hermeneutic TV aspect. Most media technologies mediate the subject–object relationship differently, and so locate themselves on one or the other 'side' of that distinction. From an interpretative position of the agent/user/subject, all media technologies can be placed on a continuum between the two extremes. The location of the web would depend on its interactive design and use of sub-media like email, mailing lists, chat groups and so on. It is a question of allowing the reader to write.

DOI: 10.1057/9781137446466.0006

McLuhan

Marshall McLuhan, as we know, was a media thinker of many fascinating, half-baked ideas. A perspective that ran through his work was present as a turning point between the old and the new; the media in a waning world of distance and a coming unifying world of inclusion and integrated meaning. However, below the grand ideas, do we find traces of a theory of the new personal media? The revival/return of an acoustic, tribal collectivist world as an effect of telecommunications, broadcasting and heretical ideas in science was touched upon in the concluding chapter of *Gutenberg Galaxy* (The Galaxy Reconfigured). In *Understanding Media*, this turn was analysed more specifically, if still in a very McLuhanesque and fragmentary manner: Let me briefly revisit McLuhan's seven rhetorically grounded (sets of) arguments or hypotheses about media and human change in *Understanding Media*, and then his four laws of media.

One: The medium is the message: '... the personal and social consequences of any medium – that is, of any extension of ourselves – result from the new scale that is introduced into our affairs by each extension of ourselves, or by any new technology' (1964, 23). This statement means several things. First, an argument about social/mental construction: that the formal or material composition of the medium will present the world differently, hence our perception of it. To understand this we should consider the media as extensions of our senses. Our consciousness will be shaped according to the formal features of our 'extended senses'. Second, there is no real content; all content consists of other media. The content of writing is speech, the content of print is the written word and the content of the telegraph is print. The use and content of media may be diverse, but it is also of little importance: '... the medium is the message because it is the medium that shapes and controls the scale and form of human association and action' (1964, 24). Third, our conventional emphasis on use and content tends to distract us from what is important about the media, and prevents us therefore from seeing the new age carried by the electric media: 'For the "content" of a medium is like the juicy piece of meat carried by the burglar to distract the watchdog of the mind' (1964, 32).

Two: Media can be classified into hot or cold/cool media (or possibly listed on a continuum between the two) The radio is hot, while

DOI: 10.1057/9781137446466.0006

telephone is cool. Movies are hot, while TV is cool. The alphabet is hot, while hieroglyphs are cool. Waltz is hot, while jazz is cool. The principle refers to the ability of the medium to involve the user. While hot media provide complete information, cool media provide little or incomplete information that must be supplied by the user. Hot media do not leave it to the user to fill in information. A related distinction is between high- and low-definition media: High-definition media fill the user with information, often towards one or few senses, while low-definition media provide incomplete information towards many senses. Low-definition, cool, less-specialised media tend to encourage participation.

Three: At later stages of the development of a medium, the effects tend to reverse from the original effects. This can be seen in the development of singular media, and in the media culture as a whole. TV and telephone begin their careers as individualistic media, but tend to turn users towards each other. With computer power, the typed word, which once was differentiated from the spoken word, now turns towards orality again. At the level of culture, tendencies of fragmentation switch towards growing social integration and 'retribalisation'. This point reappears in later publications, such as the posthumous Media Laws (see later).

Four: The media represent extensions of our senses, and precisely therefore also provide a sort of auto amputation since the media irritate some senses at the expense of others. As in the myth of Narcissus, we become numb or shocked by the composition of the media, which changes the equilibrium of the nervous system. The senses seek new equilibria depending on which senses become extended by the media. The introduction of TV is changing culture and personality everywhere, depending, however, on the existing sense ratio in each culture. For instance, in the relatively audio-tactile Europe, TV is intensifying the visual sense, and therefore making Europeans more similar to Americans.

Five: Media change must be understood as an evolution where media compete, influence and change one another: 'The interplay among media is only another name for this "civil war" that rages in our society and our psyches alike...The crossings or hybridizations of the media release great new force and energy as by fission and fusion' (1964, 57). On the one hand, a war is going on: 'When the

DOI: 10.1057/9781137446466.0006

press opened up the "human interest" keyboard after the telegraph had restructured the press medium, the newspaper killed the theatre, just as TV hit the movies and the night clubs very hard' (1964, 60–61). On the other hand, the new media constitute new relationships that change their ways: 'Radio changed the form of the news story as much as it altered the film image in the talkies. TV caused drastic changes in radio programming, and in the form of the *thing* or documentary novel' (1964, 61).

Also, this 'hybridisation', these moments of change, opens up possibilities to glimpse the structural properties of the media. Normally, media put us in a state of numbness that diverts our consciousness while the media themselves 'slam the gates of judgment and perception' (1964, 68). With the rationalism of the printing press as a recent backdrop, we may better observe the 'tribalism' of radio. Such media meetings cause ruptures, which again may enhance reflexivity: 'The hybrid of the meeting of two media is a moment of truth and revelation from which a new form is born. For the parallel between two media holds us on the frontiers between forms that snap us out of the Narcissus-narcosis. The moment of the meeting of media is a moment of freedom and release from the ordinary trance and numbness imposed by them on our senses' (1964, 63).

Six: Mechanisation is a translation of culture and personality. It used to mean translation into more explicit, specialised forms. With new technologies, we are translated into portions of information, which is much more integrated. Just as humans used to be servants of tools to survive, we are now dependent on new media. However, whereas old tools tended to be fragmentary and partial, new technologies tend to operate more inclusively and organically, and so encourage tribalisation/communality.

Seven: There is a possibility/promise that the new situation may rebalance the ratio of the senses, and so reset our rationality: 'A new stasis is in prospect' (1964, 68). All media change affects the entire system or ration among our senses. Just as our senses constitute an integrated system that changes when a sense damaged, new media that amplify or intensify the input from a sense change the entire consciousness and culture as system. There is however one immunity; art: '... the artist is indispensable in the shaping and analysis and understanding of the life of forms, and structures created by, electric technologies' (1964, 70). 'The artist is the man in many fields, scientific or humanistic,

DOI: 10.1057/9781137446466.0006

who grasps the implications of his actions and of new knowledge in his own time. He is the man of integral awareness' (1964, 71).

Having put forward these arguments more or less systematically with more examples than references to research, and with references to everything from Toynbee to Agatha Christie (and of course to James Joyce), McLuhan proceeds to discuss a wide variety of media in turn. In 25 chapters he addresses singular media from the spoken word to weapons, in relation to human senses and culture. His famous style is associative, metaphoric, filled with more assertions than arguments about media and culture, mixed with bewildering and thought-provoking examples and references.

In two overlapping works, collaborators of McLuhan have put together central ideas that McLuhan developed during the 1970s. The origins of the ideas are somewhat unclear; to what extent these ideas are developed by, or simply formulated by McLuhan's associates remains open. The tetrad is a set of four questions that can be asked with reference to all media and material things. The thinking is inspired by classic rhetoricians and others who have opposed dialectics from Aristotle to Hegel (and Marx), preferably Plato, Aquinas, Bacon, Vico and Joyce. Rather, what we have is an ongoing interaction between forms and background furthered by the media. New media bring new aspects of reality to the fore, while others move to the background. From the electromagnetic telegraph, media have tended to bring back auditive, tactile ways of perceiving the world, tipping our orientation towards the right hemisphere/part of the brain, and culturally, towards the acoustic space of involved, emotional social contact. The reader can either see the tetrad as a simple methodology for addressing media change, or (as McLuhan did himself) look at this as an alternative research paradigm concerning media change and the history of consciousness.

The four laws of media and their corresponding questions are as follows: What is extended or enhanced by a new medium (what becomes the new form)? What phenomena are made superfluous or redundant by it (what becomes 'ground')? What phenomena are retrieved or brought back (from ground to form)? What phenomena tend to end up reversed, with contrary effects (from form to new form)? Thus, all media and technologies will tend to enhance something, make something superfluous, recreate something and press something towards its opposite effect. The telephone enhances voice communication, makes the presence of the body superfluous in conversation, brings back the personal, mystical and 'telepathic' and flips over to phenomena like telephone conferences, which distance the voice from its intimacy. Electronic mail increases information transfer, makes interpretation of all mail impossible, creates new patterns of communication and taken to the extreme, will create chaos and loss of identity.

The first law/question is the McLuhan question proper, famous from *Understanding Media* (each medium will amplify or enhance distinct senses and aspects of reality at the expense of other aspects). The second law/question is basically the same question as the first, but with emphasis on what is pulled back by the new medium (e.g. print culture overshadowed by TV/film/telephone). The third law/question refers to the point that old innovations and things occasionally get a 'second life', however in a new modern, electric or digital form. What appear as clichés reappear in new shapes as new useful things. This is easy to see in fashion, typography, social rituals and all media, which all can be considered as modernisations of archaic forms of communication (consider also current concepts like 'vintage', 'classic', 'shabby-chic', 'retro', 'nostalgia', etc.). The horse-cab turns into a car-cab, mail into email, walls into Facebook walls and so on. The fourth law/question of reversal concerns unintended and unrecognised side effects: the car creates suburbs; the telephone creates skyscrapers; information overload creates illiteracy (?); cash money reverse into credit cards; bureaucracies create informal channels of communication and so on.

Not much used in media research, the laws of media are considered as determinism (no human influence), and as trivial compared to McLuhan's rather ambitious presentation ('The New Science'). Without doubt McLuhan's legacy lies in the first law, the central message of *Understanding Media*: TV and other cool, low-definition media take over for the hot, high-definition media, and are, through their acting as selective prostheses on our senses, re-enhancing a more interacting, informal, involving, Asian-like, global culture.

Modes of mediation

McLuhan's ideas carried further a media-centred perspective on media history that perhaps began with Harold Innis, and continued with Walter Ong, McLuhan and Neil Postman, Jean Baudrillard, Joshua Meyrowitz and others. A concept in this tradition subject to some debate is reme-

DOI: 10.1057/9781137446466.0006

diation. In the book *Remediation, Understanding New Media*, Jay David Bolter and Richard Grusin (1999) argue in line with McLuhan that new media convey old media as content. What they call *remediation* drives the media evolution. Remediation involves two dimensions or perspectives: *transparency* (or immediacy) and *hypermediacy*. On the one hand, transparency means that the medium withdraws itself from reality, to let the immediate, direct experience (visually and auditively) constitute the user's frame of experience. The medium hides itself, letting reality appear. On the other hand, hypermediacy derives from rejecting the idea of total mediation; it stems from graphic artificiality, tabloid layout, computer-game virtuosity and post-modern artificiality, in staging the object as unfinished, incomplete or as a model. The medium 'wants' to make the mediation explicit, and the user feels that she constantly needs to make decisions concerning what information to receive and how to receive it. The distinction between transparency and hypermediacy is a post-McLuhan way of connecting media to perception, but by exchanging hemispheres and brain functions with aesthetics. Bolter and Grusin's theory of remediation is frequently used to understand digital media.

In a similar fashion Fagerjord (2003) Fagerjord argued that each new medium carries with it particular rhetorical features or techniques, and that these are borrowed from previous (or existing) media. To understand the appearance of video, text and sound on the web, we need to address how the rhetorical forms or existing media forms are recombined in the new medium. Fagerjord's concept of 'rhetorical convergence' and Bolter and Grusin's terms 'hypermediacy' and 'transparency' all point towards different strategies in analysing conventions inherent in new media, deriving at least in part from the technology itself. For instance, in the multimodal process of remediation or rhetorical convergence on the web, both writing and images seem to receive new functions: As Bolter argues, the technology has the effect of making text graphic by representing its verbal structure graphically. On the web, the emphasis on design is radicalised. Java applets, icons and other clickable links give the writing a more visual, symbolic style.

Another useful distinction, to examine the various features of personal media, and web media in particular, is showing/telling as it is addressed in different research disciplines. Philosopher of art Susanne Langer's distinction between discursive and presentational symbols is a case in point (Langer 1942, Meyrowitz 1986, 95). Her theory of 'presentational symbolism' was influenced by Ernst Cassirer, and she argues that basically

DOI: 10.1057/9781137446466.0006

all forms of human expression could be seen as expressive, but that some were abstracted through signs/signals, and others abstracted through symbols. Symbols give expression to ideas that go beyond what can be expressed through language. A dimension of experience that cannot be accounted for discursively is dealt with non-discursively through a wide range of symbolic phenomena (myth, ritual, art, music, dreams). She also argued that iconic symbols of human emotions could be interpreted as rules similar to rules of language.

Discursive symbols are most importantly language, while presentational symbols are predominantly pictures and images. Discursive symbols are abstract and arbitrary in that they never mirror what they stand for. Also, they are discrete, which means that they carry a meaning independent of the immediate arrangement of the particular letter or word. Also, the grammatical structure of discursive symbols does not resemble the sequence and arrangements of how things actually take place. For instance, one cannot describe events simultaneously, even if they happen simultaneously in real life. She argued that many things did not fit the grammatical scheme of language, but were still of vital importance and of objective presence. Symbols take over when language must remain silent. They need to be conceived of through another symbolic schema (Langer 1942).

In contrast, presentational (non-discursive) symbols such as music, photo or video have a direct immediate resemblance with what they represent. The particular elements of a photo have no immediate meaning by themselves, only when arranged in a pattern that in some way represents objects in the world. While discursive symbols like sentences make sense only when they are organised according to an internal formal grammar and in clauses in discourse, thus independent of the actual world, presentational symbols make sense when they are arranged according to some actual 'real' external object. Consequently, the only way to make sense of a presentational symbol is to perceive it as a whole, in one act of seeing, as a gestalt. Unlike language, the photo represents itself and cannot be 'explained' by other presentational symbols. Neither can representational symbols easily be used to discuss abstract ideas and arguments without the support of discursive symbols.

Meyrowitz (1986) argues that Langer's terms may be used to specify the difference between electronic media and print media. Print media, on the one hand, exclude presentational meaning, leaving only the meaning of discursive symbols. Electronic media, on the other hand,

DOI: 10.1057/9781137446466.0006

convey a broader range of meaning in that they mediate presentational symbols along with discursive symbols. Radio conveys sounds along with verbal language, and TV adds images to verbal or printed language. Electronic media, because of their close affiliation with expressions and presentational symbols, '... tend to unite sender and receiver in an intimate web of personal experience and feeling' (Meyrowitz 1986, 96). It is worth noting that Langer did not think that presentational symbols express the emotions of the artist, but rather an 'idea' of emotions. They express illusions, virtual versions.

A similar conceptual dualism is presented by Watzlawic et al. (1967, see Meyrowitz 1986) who distinguish between 'digital' and 'analogue' symbols. Digital symbols are discrete symbols, as numbers and words, whereas analogue symbols are continuous and fluent. Watzlawic et al. argue that digital symbols convey manifest content about issues and things, whereas analogue symbols convey relational messages about feelings and other aspects that cannot easily be formalised in digital messages. Converted to the discussion of print and electronic media, Meyrowitz suggests that print media convey digital information, whereas electronic media convey both digital and analogue information.

These sets of concepts help to explain how contrasting media forms provide diverging possibilities and limitations for the media user in understanding the world. They convey different 'logics' and lead to quite different learning and interpretation processes. While presentational media encourage more personal, intimate and expressive responses, discursive media (text) appear more precise and 'scientific', but exclude feelings, impressions and personal undertones that unavoidably come to the surface in expressive information. Presentational media forms may present objects in an unambiguous and immediately understandable way, but they cannot easily convey abstract ideas or conceptions in a precise fashion. To specify such symbols more accurately, one often must rely on language (as in subtexts of photos in newspapers). They are natural and direct in their representation of the world, but still imprecise and ambiguous. They cannot present statements that can be proven true or false. Rather, they appeal to taste and affections.

Personal media may mediate their meaning through both hot and cool media (McLuhan), immediacy and hypermediacy (Bolter and Grusin), through discursive, analogue texts and non-discursive (Langer) or digital/analogue (Watzlawick) symbols. Objects and places are non-discursive by nature; they are often products of art, craft and architecture. Ne

DOI: 10.1057/9781137446466.0006

simulation-oriented media, for example, let the viewer receive the story of the object 'told' by the object in its own presentational, symbolic ways of expression, only supplemented by written text (see later). Does this imply that the viewer comes closer to the object – with more open and direct access to the object since no information in another key comes 'between' the viewer and the object? Can presentational showing do the job of written text? In most contexts the answer is negative. The information that needs to be presented is normally too complex, exact and abstract.

Undermining representation?

This discomfort relates to what we may call fear of the Simulacrum: What is at stake is the status of representation itself, the process in which representation no longer respects the object, but replaces it. The original evaporates. The concept of *hyperreality* popular in the 1980s referred precisely to the experience of vertigo: That distinctions, spaces and time differences between objects and their representations tend to implode in the simulations and simultaneity of what Castells (1997) calls the 'spaces of flows' of the media society. The world of objects dissolves into an encompassing world of models. The model world takes over for both the real world and its representations. It creates a demand for itself due to its perfect illusions and for its reference to its environment as real. The notion of hyperreality (Baudrillard) refers to the perception of something that is neither real nor fake, a stage allegedly intimately bound up with a post-modern condition saturated with media, advertising and artificial environments.

Hyperreality refers to a stage of neither the real nor the representation, but something artificially simulated. A simulation is a representation that evolves to replace what is represented. It becomes 'reality'. Such simulations may be perfect but cannot avoid the emptiness of simulation and stimulation rather than true energy and 'aura'. It is a perfect imitation into, following Baudrillard's fourth stage, a simulacrum that transcends the real and its representations with no connection to reality. A double reference or a double loop is taking place: a simulation is pretending to be unreal. Unlike virtual reality, hyperreality creates a simulation within the real, which transcends the boundaries between the two into an apparently real reality. An example in Eco (1986), and Baudrillard (1983), is Disneyland. The land is perfect artificial realism (simulation), which

DOI: 10.1057/9781137446466.0006

makes it more stimulating and attractive than reality. This makes the term unreal meaningless and leaves the illusion that only what is outside the park is real. It is a world beyond reality and fiction, beyond true and false. Other examples would be TV reality shows and entertainment parks. The problem here is that representation was based on trust that the original existed as a guarantee, as a model. But if the original is a simulation, what is left is only circuits or systems where signs refer to signs. The fear is that the authority of originals is absorbed by the hyper-real, by the Simulacra.

Situated simulation

What has been called 'augmented reality' aims at presenting a totally mediated reality, since all traces of the physical world are mediated through the medium. Icons and text are laid over objects in the physical world, as an intermediary between the user and the physical world: 'Augmented reality is hypermediated, for it makes the user aware of computer graphics as medium, even if the goal is to keep the graphics and the external object in a close registration' (Bolter and Grusin 1999, 216). This is the dream of the smart-house and the virtual classroom. However, as a consequence of the fact that the dream of the virtual world is cancelled, other more hybrid versions are developed that account for the merge of 'the actual and the virtual' into a real world of a wide variety of mediated and unmediated experiences.

Let me illustrate this point. What is called a *situated simulation* differs from both augmented reality and virtual reality (Liestøl 2009, 2011). A situated simulation requires a broadband smartphone with substantial graphics capabilities and hardware sensors for positioning and various forms of movement. In a situated simulation there is approximate identity between the user's visual perception of the real physical environment and the user's visual perspective into a 3D graphics environment as it is represented on the screen. The relative congruity between the real and the virtual is obtained by letting the camera position and movement in the 3D environment be determined by the positioning and orientation hardware. As the user moves in real space, the perspective inside the virtual space changes accordingly.

In this modified augmented reality model, a distinction between the physical world and the virtuality of computer graphics does not exist in

DOI: 10.1057/9781137446466.0006

the medium, and so it does not aspire to capture all aspects of a physical/ virtual world into itself. Instead, in its mediation of reality, a situated simulation inserts a distinction between inside and outside the window frame of the mobile device. It acknowledges the ontological distinction between physical and virtual dimensions by letting the medium itself reproduce the distinction. The reality is 'augmented', not by capturing it entirely in the medium and then enhancing it by a graphical layer or filter. Rather, the world is here 'augmented' only by letting the medium mediate a virtual window, surrounded by a physical context. The unmediated reality actively takes part in the 'augmenting'.

This design avoids both the total rejecting of the physical world as in virtual reality (virtual transparency) and the excess of much ubiquitous computing, which celebrates an entirely mediated world (virtual hypermediacy). The medium does not attempt to take control over the world of perception – it is not its 'intention' to provide complete information about the world through (actual or virtual) mediation. It is a 'cool' medium. It respects the physical world as fundamental for situated experiences. Unlike the TV viewer or the user of VR, there is an enduring, material object (environment?) to observe. The medium obeys the fundamental interchange of perspective (ontologically and practically) between the physical and the virtual.

The medium mediates through a binary code we may call physical/ virtual. By being confronted with the object in a physical and a virtual version (coinciding with the unmediated vs. the mediated), and *de facto* observing the object through the two perspectives, the user will have to be habituated to perspectival shifts as procedure. By juxtaposing the two forms of mediation into a meaningful practice, the medium offers 'binary observation'. But it also enters what it mediates. By obeying the mobility, movements and the subjective perception of the user, the object can be perceived from various directions and angles, however in a virtual and trans-historical dimension.

Situated simulation is not intensively hypermediated as Bolter and Grusin (1999) argue, because it has no ambition to encapsulate reality. Rather, it mediates dualistically (physically and virtually), which is based on a balance between the transparent and the hypermediated. Bolter and Grusin argue in line with McLuhan that new media are representations of older media in another medium. They consider this to be a defining feature of new media. Such representation can however never be entirely complete or successful. The new medium always becomes dependent

DOI: 10.1057/9781137446466.0006

on the old, in a new shape, like the encyclopaedia is represented by and transformed by an online version – which nevertheless relies on the encyclopaedia concept of presenting definitions, descriptions and so on. Following Bolter and Grusin, remediation is what allows for new media, and at the same time what stops them from being complete or pure. Since the two dimensions of mediation in our case coincide with the inside and outside of the medium (but inside the experience), it is possible to describe them separately.

On the one hand, a *transparency perspective* lies in withdrawing its mediation from reality, letting immediate, direct experience (visually and auditively) constitute the outer frame of experience. On the other hand, a *hypermediacy perspective* derives from its pulling back from the idea of total mediation in its graphic artificiality, its computer-game realism, its emphasis on the object as unfinished, incomplete or as a model. The user experiences herself as someone who needs to make a series of decisions concerning additional (textual) information. Hypermediacy stems from text 'balloons' and audio, which provide comments (Liestøl, Rasmussen, and Stenarson 2011). Finally, it stems from the presence of holding the medium while standing/walking and its very visual distinction between physical and virtual reality.

When successful, situated simulation transforms this dualism into a duality, that is, into an augmented observation. This does not imply the complete elimination of the distinction between the physical and the virtual, but rather that the two perspectives refer to one another in a harmonic (user-friendly) way in an actual observation context. Whereas remediation is denied by the transparency of direct perception, remediation is celebrated as the main aesthetic experience by the hypermediacy of it. Although surrounded by transparency, the medium and its mobile graphics lead to the conclusion that situated simulation is a predominantly hypermediacy medium or genre (form of representation?)

As stated earlier our system departs from both virtual reality and most augmented reality systems in that it encourages the distinction between on-site reality and the computer-assisted simulation. For this reason our field trials focus on precisely users' experience of this distinction. This focus derives in part from an epistemological idea about the construction of meaning through differences. Our ambition is that the meaning of the experience does not derive from the simulation of the object, but from the distinction between simulation and the direct observation of the object. However, our intentions are worth little if the users

DOI: 10.1057/9781137446466.0006

feel seduced or alienated under the abstract spell of the simulacrum (Baudrillard 1994). Our field trials and user workshops test to what extent the difference-principle actually works as intended, to what extent the unmediated reality serves as a reality check vis-à-vis the simulation. However, equally important is to learn whether the simulation is sufficiently sophisticated as to enter into an interaction with the real. Much more than letting the simulation of the real undermine the *real* real, we search for a way closer to Lewis Carroll's map that had 'the scale of a mile to the mile': By letting the real and its simulation constitute a double description, the real is getting a chance to guide itself *about* itself, simplify itself and provide information about itself.

This follows the line of the well-known ideas of Gregory Bateson (1979). He draws on a wide variety of ideas from systems theory, biology, pragmatism and social anthropology. Bateson addresses how to identify homologies beyond scientific categories (similarities between a lobster and a crab). His famous phrase 'pattern which connects', refers to ongoing interaction between ways of perception, producing a rich vision and context for meaning. His relational view places conventional science in a context, as a rational way of perception, but it cannot avoid referring to its perception (itself) and can never prove scientifically. Information recursively feeds back to previous observations of an object made by the system, potentially correcting or calibrating classes of observations. Information emerges as a result of interaction between two sites or viewpoints, supplying depth and width to the observed, as in bilingual view, bilingualism, and being trained in two related disciplines and so on. The system may adapt its view of the object depending on its degree of flexibility and stability.

Oscillation between originals of the past and synthetic information of today may give experiential insight into an object that can no longer present itself in full because of time. Augmented reality provides double descriptions by adding a model world to the physical world – a twin world for adding perspective and comparative knowledge. The viewer now has two sources of information, which converge or fuse to form a single, however rich, object, an 'extra dimension of seeing' (Bateson 1979, 70). This however is only possible if true oscillation takes place. If successful this medium may help the user to establish an interchange between the real and the synthetic so as to create another dimension of information 'of depth', beyond what is actually presented. If they are accepted as exemplars of the same type, that they disclose different

DOI: 10.1057/9781137446466.0006

descriptions about the same type, they belong together and may be combined to enrich or enlarge one's view on the phenomenon. Double descriptions, if successful, create a *third* description, a synthetical inferential mode of information.

Convenient media

The network development, improved user interfaces along with further individualisation, brought media change to the current stage of digital personal media. The main forms of online activity tended to be chatting, through emailing, chat rooms, the mobile and SMS and messaging services. Increasingly, software allowed young people to create content for web-based sites. The change was quick, research of advanced personal media user groups ended up as relatively representative sample of young people in Western Europe. What were minor and peak phenomena at the beginning of the millennium is now mainstream. The affordability and improved user interfaces of multi-functional mobiles, laptops and mini-computers increased the competence and consciousness of both technologies and services on the Internet.

From the mid-1990s a series of media appeared on the Internet as channels of self-performance and self-presentation. The key to them all was management of personal information and social relationships. Now users present themselves in distinct and purposive ways that in accumulated form appear as social databases. Interaction of different sorts among users are stimulated and organised. There is little or no need for specialised computer or network competence. Along with creativity it is rather channelled towards writing, photography and video filming, which now can be made available in public spaces like Youtube.

As digital personal media proliferated, the avant-garde (that early research was based on) became a minority. Young people with digital media experience brought their everyday life into their new mediated forms. The new media were not simply alternative channels for interaction and expression; they were media for the very social life they lived among friends, family and associates. For instance, Lin Prøitz demonstrated how young people use mobile text messages and camera-phone images in their performance of sexuality and gender relations (Prøitz 2005, 2007; Lüders 2007). The same goes for the use of mobile telephony that exploded as a tool for coordination of daily life from the mid-1990s.

DOI: 10.1057/9781137446466.0006

Its use was predominantly associated with maintaining existing social relationships. We are thus not talking about separate realities and identities, but contexts of online and offline communication combined. As a general rule therefore, online activity should be seen as interdependent with offline life. Blogs, for instance, appear as individual, even intimate forms of self-expression through text, photos and videos, but are also a way of maintaining social interaction with others. Users create profiles dedicated to online and offline friends and visualise networks of relationships, all of which have real social effects.

The mediated and the unmediated are not different ontologies, nor are they different social spheres. Various media influence communication and interaction in different ways, but they all support the individual in his/her everyday interaction and meaning-production. On the one hand, unmediated face-to-face interaction is probably considered to have a prominent, ideal–typical status among most people. On the other hand, there is no reason to consider the unmediated as a pure or ideal form, isolated from the diversity of media use. Mediated interactions are as real as unmediated communication – it is influenced by both in terms of interacting persons, topics for communication and as a way for friendships and relationships to develop (Tanis and Postmes 2003, Brandtzæg and Stav 2004).

Viewing everyday life in a social network perspective helped to see this. Barry Wellman, Carolyn Haythornthwaite (1998) and others have pointed out that personal media support personal networks among friends and family. Seeing social relationships in a social networks perspective is an analytical key that neither exaggerates the role of distinct media, nor views social relationships as virtual communities. Personal media supports distributed patterns of communication in social networks, and people begin to use such media for social reasons. The more social relations one tends to have, the more diverse use of personal media is likely to be found (Haythornthwaite 2002). The stronger the tie, the more different media are in use in a particular relationship (Haythornthwaite and Wellman 1998). Thus, media choice is to a large extent influenced by the nature of the social relationship (Licoppe and Smoreda 2005). Or in a media-pragmatic perspective, relationships are formed by the social and material conditions at hand.

As we have reached well into the second decade of the new millennium, new technologies for perception, interaction, publication and archiving have been absorbed to a large extent and embedded in everyday

DOI: 10.1057/9781137446466.0006

practices. To most people in countries far beyond the developing part of the world, the mobile telephone has become simply the 'mobile', and the personal computer is the 'laptop'. Both are devices for a multitude of obvious and mundane tasks in daily life. They are themselves of less interest as their essential use is related to functions and services on the Internet and telecom networks.

At this stage, the media research agenda is society itself, as it takes different directions through its use of mundane media. Technologies and society are fundamentally intertwined and integrated. But at the same time we need to keep the two concepts analytically separate in order to see how technologies influence everyday life and vice versa. The view here is that personal media enhance particular forms of social change in modern society, and that they both accelerate certain changes and compensate for roads not taken. This has always been the case with media technologies – what is new is that these forms of social regulation have reached the private realms of the individual in a fundamental way. Social interaction is to a greater extent than before the responsibility and the possibility of the individual. The freedom and responsibility of mediated communication belong to most people in the world.

Rather than focusing on singular media with their distinct functions and purposes, a media-pragmatic approach addresses communicational selectivity and practicability. With this I refer to the constant social–technological interplay, which establishes routine preferences and choices as a pragmatic, mundane everyday practice by skilled social actors. Personal media belong to the social lives of people who are much more than 'users'. The person and their personal media knit a complicated web of meaning, where face-to-face contact plays the most prominent role. Face-to-face interaction, the fixed telephone, the mobile, the email, SMS and a wide range of other media are entangled and continue to approach one another and our various social ties in our individual life world. From a media-pragmatic perspective, this range of media alternatives and supplements are not only channels to a wider world, but also in the personal world of meaning-making, and of things present and absent, practical and impractical, convenient and inconvenient, impulsive and calculating. This is why much research on the use of personal media tends to report observations with limited generalisation value.

DOI: 10.1057/9781137446466.0006

6
Social Capital and Social Media

Abstract: *This chapter examines the accumulation and dislocation of social capital in everyday life and the intermediary role of personal media, particularly social media. The concept of social capital, it argues, helps to achieve a nuanced view on mediated social relationships in everyday life. Various approaches on social capital are addressed (Bourdieu, Coleman, Putnam, Granovetter and Burt). A balance between a conception of the 'undersocialised' and 'oversocialised' individual is examined through the concepts of skills, social capital and social network. It refers to research that illustrates the relevance of the concept in various situations and for distinct types of media.*

Keywords: communication theory; digital media; everyday life; lifeworld; media theory; personal media; social capital; sociology

Rasmussen, Terje. *Personal Media and Everyday Life: A Networked Lifeworld.* Basingstoke: Palgrave Macmillan, 2014. DOI: 10.1057/9781137446466.0007.

DOI: 10.1057/9781137446466.0007

People not only enjoy being in touch with others, they also gain from it, intentionally or unintentionally. Increasingly, social ties are a source for resources of various kinds and increasingly, these ties and connections are digitally mediated. This chapter aims at broadening the understanding of personal digital media in everyday relationships with the aid of the term 'social capital'. With Portes and many others, I generally understand the term 'social capital' as the ability to secure benefits through membership in networks and other social structures (Portes 1998, 8). I will provide a definition relevant for personal media later in the chapter. Suffice to say here that social capital refers to features that appear as resources for individuals and groups, and that are produced collectively. The term may also refer to the 'energy' that stems from more or less stable social relationships, and that enables the individual to reach certain more or less shared aims. It emerges from the structure of social relationships, but appears as individual characteristics.

In this chapter, I address the significance of personal media in everyday social networks by making use of the notion of social capital to make sense of people's media priorities, uses, and non-uses, as well as their views and norms regarding their mediated relationships. Skills and access related to the use of the broadening range of personal media play an increasing role in the shaping of young people's social life. With the growing diversity of personal media, the how will be more important than the how much: qualitative priorities concerning media and people will be at the centre of our interest, rather than time spent. If specified well, 'social capital' is a suitable concept in examining this, because it addresses the relationship between power, skills and social networks in everyday life.

Generally, the use of digital personal media in social networks (from mobile telephony to social media) tends to support social capital of groups, because such media allow for keeping social relationships in spite of individualisation and a hectic and mobile everyday life. (In certain cases, they actually reduce social capital as in the case of computer-game addicts, who pull out of important social networks.) In general, however, it is difficult to identify causal relationships between technology and social capital because social networks are virtual-actual: face-to-face contact and media contact interweave contexts, intersect and maintain social ties together.

A broadening repertoire of personal media provides the individual with a varied set of alternatives for interaction. Personal media have simply become decisive in achieving the values and objectives that we

DOI: 10.1057/9781137446466.0007

appreciate in life. The mobile and Internet media, with their features so very suitable for acting out one's (culturally informed) will and decisions, have become artefacts of welfare. Social capital has increased as a consequence of Internet-based social networks. What Lin (2001) calls 'cyber-networks' are constructed through email, chat rooms, blogs and so on, which have experienced astonishing growth. To the question of the implications of cyber-networks' growth for the study of social networks and social capital, Lin's short answer is: incredible – we are witnessing a revolutionary rise of social capital: 'In fact, we are witnessing a new era in which social capital will soon supersede personal capital [in face-to-face interaction] in significance and effect' (Lin 2001, 214). Quite clearly 'cyber-networks' mediate social capital in various ways. A simple exchange through email with another person may create weak ties. Network sites specialise in establishing latent contacts, which then can be actualised when appropriate. From social interaction on the Internet, numerous campaigns and movements have emerged, as have entrepreneurial start-ups in the new economy. And not least within the sciences new constellations are formed that produce new published knowledge. Through the Internet, access to people and information is possible with less effort. More informal relationships are possible, which thereby enable cooperation. Personal media and mediated social networks help everyday interaction to go on in spite of a hectic life of obligations and demands, and at the same time reproduce the stability of the network (Sproull and Kiesler 1991). It is the network aspect which is particularly important here. Danah Boyd (2011, 39–43) understands social media like Facebook as a genre of network publics. Network publics are publics that are constituted by network media in that they are constructed space and an imagined collective that emerge from the intersection of people, technology and practice. This hybrid term is meant to refer several functions that cover both networked and audience aspects. Individuals are allowed to construct profiles, produce a list of connections, and view other viewer's profiles and their list of connections. All these can be contacted interpersonally of in a (semi)public fashion. The main features are thus profiles, friends and public connecting features along with stream-based updates. Such features gradually form the basis of important aspects of everyday sociability. They form the infrastructure of social habitual contact. Of importance here is how they are suited for obtaining particular resources from particular others in order to harvest particular benefits in particular contexts.

DOI: 10.1057/9781137446466.0007

Elements of social capital

In addressing social capital, observers generally tend to distinguish between structural aspects, individual aspects and the benefits in question. Some emphasise norms and trust, others focus on the individual as agent. For instance, Lin (2001) argues that social capital has three segments: (1) individual position in networks (causes), (2) access and use of resources (processes, skills) and (3) the effects or outcomes. Naahpiet and Ghosal (1998) suggest three dimensions (structural, cognitive and relational) of social capital: (1) patterns of ties in networks, (2) personal relationships of individuals who influence their actions, motives, aspiration and so on and (3) resources that provide shared representations and norms, and systems of meaning in the network. Similarly, Huysman and Wulf (2004) distinguishes between structural opportunity (who shares knowledge and how), cognitive ability (understanding) and relation-based motivation (trust, reciprocity, respect). Portes (1998, 8) distinguishes between the actors possessing or claiming social capital, the sources of social capital, which is also a source of social control, support and trust (the group or network), and the resources or benefits themselves, usually information in some form. Licoppe and Smoreda (2006) argue that we need to keep two forms of complexity separate: the contents, genres, ties and formats of interaction, and the technical means for which such interactions can be used.

As noted by Ellison et al. (2007), social capital is not something an individual (or group) possess (as is the case with financial, cultural, human capital) but rather something that emerges from interaction and communication in some form of social organisation. Therefore the term is social capital. That is why the term can refer to both individual and collective processes. Social capital stems from the dynamics of social organisation, for instance, a social network, and is identified at the individual level. Social capital is an abstract concept in that it can be observed as something more specific like information, influence, goods, high status and so on. Also, as it derives from membership in a greater social entity, its structural aspects are of some importance, particularly in our case its technological mediation. With Huysmann and Wulf (2004), I see the technological alternatives applied by the social network as interdependently embedded in the network. The choice of medium is in effect often a question of choice of interaction partner and context, and

DOI: 10.1057/9781137446466.0007

vice versa. Social interaction is pragmatic, flexible and malleable, and carries with it rationalities about suitable media for various occasions.

I define social capital as the outcome of resources shared through skilled membership and position in a social network. Thus, I distinguish between three elements of social capital:

1   The (structural) social organisation (the social network structure) including personal media, which temporally, spatially and otherwise influences capital distribution and accumulation. This structural component relates to technologies, demography, transport and much more. Regarding personal media, questions regarding their handling of meaning as texts, sounds or images, their dialogical character, or their interconnection with other media and so on are of interest. Media studies and related disciplines would emphasise this element.

2   The skills and positions of singular nodes (individuals or groups) of the social network. The study of human nodes and their position in networks refers to the nature of embodied personalised or organisational power in particular positions vis-à-vis others, their size and centrality in the network, and the strategies applied in order to accumulate resources.

3   The actual resources that the nodes may receive as a result of membership in the network and that are used and converted into social capital, which intentionally or unintentionally leads to benefits, which are then reinserted into the network and so contribute to its reproduction. We may draw on Lin (2001) who argues that network media enable the accumulation of social capital in the form of several kinds of resources:

(a)   Information of many forms, for instance, about job vacancies as was demonstrated by Granovetter (1973) in face-to-face encounters or in dedicated media networks such as LinkedIn.

(b)   Influence, such as in lobbying. Political party networks are another example, where party membership leads to party network access and potential influence.

(c)   Credibility and reputation: In sociology, this was probably first commented upon by Weber, who in his writings on religion in America refers to a man who wanted to open a bank found it necessary to join the Adventist community to achieve high status and credibility in the bank. Still membership, whether

DOI: 10.1057/9781137446466.0007

formal or informal, in certain organisations in politics, charity, sports and so on, leads to a rise in respectability.

(d) Self-recognition: As we have seen, Michel Foucault (1994, 223) writes about Technologies of the Self (such as the notebook and the letter), which assist the individual in 'self-caring', that is, in reaching a morally accepted level of self-esteem and self-identity. Personal blogs in particular would be a good case in point in that they constitute the Self as an object for reflection in and through.

(e) Reciprocity: To these, I would like to add a fifth kind of resource, which not only underlines the fundamentally human need for appreciation and trust, but also focuses on the individual contribution to qualitative dimensions of the reproduction of the network. The observed needs to respond to others, appearing from other's requests, regards and so on. This corresponds to Malinowski's observations that receiving gifts creates debt, an obligation to give back. All personal media dedicated to dialogue in some sense would encourage – if only passively, reciprocity, due to the low threshold for response. In social media, technology enters in assisting reciprocity more actively, in that the system provides hints, reminders and notices, which trigger new responses from the users.

Capital in personal media

The term 'social capital' designates several basic sociological insights, but at the same time it needs to be specified according to its empirical use and context. Several studies a decade back questioned whether use of the Internet can enhance community involvement (Kraut et al. 1998, see also Shah et al. 2001, 141). Data from United States and the Netherlands suggest that users of the Internet not only seem to have a more active life than others, but they also travel more and work more. Activity leads to more activity (Robinson and Haan in Kraut et al. 2006). In the late 1990s, Kraut et al. (2006) argued that Internet, like TV, implies physical inactivity and limited social face-to-face social interaction. They found that Internet use leads to declining sociality and increasing loneliness and depression. Most such studies, however, did not focus on particular forms of use. The Internet was viewed as

DOI: 10.1057/9781137446466.0007

one single medium, hiding distinct forms of use with widely different social effects. As we know today, 'internet use' is not a much better term than 'technology use' as it presents a far too crude and undifferentiated view of social activities.

A growing focus on social capital has helped to understand under what conditions specific kinds of Internet use are related to social trust and civic activity (Shah, Kwak and Holbert 2001, 142). Social capital often refers to how various forms of sociality help to generate cooperation and social change, and naturally the Internet in its distinct media forms enters as a vital factor, in that it can connect people and help them to acquire information and discover opportunities in conjunction with others. People with stronger social networks tend to be healthier and happier than others (Kraut 2006, 7). Time spent on the Internet does not reduce offline sociability (Gershuny 2003). Data from Blacksburg, Virginia, indicate that people who belong to more than one community group are better educated, more informed and more extroverted. They have higher levels of participation, trust and community attachment than others (Kraut et al. in Kraut 2006, 180). The notion of 'bridge' between social networks is crucial. In the hands of human bridges, they argue, the Internet is 'a tool for maintaining social contact and relations and increasing face-to-face interaction, all of which help to build both bonding and bridging types of social capital in communities'. And conversely, households without Internet access are generally those who are already disadvantaged in other ways as well (Anderson et al. 2007, 40).

However, the ability to use and gain from Internet use is socially differentiated according to a number of external factors such as motivation and knowledge among parents and friends. Research also indicates that social ties created online are more fragile. People spend less time with, and are less committed to, online friends than to offline friends (Cummings, Lee and Kraut, in Kraut 2006, 266). Networks of relatives are more stable than networks of friends. Friends may shift status from central to peripheral because the nature of relationships is only decided by the involved. Family and friends offer the comfort of the familiar (Blokland 2003, 77) at least as much as confidentiality. Friendships may exist without involving one biography in detail for the other. They may exist in the present, for a present. Some friendships exist best as a two-person relationship while others thrive best within a group. Naturally such complex social–psychological features would decide the use of personal media for social contact. While social media and email may

DOI: 10.1057/9781137446466.0007

be used to involve others, the mobile conversation and SMS are better suited for twosome relationships.

Shah, Kwak and Holbert (2001) addressed Internet use according to four types of use patterns and different facets of social capital, and found that use of the Internet for social recreation (e.g. participation in chat rooms and game playing) was consistently and negatively related to engagement in civic activities, trust in other people and life contentment. In contrast, usage of the Internet for information exchange had positive impact on the same variables (Shah, Kwak and Holbert 2001, 149). Their decade-old results suggest that the connection between Internet use and civic activities, interpersonal trust and life contentment was highly contextual.

The actual capital-enhancing role of the Internet use is very difficult to identify, precisely because it is so embedded in social life. It also seems vital to distinguish between forms of use along and with degrees of use. In neither case is the Internet a causal agent, but a medium in all senses of the word – an intermediary variable between social networks and the individual, which may encourage or discourage forms of use. For example, trust refers to an essential worldview developed during a harmonious childhood and cannot be changed by the Internet. As Uslaner (2004) reminds us, trust refers to an attitude towards strangers established long before the first Internet experience. But Internet availability may lead to the exercising of trust. The net makes things easier for those with many friends than for those with few. As Uslaner notes: 'The World Wide Web is very much like the world. It makes things better in some ways and worse in others. But it is not transforming. If you want to make a revolution, you have to go offline' (Uslaner 2004, 239). After the Arab spring, this statement probably still holds.

The nature of the medium may invite specific forms of social interaction. Sproull and Kiesler's 'Reduced social cues model' (1985) were intended to demonstrate that reduced social cues produce a less gratifying communication experience, resulting in a de-individualising effect, and inducing behaviour that is more self-centred and less socially regulated. Examples would be racist statements and 'flaming' in chat rooms. Thus, the use of various media can in some instances be taken as a statement of closeness (Licoppe and Smoreda 2006, 298). Media activating the human voice without delay would signal intimacy, whereas email indicates a somewhat larger distance or thinner tie. Late replies are also indication of a relationship less close than a relationship where SMS or

DOI: 10.1057/9781137446466.0007

emails are exchanged with greater frequency. As Licoppe and Smoreda (2006, 298) noted, 'the differential use of particular means of communication thus lays down a space of relational practices in which ties of similar closeness are treated in a similar way, and in which this degree of closeness is publicly expressed and negotiated'. If an announcement is addressed to one or more recipients, whether it arrives via someone else and whether it is simple/short or complicated/long are other variables (Licoppe and Smoreda 2006, 299).

Of course, time is an inherent dimension of sociability, and the choice of technical media is a way to use time to organise sociability. And as more than one person is involved in this organisational activity, the process takes the form of a meta-process of negotiating time. For example, friends may have different expectations with regard to frequency of chatting and choice of media, which influence the dynamic structure of the dyadic tie or the greater network. And yet dyads or social networks involving more people will tend to order themselves in rhythms and workable social distances. Although social relationships may vary in closeness and frequency (friends may become distant contacts and vice versa), they seem to be relatively robust and able to reshape themselves. Most friendships operate on a second-order level involving at least some vague reflection on the relationship, which sorts out how the relationship should be maintained. Such more or less reflexive preferences would involve activities, interaction under what circumstances and contexts and with what media. The mobile, for instance, serves as a channel of trust in spite of mobility. As Deborah Chambers (2006, 151) argues, the mobile is the ideal technology for the exploration of intimacy, in the form of loyalty and privacy as well as solidarity. The mobile helps to enhance strong tie networks, based upon individualisation. It is network-oriented rather than community-oriented (Licoppe and Smoreda 2006).

Investing in the mobile as 'Link-up'

Among teenagers, face-to-face contact tends to be so frequent that mediated contact functions as extending the presence of the other. Among adults and especially after many years of friendship, a phone call or an email serves to keep the relationship warm. In both cases, physical and mediated togetherness are interwoven. The mobile is of

DOI: 10.1057/9781137446466.0007

particular importance in this respect. In all parts of the world, the mobile is an embedded tool for coping. Particularly among low-income cultures, connectivity is a condition for surviving. In many poor cultures, the very fact of being in active and negotiating relationships with others is a major source for income. In poor countries (and in contrast to the Scandinavian countries), social capital is more important than cultural capital.

In their analysis of the use of mobile in Jamaica, Horst and Miller (2006) demonstrate how what they call Link-up through the mobile has become an essential part of everyday life. The almost global spread of the mobile has in many places led to personal networks (ego-centred networks), which tend to become an essential form of sociality, at times at the expense of more communal forms of sociality. The mobile has become the main technological tool for personal networks, which contribute significantly to changes in sociality. The phone is used to actively be involved in the lives and troubles of friends and relatives, and to exchange favours and services, which make life easier. The mobile phone list not only contains the names of family, friends and acquaintances, but also those distant contacts who may help out with possible favours. The mobile is heavily integrated in the informal and black economy, which is essential for survival in many low-income cultures.

Horst and Miller also show that the mobile is used to keep social relationships separate and to influence flows of information. It is a tool for empathy, trust and care, but also for (within households) deceiving and administrating sexual relationships. Link-up involves, according to Horst and Miller (2006, 96), a high number of very short calls to keep in touch, and to accumulate a high number of contacts in the SIM card. As an essential form of social interaction in mobile, low-income societies like in Jamaica, the mobile enhances social networks that do not always have much meaningful content, but are essential all the same for coping. Link-up is a social pattern of interaction and demonstrates how the mobile has become appropriated into all aspects of everyday life of ordinary Jamaicans. The essence of the social role of the mobile lies not in the conversations as such, but in the ongoing overlapping complexity of actual and potential connections and encounters. Horst and Miller (2006, 101) call Link-up a genre which may involve a host of emotions (suspicion, love), but where each call is most essentially a series of confirmations of liaisons.

DOI: 10.1057/9781137446466.0007

Skills

As the Link-up case illustrates, social skills produced in and through the individual lifeworld play an important differentiating role. Skills concern how and to what extent one makes use of resources to reach certain ends and to perform in the reproduction of social networks. Social capital is structured through membership in a social organisation, and through the individual skills. Agre (2004, 202) argues that it is important to separate out social skills that to a variable degree enable the actor to take advantage of his or her access to the resources of the group. A notion of social skills, social competence, digital literacy, agency or simply *habitus*, refers to the actual operation of social capital as a social mechanism influencing inequalities and exclusions in status and information. Social skills transform resources of networks into social capital for the individual or group. Social skills and social capital are thus interdependent properties of the social network. It is the interplay between individual skills and network that builds social capital, and that subsequently may benefit both skills and networks.

The discussion has mostly addressed what mechanisms of social structure tend to give access to social capital, such as the nature of trust mechanisms, and the difference between open and closed networks. The term tends to ignore aspects that may explain the variation in the ways actors make use of their opportunities, such as cultural capital, social skills and moral norms. I follow Agre (2004, 202) and Coleman in that social skills are a form of capital of their own, usually coined human capital. Social capital is a resource for those who already possess the skills to gain access to social networks, and make use of the resources obtained from those. Conversely, access and central positions in social networks are a result of skills that are in part learned through contacts in social networks such as the family. In this way, the dynamic of social capital and social skills is a self-enforcing resource.

However, the obtaining of skills is also a resource that derives from wider social networks such as political communities or colleagues. This explains why people of excellence in terms of knowledge and competence are sometimes left to see others without the same qualities make careers.

However, skills also refer to the sensible operation of the actual personal medium like the mobile or the web. There are considerable differences in what functions and options we actually apply in our devices, and quite

DOI: 10.1057/9781137446466.0007

a lot of people refrain from using the web altogether. By social skills, we also think of the abilities to handle the available repertoire of personal media in socially advantageous ways on the part of the user and the network as a whole. This involves selecting specific media for distinct purposes and communication partners, and steering away from the social and ethical pitfalls that follow in the footsteps of all media. Social capital involves acting responsibly vis-à-vis oneself and the network. This means, for example, to reply promptly on SMS, to act civilly, to refrain from uploading intimate information and so on. Increasingly, the failure to handle our new wide-reaching personal media with care may have serious implications for the social life of the individual.

The quality and usability of a website for an organisation or association influences the nature of trust in the network, by sharing information, obligations, trust, norms, arguments, ideas and so on. This is often seen as elements of *literacy*. Particularly personal media literacy is of relevance. Personal media literacy refers to 'the interpretative and writing skills necessary to communicate effectively via online media' (Warschauer 2004, 117). This includes the internalisation of a range of informal and unwritten rules, from the netiquette of civil communication to the pragmatics of effective argumentation according to the topics discussed, the nature of the media and the participants. It includes how to write emails in an effective and civil way, and how to make a personal homepage personal but not embarrassingly private. In the case of homepages, blogs and digital storytelling, skills refer to the ability to compose appropriate narratives. But personal media literacy also includes avoiding flaws (such as using the 'reply to all' button when replying personally to a widely distributed email.) It refers to how to establish and continue online relationships for the benefit of oneself and others. Such mastering is normally learnt through various social networks and settings, from school, family and friends along with experimentation (trial and error).

Capital dynamics in social media

Regarding 'social' media like Facebook, LinkedIn, Google+ and so on, a number of social issues are relevant for research on social capital. These include issues such as *general media use*: concern about how people are incorporating social media in their everyday life, in relation to their activities and their use of other media, changes between age groups and

DOI: 10.1057/9781137446466.0007

life phases and so on, as a foundation to understand changes of everyday life. Also i*dentity* themes concern how social media are used as a looking glass, as a façade, as impression management and so on, and as technology of the Self for the care of oneself. It concerns the ways the individual handles pride and shame (along with rejection, insecurity acceptance, etc.) as fundamentally relational emotions.

In order to understand how social media produce social capital, I would first like to indicate how social media create social capital structurally, and then address how social media appear as a social system or circuit of activities on both individual and structural levels, making mediated social networks into something different than the sum of its members. Social media networks generate social capital through a number of structural features, often conceptualised as the 'architecture' or 'topography' of networks. From the insight of network theory, I will mention four such structural features drawn from network analysis (Rasmussen 2008):

> *Clusters:* By mediating clusters of strong ties, and with high density of connections along with unifying norms and trust, social media mediate small community-like groups of sociality and loyalty. The effect of such bonding groups is a high degree of homogeneity. Such groups provide direct links to others, who each have links out of the group. However, such groups are relatively introverted, with relatively few connections out of the group compared to the connections inside the group. In other words, the connections are quite far from random-like. The redundancy is high inside the group, but low out of the group. The kind of social capital from such groups (best described by Coleman) is also called 'thick' social capital. Such clusters inhibit small, world connections for the individual of the group. But when such clusters appear as *nodes in larger networks,* they serve a 'small world effect' from the local level.

> *Short-cuts/redundancy:* In networks of relatively random-like connections between the nodes, enabled by a large share of weak ties, bridges will also develop between networks. In large, random-like networks, there are fewer clusters and more random-like connections, and therefore a shorter path distance than in a world of clusters. For example, a large share of my connections also know someone I do not know, and some of them serve as bridges to other networks. The network is more individualistic, redundant and heterogeneous. It more easily connects different groups.

> *Supernodes:* Online and offline networks tend to generate a certain bias, favouring the nodes that enter the network early or possess other advantages. Thomas Merton called this the Matthew effect. The long tail thesis actually shows the same thing, although the argument is different. The web-topology

DOI: 10.1057/9781137446466.0007

develops supernodes, relatively few extraordinarily popular sites, and a very large number of smaller sites. Web use creates 'mountain-peaks' in the horizon, which everyone sees regardless of where they are positioned, and which dramatically reduce the number of steps between randomly selected nodes. Power-law distributions emerge, due to knowledge, conformity and time. Herbert Simon pointed towards time and attraction as the two central mechanisms that tend to create bias. A self-enforcing differentiation takes place, which is strategically developed, as in Google's search method, and in rating methods (Slashdot, Digg). Popularity leads to more popularity.

Cascades: Increasing exposure of practices of others with lower threshold than oneself leads for socio-psychological reasons of conformity to lower thresholds for joining campaigns, petitions, spreading 'memes' (jokes, images) and so on. Snow-ball effects emerge and may appear in virus-like phenomena due to the speed and reach of information. This is particularly true for information, which seems important or provocative. As accumulated side-effects, certain forms of information are imitated and duplicated locally, and then escalate widely.

Successful social media allow for all these features in a productive combination. They help users to navigate locally and long-distance, to identify changes and pick up news and groups, and to establish new connections. They potentially magnify effects of individual actions and so instigate social change. But they all remain dependent on individual activity on the mobile or the laptop keyboard.

To see individual action and structural features together, and also with both social and technological features, we may see social media as a complex socio-technical system (of systems). We may distinguish between an individual level of social activity (publish profiles, click on likes, poke others, read others' profiles and other people's feeds about what they do or think now, post comments, hyperlinks, photos and so on on the group walls, accumulate friends) and technological operations (suggesting friends, groups, who to poke, birthday reminders, helping to search for friends, keeping score on requests, friends, updating profiles etc.), and a structural level of social (social control, trust, moral, critical mass) and technological phenomena (control, oversight, stability). Various forms of techno-social activity circulate between the two levels and between the social and the technological into a mediated social network (consisting of thousands of interconnected networks) of stable change.

From this, it is evident that social media like Facebook are not only spaces or sites for communication, but also in fact 'avatars', which interact with the users. The success lies in the combination of the similarity with the social world (communication) and the difference from it (effortless and compressed). The result is a world of social density worthwhile spending time in. Network media minimise/shrink/compress the social world by way of technological code. They make the social world of the individual into a convenient entity, almost a material unit that can be observed and handled in different ways. They combine the simplicity and oversight of the map with the social reality of the world. In integrating the model and the reality, social media visualise social patterns. The net result is more sociability with less effort (lower costs and thresholds).

Clearly the notion of unintended consequences plays a role here. Social media like Facebook can be considered as a 'social fact' in a durkheimian sense, as a durable, collective social phenomenon external to and influencing the individual, and still reproduced through individual practices. Social facts (material and immaterial) are sets of values and norms in a society, social community or social integration in various spheres of society or in society in general. These social facts can be identified through sociological method and vary among cultures and over time. The main point here is that the social fact is external to the individual, in the sense that it is an unintended (and often unrecognised) effect of everyday practices, which are to some degree defined by custom, tradition or norms. A similar sociological argument is Giddens' structuration argument that structures (I think to a certain extent comparable to Durkheim's social fact) are a medium and outcome of practices. However, as is noted by many sociologists, Durkheim overstated cultural authority over individual practices. On the other hand, Giddens tended to understate both collective and material powers. However, with different emphases, both enable us to think about social structures like Web 2.0 phenomena as a collective and unintended construction made by innumerable individual acts. The more social network sites depend on user-generated initiatives (as in the step from Web 1.0 to Web 2.0), the more essential this argument is to understand their stability and transformation.

In commercial Web 2.0 sites like Facebook, user activity serves individual and collective needs and interests, and provides value to adverts and the exchange value of goods they advertise by stimulating the demand for them. It seems that with Web 2.0 we have reached a new level in the gradual convergence of the roles as citizen and consumer. With the historical coexistence of individualisation and liberalisation, consumption is regarded as the crux of autonomy, as the epitome of individual freedom. Only the economical and political autonomous

DOI: 10.1057/9781137446466.0007

subjects can freely exercise choice among products and services. Also, unrestricted consumption is seen as self-expression and as an identity-building practice. Therefore, advertising may coexist with meaningful communication and interaction. Or conversely, in Web 2.0, highly efficient and flexible systems for private and public interaction are made possible by the commoditising and monitoring of the same interaction.

Web 2.0 services like Facebook make use of innovative technologies (Javascript, XML, Flash) that allow for a wide variety of social interaction. The concept of Web 2.0 refers to a combination of innovative technologies and social networks. As Cormode and Krishnamurti (2008, 1) argue, 'Web 2.0 is both a platform on which innovative technologies have been built and a space where users are treated as first class objects'. The main difference, they argue, is that in Web 2.0 the content creators consist of the majority of the users of the site. Design and features are created to make every user a creator of content, ranging from 'like' to uploading software. From 2007, other applications that can be added to user accounts in Facebook were supported through the opening of APIs. This opened up the possibility of widespread use. Cormode and Krishnamurti (2008, 9) suggest the following classes of practices on Web 2.0 sites, from the most simple and quick, to the more skilled: Clicks and connections (simple one-click actions, such as a rating, accepting a friend request, voting), Comments (adding brief responses and comments), Casual communication (sending messages), Communities (joining and interacting in larger groups) and Content creation (uploading original content, such as photos, movies).

Web 2.0 provides a simple user interface for a wide range of forms of interaction and expression enabled by recent advancements in web technology. Web 2.0 also refers to a particular innovation model, as it signifies an architecture that gives user-generated content first priority. 'This burgeoning phenomenon suggests that users are gratified in significant ways by the ability to play an active role in generating content, rather than only passively consuming that which is created for them by others' (Harrison 2009, 157). It seems logical to see Web 2.0 as a radicalisation of the 'participatory culture' (Jenkins 2006) of collaborative consumer communities enabled by the new media. As Harrison and Barthel (2009, 174) conclude: '... new media technologies now enable vastly more users to experiment with a wider and seemingly more varied range of collaborative creative activities'. The various features in Web 2.0 media constantly create incidents, changes, events

DOI: 10.1057/9781137446466.0007

and other novelties, which serve as new reasons for entering and inter-acting, which reproduce patterns of social interaction. From innumer-able singular and trivial practices (notices, pokes, likes, greetings and so on), the system generates large-scale patterns of movement. Individual practices are transformed into collective and ordered subsystems of walls and groups.

An aspect of Facebook, compared to other social media like Wiki-pedia and Slashdot, is its extremely decentred user structure combined with a strong command centre for all technological and economic issues. There is no central idea or ideology, no human moderation, no hierarchy between ranks and no differentiation of status. This structure is imple-mented to reduce tension between individual freedom of expression and collective interest in relevance and order. In Facebook, control features are handled in decentred and technological ways.

How do technological and social aspects, software and meaningware of Web 2.0 interact in order to generate so much activity? How is the free rider problem solved? Web 2.0 partially avoids the Free Rider problem by allowing for large number of free riders as long as the number of 'paying riders' is sufficiently high. Millions of free riders in, for example, Slashdot, GNU/Linux and Wikipedia can be tolerated and do not erode the system as long as the number of active participants counts in the thousands. In fact, the free riders are considered as sensible users or supporters and do not bother the active participants. This suggests that Facebook either has solved the Free Rider problem or that the Free Rider problem is not relevant for Facebook. Hetcher (2009, 996) prefers to call Facebook a 'spontaneous order' and 'a spontaneous informal ordering': It does not aim for one single outcome and is not a common project, but still it is highly social.

The collective action is not a collective action mystery, because we are not talking about altruism, but sociality (Hetcher ??995). Facebook does not rely on peer production as in Wikipedia, since people tend to approach places of sociality like the city market or village square. It is simply experienced as in one's own interest to participate. The system operates without being dependent on altruism or idealism, thus provid-ing a more robust structure than for example Wikipedia. The normative expectations towards the system are relatively low and thus also the level of disappointments. For example, in spite of several well-known Face-book attempts to exploit privacy information commercially, people seem not to defect – yet.

DOI: 10.1057/9781137446466.0007

As both a typical and exceptional Web 2.0 site, the interface technology of Facebook puts the user first in terms of interaction and creation (profiles, including comments from other users, simple connections to 'friends', simple ways to post various material and to rate other's posts, simple ways of creating groups, walls, public APIs and embedding of rich content (Flash videos), and RSS feeds and email (Cormode and Krishnamurti 2008, 3). Contrary to Web 1.0 sites (like Craig's list, Amazon, Slashdot etc.), Web 2.0 sites are entirely dependent on these features, and share many of the features of offline social networks. This also means that each individual user appears as the centre of the site universe, as is the case in the offline dimension of our lifeworld.

Jarrett lists the following interactive features of Web 2.0: *Flexible time* (in contrast to broadcast 'push' time), *Creative capacity* (tagging, uploading personal photos and music, creating profiles etc.), *Body–object articulation* (creative self-expression never fully controlled or shaped by the actual site), *Intensive use* (no exhaustive use of the technology – features like tagging and folksonomies help the user to make use of tiny, selected content of the site), *Concealment of expertise* (strategic denial of authority by the corporate owner to signal full authority and freedom of the user) (Jarrett 2008, 5).

A possible negative outcome of this is that a wide variety of activity through various media forms may lead to *portalisation* (Cormode and Krishnamurti 2008, 1). This implies that sites try to minimise reasons for leaving the site through detecting users' browsing habits. Based on this, a broad range of intra-site features and other media features like blogging, email, search, hosting of photos and video are provided. The Facebook API allows for a number of features to be imported to profile pages. That an increasing share of users' online communication takes place through the portal of one social network may lead to 'balkanisation', making it into a network within the Internet. Such intra-network communication is not reachable from other social networks, nor searchable with search engines.

Users do not use Facebook 'for free'. The relationship between users and the company is both of economic and social character. By spending time, attention and activity on Facebook, by exposing themselves to ads and information-processing algorithms, every user contributes to the company's profit. Since there is no money involved from users' hands, the transaction is not considered as such, only as social activity. There are some user terms to 'OK', but no labour contract. The peculiar

DOI: 10.1057/9781137446466.0007

situation here is that there is no abstract labour. Information goods are produced through social activity (attention and interaction). From this the forces of production (computers, the Internet, clever software and big data) aggregate this in various ways and make externalities become evident for advertisers. Big data are translated into big money. The 'prosumer' (Toffler 1980), the users-as-producers, has now lifted portions of their sociality and knowledge-production into systems of production *and* consumption. There is little use in withholding the distinction between forces and relations of production in this world. Production is based on consumption and vice versa. Commodities are extracted from lifeworld practices of friendship, love, trust and social protest, and reversibly, the lifeworld is reproduced through social media.

The problem of trust

As Field et al. (2000) point out, the concept of social capital also reinserts issues of value into social and media research. Trust, reciprocity and norms are all central concerns for adequate action. However, in spite of Putnam's and partly Coleman's emphasis on community and solidarity, the interest in social networks and social capital also bear witness to a crisis of the term 'community'. This term has traditionally signified a value-based collective of consensus building, solidarity and loyalty. As Fernbacx (2007) notes, from early sociology and social anthropology, the notion of strong, place-based solidarity through rituals has dominated.

Certainly, this notion is of relevance for certain organised groups and associations. However, for the practices of social media, the term suggests too much fellowship and cohesiveness, while saying little about the descriptive nature of interaction and communication. An extended interpretation is needed that (a) keeps an eye on the media dimension without discriminating ontologically between online and offline interaction, (b) that accounts for the building and transformations of multiple and overlapping networks, without losing sight of the reciprocity and stability of everyday interaction and (c) that accounts for both purposive/instrumental, affective and expressive practices. As Castells (2000) and others have noted, the ritualistic and cultural dimension should be toned down. The point here is that one should not normatively assume cohesiveness as an a priori value of communities. While Fernbeck (2007) attempts to

DOI: 10.1057/9781137446466.0007

compensate this with ideas from Symbolic interactionism, insights from network analysis are an alternative. While a social community consists of a group of people interacting over time within a common frame of reference, social networks of the kind we study are more variable in terms of interaction intensity. By using the term network, we also intend to emphasise *the nature of relationships* more than individuals themselves.

The individuals are not so much influenced by norms and knowledge as that depend on multidirectional relationships. The common arrangements of both practical and normative kinds are less cohesive than in community-oriented groups. Compensatory mechanisms that may ensure stability of social relationships in spite of distances, mobility, heterogeneity and other risks are at play. More than previously, a lot depends on the communication context and infrastructure of the networks. Among other factors, the user interface of personal media may be seen as a functional equivalent for the normative cohesion of face-to-face settings. This indicates the pivotal role of media technologies, as normative cohesion evaporates. Only in the last decade, a wide range of personal media using both the Internet and the telephone network have been adopted by the majority of the populations in OECD countries, precisely because of increasing transparency, reach, simplicity, flexibility, adaptability and so on. The 'domestication' process analysed by Silverstone and others has proceeded towards 'personalisation' both on the web and the phone platforms. Media have lowered their threshold for use, and by this have approached the threshold for communication as such. They have become personalised by narrowing the gap between the idea of communicating with someone and actually applying a technical device to do so.

Another common term is *Communities of practice* (Wenger 1998), which refers to social networks that are engaging in similar activities and learn from each other along the way. The term and its following theoretical insights are for the most part applied in professional contexts such as working places and schools, but the term may also apply to groups of friends and families. It is a term that draws on social capital, as it refers to informal learning as a consequence of collective activities, such as argumentation and discussion, giving feedback, sharing facts and so on in communities. Families turn into communities of practice when they work in the garden or learn a new card game and when people meet to help a friend move to a new flat.

The web provides an efficient way to get in touch with not only weak ties like a plumber or the sports club, but also strong ties like old school friends. The mobile is indispensable for keeping daily contact with friends and family. Importantly, these new channels for social ties tend to complement other forms of social contact (Hampton and Wellman 1999, Wellman et al. 2003, see Agre 2001). More and more social groups tend to communicate through a broader range of media in addition to face-to-face encounters, such as email, phone, discussion-lists and so on. Networks make themselves more flexible and robust by the appropriation of the web, email, social media and so on.

Trust as a dimension of social capital is essential not only in Coleman, Putnam, Fukuyama but also in Bourdieu. As an equivalent of the lack of demand for explicit instrumental information in expressive information, an atmosphere of mutual trust must emanate from the network. Thus trust, as a platform for motivation, is more required in friendship networks than in organisation networks.

According to Fukuyama (1999), social capital is 'an instantiated informal norm that promotes cooperation between two or more individuals. The norm that constitutes social capital can range from a norm of reciprocity between two friends, all the way up to complex and elaborately articulated doctrines like Christianity and Confucianism. They must be instantiated in an actual human relationship: the norm of reciprocity exists in potential in my dealings with all people, but is actualized only in my dealings with my friends'. By this definition, trust, community and civility are fundamental. Generalising a certain amount of trust in strong and weak ties enables an undisturbed exchange of information. The argument about trust may in certain instances be overstated. In networks of weak ties, a bottom line of confidence is needed, but the real reproducing driving force is much more the actual results from being a member of the network – what is actually learnt through the status as a node. Trust is a variable that is mobilised quite differently in different sorts of networks – independently of the online–offline distinction.

Trust is a belief or an attitude towards strangers, which indicates that they are similar to oneself in terms of values, that they are friendly. This makes people less hesitant or afraid to get in touch with strangers offline or online. They would be less worried about interacting with new acquaintances. However, trust is only *one* personal factor that influences communication with strangers, and a hypothesis is that it will have only moderate influence on online behaviour. There are also factors that may compensate for lack of trust.

DOI: 10.1057/9781137446466.0007

Resource distribution

I have so far not touched upon John Urry's concept of network capital, although it resembles social capital (Urry and Elliott 2010). Urry's argument is that capital in the field of what he calls 'mobilities' is of increasing importance in social stratification, at least in the rich parts of the world. Mobility is central for the individual to reach goals and to avoid misfortune. Network capital involves a number of resources that are a prerequisite to life in the rich North (Urry and Elliott 2010). Network capital enables mobilities, which may engender and sustain social relations with distant people and which generate emotional, financial and practical benefit. More explicitly than other scholars of social capital, Urry emphasises physical mobility and transport, however, fundamentally dependent on communication technologies for coordination.

Urry's most important contribution, however, concerns the role of network capital on widening regional- and class-based divides. As is the case with other forms of capital, network capital tends to reproduce and reinforce social differences (Urry and Elliott 2010). That there is a 'Matthew law effect' regarding social capital has been confirmed by most research in the area that I have referred to above. Groups that enjoy much network capital benefit from the making and remaking of social connections. Resources tend to generate more resources. As personal media in general, and social media in particular, are used by the majority of the population in rich countries, the share of passive users with little or no motivation in generating social capital through their media use are likely to increase. Social media are dedicated to the accumulation of social capital. This is most easy to see in sites like LinkedIn, which is oriented towards career-stimulating connections, but also evident in Facebook, where the benefits are many: friendship, specialist knowledge (re)discoveries of memories, sharing of images, as well as political campaigning. The potentials are astonishing but very unevenly exploited by users. Further research is needed to identify not only the social implications of social networks, but also the necessary social conditions among users that stimulate social capital accumulation.

To conclude, unlike certain studies of domestication (see Kraut et al. 2006), social capital is here not simply viewed as social 'effects' and 'impacts' of digital media on everyday life, but more carefully concerning the implications and significances of social networks. Personal media, through processes of personalisation, become embedded in networks

DOI: 10.1057/9781137446466.0007

where effects and impacts cannot be distinguished from their causes. Rather, of interest for social research should be changes in everyday life with emphasis on its communication networks, which may have implications for individual life qualities as well as for civil life and social change (see Wittel 2001). In this, the media will play a role as structural resource. There is plenty to say about the mobile and computer as communication devices, as privacy zones, as socialisation spheres, as network facilitators, and as infrastructure for the public sphere and for social integration in general. But they cannot be empirically isolated from shifting norms, living conditions, education, family patterns, habits and a number of other variables that also undergo change. In observing communication in daily life situations, the medium is only one aspect of the message.

In social capital studies, individuals tend to have both weak and often widely scattered ties and strong ties within closed networks. At the outset, both the bonding and bridging approaches, developed by Coleman, Putnam, Granovetter and Burt, need to be represented. Some relations enable the individuals to receive trust and support on intimate matters, while weaker ties are beneficial in terms of receiving information and sharing political or moral concerns. In all cases, the individual receives collective benefits in a wide sense, which unintentionally and intentionally contribute to identity and meaning-making, which harmonises realistically with given external possibilities. And yet, the concept of social capital needs refining in order to serve as a useful tool for research on mediated social relationships in daily life. Rather than assuming cohesive civic communities and dense family bonds, the starting point for research on social capital ought to open for diverse and rather loose, ego-centric networks, in part due to geographically disperse contacts. Particularly, it is of interest to explore whether the mastering of digital media gives new possibilities to individuals who do not have much social capital through their networks, or whether they simply facilitate existing networks among those who already are 'social capitalists'. Clearly such questions are important when digital media become widely applied channels for not only friendship and trust, but also for learning, civil organisation and social change.

DOI: 10.1057/9781137446466.0007

Bibliography

Adam, F. & Ronkevik, B. (2003) 'Social capital: Recent debates and research trends'. *Social Science Information* 42(2): 155–183.

Adamic, L. A. & Adar, E. (2003) 'Friends and neighbours on the web'. *Social Networks* 25: 211–230.

Agar, J. (2003) *Constant Touch. A Global History of the Mobile Phone.* Cambridge: Icon books.

Agre, P. (2004) 'The practical republic: Social skills and the progress of citizenship', in A. Andrew Feenberg & D. D. Barney (eds) *Community in the Digital Age*, Rowman and Littlefield.

Anderson, B., Brynin, M., Gershuny, J. & Rabian, Y. (eds) (2012) *Information and Communication Technologies in Society. E-living in Digital Europe.* London: Routledge.

Aronson, S. (1971) 'The sociology of the telephone'. *International Journal of Comparative Sociology* 12: 153–167.

Bakardjieva, M. (2006) 'Domestication running wild. From the moral economy of the household to the mores of a culture', in T. Berker, M. Hartmann, Y. Punie & K. Ward (eds) *Domestication of Media and Technology*, pp. 62–79. Maidenhead: Open University Press.

Bankston, C. L. & Zhou, Z. (2002) 'Social capital as process: The meanings and problems of a theoretical metaphor'. *Sociological Inquiry* 72(2): 285–317.

Barnes, Stuart J. & Sid, Huff (2003) 'Rising sun: iMode and the wireless internet'. *Communications of the ACM* 46(11): 79–84.

Baron, S., Field, J. & Schuller, T. (2000) *Social Capital. Critical Perspectives.* Oxford: Oxford University Press.

Bateson, G. (1979) *Mind and Nature: A Necessary Unity*. New York: E. P. Dutton.

Baudrillard, J. (1983) *Simulations*. New York: Semiotext(e).

Baudrillard, J. (1994) *Simulacra and Simulation*. Ann Arbor: The University of Michigan Press.

Bauman, Z. (2000) *Liquid Modernity*. Cambridge: Polity Press.

Baym, N. K. & Burnett, R. (2008) *Amateur Experts: International Fan Labor in Swedish Independent Music*. Paper prepared for Internet Research 9.0, Copenhagen, Denmark.

Baym, N. (2010) *Personal Connections in the Digital Age*. Cambridge: Polity.

Beck, U. & Beck-Gernsheim, E. (2002) *Individualization*. London: Sage.

Beck, U., Giddens, A. & Lash, S. (1994) *Reflexive Modernization*. Cambridge: Polity Press.

Becker, B. & Wehner, J. (2001) 'Electonic networks and civil society: Reflections on structural changes in the public sphere', in Ess, Charles (ed.) *Culture, Technology, Communication. Towards an Intercultural Global Village*. Albany: State University of New York Press.

Bell, D. & Hollows, J. (2005) *Ordinary Lifestyles: Popular Media, Consumption and Taste*. Maidenhead: Open University Press.

Benkler, Y. (2006) *The Wealth of Networks. How Social Production Transforms Markets and Freedom*. New Haven: Yale University Press.

Berkenkotter, C. & Huckin, T. N. (1993) 'Rethinking genre from a sociocognitive perspective'. *Written Communication* 10(4): 475–509.

Berker, T., Hartmann, M., Punie, Y. & Ward, K. J. (eds) (2006) *Domestication of Media and Technology*. Maidenhead: Open University Press.

Bernstein, R. (ed.) (1985) *Habermas and Modernity*. Oxford: Blackwell.

Blokland, T. (2003) *Urban Bonds: Social Relationships in an Inner City Neighbourhood*. Cambridge: Polity Press.

Bolter, J. D. (1991) *Writing Space. The Computer, Hypertext, and the History of Writing*. Hillsdale: LEA.

Bolter, J. D. & Grusin, R. (1999) *Remediation. Understanding New Media*. Cambridge, MA: The MIT Press.

Bourdieu, P. (1984) *Distinction. A Social Critique of the Judgement of Taste*. London: Routledge and Kegan Paul.

Bourdieu, P. (1986) 'The forms of capital', in J. Richardson (ed.) *Handbook of Theory and Research for the Sociology of Education*. New York: Greenwood.

DOI: 10.1057/9781137446466.0008

Boyd, D. (2006) 'Friends, friendsters, and top 8: Writing community into being on social network sites'. *First Monday* 11(12).

Boy, D. (2011) 'Social network sites as network publics: Affordances, dynamics, and implications', in Z. Papacharissi (ed.) *A Networked Self. Identity, Community, and Culture on Social Network Sites.* New York: Routledge.

Brake, D. (2007) 'Personlige webloggere og deres publikum: Hvem tror de egentlig at de snakker med?', in M. Lüders, L. Prøitz & T. Rasmussen (eds) *Personlige Medier: Livet Mellom Skjermene*, pp. 141–163. Oslo: Gyldendal.

Brandtzæg, P. B. and Stav, B. H. (2004) Barn og unges skravling på nettet – sosial støtte i Cyberspace? [Social support in Cyberspace among children and young people?] *Tidsskrift for ungdomsforskning* 4(1) 27–47.

Brody, F. (2000) 'The medium is the memory', in P. Lunenfeld (ed.) *The Digital Dialectic. New Essays on New Media.* Cambridge, MA: The MIT Press.

Burt, R. (1992) *Structural Holes: The Social Structure of Competition.* Cambridge, MA: Harvard University Press.

Burt, R. S. (2000) 'The network of social capital', in R. I. Sutton & B. M. Staw (eds) *Research in Organisational Behavior.* 22 Greenwich, CT: JAI Press.

Calhoun, C. (1995) *Critical Social Theory.* Oxford: Blackwell.

Cardon, D. & Granjon F. (2004) 'Social networks and cultural practices. A case study of young avid screen users in France'. *Social Networks* 27: 301–315.

Casalegno, F. (2006) 'Connected memories in the networked digital era: A moving paradigm', in P. Purcell (ed.) *Networked Neighbourhoods: The Connected Community in Context.* London: Springer.

Casey, E. S. (2000) *Remembering: A Phenomenological Study.* Indiana University Press.

Castells, M. (1997) *The power of identity.* Oxford: Blackwell.

Castells, M. (2000) 'Toward a sociology of the network society'. *Contemporary Sociology* 29(5): 693–699.

Castells, M. (2009) *Communication Power.* Oxford: Oxford University Press.

Castells, M. (ed.) (2004) *The Network Society. A Cross-cultural Perspective.* Cheltenham: Edward Elgar.

DOI: 10.1057/9781137446466.0008

Chambers, D. (2006) *New Social Ties. Contemporary Connections in a Fragmented Society.* Houndmills: Palgrave.

Chambers, D. (2012) *A Sociology of Family Life. Change and Diversity in Intimate Relations.* Cambridge: Polity Press.

Chambers, D. (2013) *Social Media and Personal Relationships. Online Intimacies and Networked Friendship.* Houndmills, Basingstoke: Palgrave Macmillan.

Chandler, D. (1997) *Writing Oneself in Cyberspace.* Retrieved April 2014 http://www.aber.ac.uk/media/Documents/short/webident.html

Cherny, L. (1999) *Conversation and Community: Chat in a Virtual World.* New York: CSLI Publications.

Chesbrough, H., Vanhaverbeke, W. & West, J. (2005) *Open Innovation. Researching a New Paradigm.* Oxford: Oxford University Press.

Choi, J. H. (2006) 'Living in cyworld: Contextualising cy-ties in South-Korea', in A. Bruns & J. Jacobs (eds) *Use of Blogs (Digital Formations),* pp. 173–186. New York: Peter Lang.

Coleman, J. S. (1988) 'Social capital in the creation of human capital'. *The American Journal of Sociology* 94: 95–120.

Coleman, J. S. (1990) *Foundation of Social Theory.* Cambridge, MA: Harvard University Press.

Cormode, G. & Krishnamurti, B. (2008) 'Key differences between Web 1.0 and Web 2.0'. *First Monday* 13(6).

Crapeau, S. & Kretz, F. (1987) 'Methodological analysis of experiments with communication services', in L. Qvortrup et al. (eds) *Social Experiments with Information Technology and the Challenges of Innovation.* Dordrecht: D. Reidel Publ.

Crook, S. (1998) 'Minotaurs and other monsters: Everyday life in recent social theory'. *Sociology* 32(3): 523–540.

Crossley, N. (1996) *Intersubjectivity: The Fabric of Social Becoming.* London: Sage.

Cubitt, S. (2001) *Simulation in Social Theory.* London: Sage.

Dasgupta, P. & Serageldin, R. (eds) (1999) *Social Capital: A Multifaceted Perspective.* Washington, DC: World Bank.

de Certeau, M. (1984) *The Practice of Everyday Life.* Berkeley: University of California Press.

Delanty, G. (2003) *Community (key Ideas).* New York: Routledge.

Dhavan V. S., Kwak, N. & Holbert, R. L. (2001) ' "Connecting" and "disconnecting" with civic life: Patterns of internet use and the production of social capital'. *Political Communication* 18: 141–162.

DOI: 10.1057/9781137446466.0008

Döring, N. (2002) 'Personal home pages on the web: A review of research'. *Journal of Computer-Mediated Communication* 7(3).

du Gay, P. et. al. (1997) *Doing Cultural Studies: The Story of the Sony Walkman*. London: Sage.

Goffman, E. (1981) *Forms of Talk*. University of Pennsylvania Press.

Goffman, E. (1983) ' "The interaction order" American Sociological Association, 1982 presidential address'. *American Sociological Review* 48(1): 1–17.

Eco, U. (1986) *Faith in Fakes: Travels in Hyperreality*. London: Minerva.

Eisenstein, E. L. (1983) *The Printing Revolution in Early Modern Europe*. Cambridge: Cambridge University Press.

Ellison, N. B., Steinfield, C. & Lampe, C. (2007) 'The benefits of Facebook "friends:" Social capital and college students' use of online social network sites'. *Journal of Computer-Mediated Communication* 12(4): 1143–1168.

Etzioni, A. (1996) 'The responsive community: A communitarioan perspective'. *American Sociological Review* 61: 1–11.

Fagerjord A. (2003) "Rhetorical Convergence. Earlier Media Influence on Web Media Form." Oslo: Faculty of the Humanities, University of Oslo.

Feenberg (1991) *Critical Theory of technology*. Oxford: Oxford University Press.

Fernback, J. (2007) 'Beyond the diluted community concept: A symbolic interactionist perspective on online social relations'. *New Media and Society* 9(1): 49–69.

Field, J., Schuller, T. & Baron, S. (2000) 'Social capital and human capital revisited', in S. Baron, J. Field & T. Schuller (eds) *Social Capital: Critical Perspectives*, pp. 243–263. Oxford: Oxford University Press.

Fisher, C. S. (1992) *America Calling: A Social History of the Telephone to 1940*. Berkeley: University of California Press.

Foucault, M. (1988) *Technologies of the Self.* Cambridge, MA: University of Massachusetts Press.

Foucault, M. (1994) 'Technologies of the self', in P. Rabinow (ed.) *Essential Works of Foucault 1954–1984*. Vol. 1. London: Penguin.

Foucault, M., (1994) *Ethics. Essential works of Foucault 1954–1984*, vol.1. P. Rabinow ed. London: Penguin

Frane, A. & Ronkevik, B. (2003) 'Social capital: Recent debates and research trends'. *Social Science Information* 42(2): 155–183.

Fukuyama, F. (1995) *Trust: The Social Virtues and the Creation of Prosperity*. New York: The Free Press.

DOI: 10.1057/9781137446466.0008

Fukuyama, F. (1999) 'Social capital and Civil Society'. IMF conference on Second generation Reforms. http://www.imf.org/external/pubs/ft/seminar/1999/reforms/fukuyama.htm#1

Garton, L., Haythornthwaite, C.& Wellman, B. (1997) 'Studying online social networks'. *Journal of Computer-Mediated Communication* 3(1).

Gershuny, J. I. (2003) *Changing Times: Work and Leisure in Postindustrial Society*. Oxford University Press.

Gershuny, J. (2003) *Time, through the Lifecourse, in the Family*. Institute for Social and Economic Research, University of Essex.

Gershuny, J. (2003). 'Web use and net nerds: A neofunctionalist analysis of the impact of information technology in the home'. *Social Forces* 82(1): 141–168.

Geser, H. (2004) *Towards a Sociological Theory of the Mobile Phone*. University of Zurich. http://socio.ch.mobile/t_geserl.htm.

Giddens, A. (1991) *Modernity and Self-Identity*. Cambridge: Polity Press.

Goffman, E. (1959) *The Presentation of Self in Everyday Life*. NY: Doubleday Anchor.

Goffman, E. (1967) *Interaction Ritual: Essays on face-to-face interaction*. Oxford: Aldine.

Granovetter, M. (1973) 'The strength of weak ties'. *American Journal of Sociology* 78: 1360–1380.

Granovetter, M. (1978) 'Threshold models of collective behavior'. *The American Journal of Sociology* 83(6): 1420–1443.

Granovetter, M. (1983) 'The strength of weak ties: A network theory revisited'. *Sociological Theory* 1: 201–233.

Granovetter, M. & Swedberg, R. (2001) *The Sociology of Economic Life*. Boulder, CO: Westview Press.

Green, N. (2002) 'On the move: Technology, mobility and the mediation of social time and space'. *The Information Society* 18: 281–292.

Gross, N. (2005) 'The detraditionalization of intimacy reconsidered'. *Sociological Theory* 23(3): 286–311.

Habermas, J. (1984) *The Theory of Communicative Action*, Vol. I. London: Heinemann.

Habermas, J. (1987) The *Philosophical Discourse of Modernity*. Cambridge, Mass.: The MIT Press.

Haddon, L. (ed.) (2005) *Everyday Innovators: Researching the Role of Users in Shaping ICTs* (Vol. 32). London: Springer.

Hadot, P. (2000) 'Reflections on the idea of "cultivation of the self"'', in P. duGay, J. Evans, & P. Redman (eds) *Identity: A Reader*, pp. 373–379. London: Sage.

DOI: 10.1057/9781137446466.0008

Hampton, K. N. & Wellman, B. (1999) 'Netville online and offline: Observing and surveying a wired suburb'. *American Behavioral Scientist* 45(3): 477–496.

Harper, R., Palen, L. & Taylor, A. S. (eds) (2005) *The Inside Text: Social, Cultural and Design Perspectives on SMS* (vol. 4). London: Springer.

Harrison, T. (2009) 'Wielding new media in Web 2.0: exploring the history of engagement with the collaborative construction of media products'. *New Media & Society* 11(1–2): 155–178.

Haythornthwaite, C. (1998). "A social network study of the growth of community among distance learners." *Information Research*, 4 (1).

Haythornthwaite, C. (2000) 'Online personal networks', *New Media and Society* 2(2): 195–226.

Haythornthwaite C. (2002) "Strong, Weak and latent ties and the impact of new media." *Information Society* 18, 385–401.

Haythornthwaite C. and Wellmann B. (eds) (2002) *The Internet in Everyday Life* Malden MA: Blackwell.

Haythornthwaite, C. (2002) 'Building social networks via computer networks: Creating and sustaining distributed learning communities', in K. A. Renninger & W. Shumar (eds) *Building Virtual Communities: Learning and Change in Cyberspace*, pp. 159–190. Cambridge, UK: Cambridge University Press.

Herring, S. C., Scheidt, L. A., Wright, E. & Bonus, S. (2005) 'Weblogs as a bridging genre'. *Information Technology and People* 18(2): 142–171.

Hess, C. & Ostrom, E. (eds) (2007) *Understanding Knowledge as a Commons: From Theory to Practice.* Cambridge, MA: The MIT Press.

Hetcher, S (2009) "Hume's Penguin, or, Yochai Benkler & the Nature of Peer Production." *Vanderbilt Journal of Entertainment and Technology Law* 11(4), 995–1000.

Highmore, B. (2001) *Everyday Life and Cultural Theory.* London: Routledge.

Hodkinson, P. (2007) 'Interactive online journals and individualisation'. *New Media and Society* 9(4): 625–650.

Horst, H. A. & Miller, D. (2006) *The Cell Phone. An Anthropology of Communication.* Oxford: Berg.

Huffaker, D. A. & Calvert, S. L. (2005) 'Gender, identity, and language use in teenage blogs'. *Journal of Computer-Mediated Communication* 10(2). URL (consulted 7 March 2009): http://jcmc.indiana.edu/vol10/issue2/huffaker.html.

DOI: 10.1057/9781137446466.0008

Hui, J., Cashman, T. & Deacon, T. (2008) 'Bateson's method: Double description. What is it? How does it work? What do we learn?', in J. Hofmeyer (ed.) *A Legacy for Living Systems. Gregory Bateson as Precursor to Biosemiotics.* Copenhagen: Springer.

Huysman, M. & Wulf, V. (eds) (2004) *Social Capital and Information Technology.* Cambridge, MA: The MIT Press.

Ihde, D. (1990) *Technology and the Lifeworld. From Garden to Earth.* Bloomington: Indiana University Press.

Ihlström, C. & Henfridsson, O. (2005) 'Online newspapers in Scandinavia. A longitudinal study of genre change and interdependency'. *Information Technology and People* (2): 172–192.

Illouz, E. (2006) *Cold Intimacies: The Making of Emotional Capitalism.* Cambridge: Polity Press.

in Japanese Life. Cambridge, Mass.: The MIT Press.

Innis, H. (1951) *The Bias of Communication.* Toronto: University of Toronto Press.

Innis, H. (1986) *Empire of Communication.* Victoria: Press Porcepic.

Ito, M , Okabe, D. & Matsuda, M. (2006) *Personal, Portable, Pedestrian: Mobile Phones in Japanese Life.* Cambridge, MA: The MIT Press.

Jamieson, L. (1999) 'Intimacy transformed? A critical look at the "Pure Relationship"'. *Sociology* 33(3): 477–494.

Jarrett, K. (2008) 'Interactivity is evil! A critical investigation of Web 2.0'. *First Monday* 13(3).

Jauss, H. R. ([1967] 1982) *Toward an Aesthetic of Reception.* Minneapolis: University of Minnesota Press.

Johns, A. (1998) *The Nature of the Book.* Chicago: The University of Chicago Press.

Kasesniemi, E.-L. (2003) *Mobile Message: Young People and a New Communication Culture.* Tampere: Tampere University Press.

Kavanaugh, A. L., Reese, C., Carrol, J. M. & Rosson, M. B. (2005) 'Weak ties in network communities'. *The Information Society* 21: 119–131.

Kitzmann, A. (2004) *Saved from Oblivion: Documenting the Daily from Diaries to Web Cams.* New York: Peter Lang.

Knorr Cetina, K. (2001) 'Post social relations: Theorizing sociality in a post social environment'. *Handbook of Social Theory* 520–537.

Kohiyama (2005) 'A decade in the development of mobile communication in Japan (1993–2002)', in M. Ito, D. Okabe & M. Matsuba (eds) (2005) *Personal, Portable and Pedestrian: Mobile Phones in Japanese Life.* Cambridge, MA: MIT Press.

DOI: 10.1057/9781137446466.0008

Kraut, R., Brynin, M. & Kiesler, S. (2006) *Computers, Phones and the Internet. Domesticating Information Technology.* Oxford: Oxford University Press.

Kraut, R., Kiesler, S., Boneva, B., Cummings, J., Helgeson, V. & Crawford, A. (2002) 'Internet paradox revisited'. *Journal of Social Issues* 58(1): 49–74.

Küchler, S. & Melion, W. (eds) (1990) *Images of Memory: On remembering and Representation.*

Kuhn, A. ([1995] 2002) *Family Secrets: Acts of Memory and Imagination.* London: Verso.

Langer, S. (1942) *Philosophy in a New Key. A Study in the Symbolism of Reason, Rite, and Art.* Boston: Harvard University Press.

Lefebvre, H. (1991) *Critique of Everyday Life:* Vol. 1. London: Verso.

Levi, M. (1996) 'Social and unsocial capital: A review essay of Putnam's making democracy work'. *Politics and Society* 24(1): 45–55.

Licoppe, C. & Smoreda, Z. (2005) 'Are social networks technologically embedded? How networks are changing today with changes in communication technology'. *Social Networks* 27: 317–335.

Licoppe, C. & Smoreda, Z. (2006) 'Rhythms and ties: Toward a pragmatics of technologically mediated sociability', in R. Kraut, M. Brynin & S. Kiesler (eds) *Computers, Phones, and the Internet: Domesticating Information Technologies,* pp. 296–324. Oxford: Oxford University Press.

Liestøl, G. (2009) 'Notes on mobility, localization & the possibility of genre design', in I. Wagner et al. (eds) *Exploring Digital Design.* New York: Kluwer Academic/Plenum.

Liestøl, G. (2011) 'Situated simulations between virtual reality and mobile augmented reality: Designing a narrative space', in B. Furht (ed.) *Handbook of Augmented Reality.* Springer.

Liestøl, G., Rasmussen, T. & Stenarson, T. (2011) 'Mobile innovation: Designing & evaluatiing situated simulations', in *Digital Creativity* 22(3), pp. 172–184. Abingdon: Routledge, Taylor & Francis Group (2011).

Lin, N. (2001) *Social Capital. A Theory of Social Structure and Action.* Cambridge: Cambridge University Press.

Ling, R. (2004) *The Mobile Connection: The Cell Phone's Impact on Society.* San Fransisco: Elsevier.

Ling, R. (2008) *New Tech, New Ties. How Mobile Communication is Reshaping Social Cohesion.* Cambridge, MA: The MIT Press.

Ling, R. & Haddon, L. (2001) 'Mobile telephony and the coordination of mobility in everyday life'. *Telenor FoU,* R16.

DOI: 10.1057/9781137446466.0008

Livingstone, S. (2002) *Young People and the New Media. Childhood and the Changing Media Environment*. London: Sage.

Lüders, M. (2007) *Being in Mediated Spaces. An Enquiry into Personal Media Practices*. PhD-thesis. Oslo: University of Oslo.

Lüders, M. (2008) 'Conceptualising personal media'. *New Media and Society* 10(5): 683–702.

Lüders, M., Prøitz, L. & Rasmussen, T. (2010) 'Emerging personal media genres', in *New Media and Society* 12(6): 1–17.

Luhmann, N. (1990) *Essays on Self-reference*. Stanford: Stanford University Press.

Luhmann, N. (1996/2000) *The Reality of the Mass Media*. Stanford: Stanford University Press.

Luhmann, N. (1998) *Observations on Modernity*. Stanford: Stanford University Press.

Luhmann, N. (2012) *Introduction to Systems Theory*. NJ: Wiley.

Madianou, M. & Miller, D. (2013) 'Polymedia: Towards a new theory of digital media in interpersonal communication'. *International Journal of Cultural Studies* 16(2): 169–187.

Manovich, L. (2001) *The Language of New Media*. Cambridge, MA: The MIT Press.

Martin, J. R. (1989) *Factual Writing: Exploring and Challenging Social Reality*. Oxford: Oxford University Press.

Martin, J. R. (1992) *English Text: System and Structure*. Philadelphia/Amsterdam.

Matsuda, M. (2005) 'Discourses of *Keitai* in Japan', in M. Ito, D. Okabe & M. Matsuba (eds) *Personal, Portable and Pedestrian: Mobile Phones in Japanese Life*. Cambridge, MA: The MIT Press.

McLuhan, M. (1964) *Understanding Media: The Extensions of Man*. New York: Signet.

McLuhan, M. & McLuhan, E. (1988) *Laws of Media: The New Science*. Toronto: University of Toronto Press.

Meyrowitz, J. (1986) *No Sense of Place*. Cambridge, MA: The MIT Press.

Misztal, B. A. (1996) *Trust in Modern Societies. A Search for the Base of Social Order*. Cambridge: Polity Press.

Mitchell, W. (2003) *Me++*. Cambridge, MA: MIT Press.

Petersen, S. M. (2008). 'Loser generated content: From participation to exploitation'. *First Monday* 13(3).

DOI: 10.1057/9781137446466.0008

Naphapiet, J. & Ghosal, S. (1998) 'Social capital, intellectual capital and organisational advantage'. Management research papers 97/6. Oxford: Oxford Centre for Management Studies.

Norris, P. (1996) 'Does television Erode social capital? A reply to Putnam'. *Political Science and Politics* 29: 474–479.

Okada T. (2006) 'Youth culture and the shaping of Japanese mobile media: Personalization and the *Keitai* internet as multimedia', in M. Ito, D. Okabe & M. Matsuba (eds) (2005) *Personal, Portable and Pedestrian.*

Ong, W. (1982/1991) *Orality and Literacy: The Technologizing of the Word.* London: Routledge.

O'Reilly, T. (2005) 'What is web 2.0. Design patterns and business models for the next generation of software" http://OReilly.com

Papacharissi, Z. (ed.) (2011) *A Networked Self. Identity, Community, and Culture on Social Network Sites.* New York: Routledge.

Pichault, F. (1978) 'Social experiments with IT from the initiator's point of view', in L. Qvortrup et al. (eds) *Social Experiments with Information Technology and the Challenges of Innovation.* Dordrecht: D. Reidel Publ.

Portes, A. (1998) 'Social capital: Its origins and applications in modern sociology'. *Annual Review of Sociology* 24: 1–24.

Poster, M. (1995) *The Mode of Information.* Cambridge: Polity Press.

Prøitz, L. (2005) "Cute Boys or Game Boys? The Embodyment of feminity and masculinity in young Norwegians' Text-message love projects" *Fibreculture Journal* No. 6.

Prøitz, L. (2007) 'The mobile phone turn – a study of gender, sexuality and subjectivity in young people's mobile phone practices'. University of Oslo: *Acta Humaniora*, Unipub Press.

Putnam, R. (1995) 'Tuning in, tuning out: The strange disappearance of social capital in America'. *Political Science and Politics* 28(4): 664–683.

Putnam, R. et al. (1993) *Making Democracy Work: Civic Traditions in Modern Italy.* Princeton, NJ: Princeton University Press.

Quan-Haase, A. & Wellman, B. (2004) 'How does the internet affect social capital?' in M. Huysman & V. Wulf (eds) *Social Capital and Information Technology.* Cambridge, MA: The MIT Press.

Qvortrup, L. et al. (eds) (1987) *Social Experiments with Information Technology and the Challenges of Innovation.* Dordrecht: D. Reidel Publ.

Rasmussen, T. (1996) *Communication Technologies and the Mediation of Social Life.* Oslo: The University of Oslo.

DOI: 10.1057/9781137446466.0008

Rasmussen, T. (2000) *Social Theory and Communication Technology.* Aldershot: Ashgate.

Rasmussen, T. (2003) *Luhmann. Kommunikasjon, medier, samfunn.* Bergen: Fagbokforlaget.

Rasmussen, T. (2007) *Nettverksformelen. Hvordan det sosiale livet henger sammen.* Oslo: Unpub.

Rasmussen, T. (2003) 'On distributed society: The internet as a guide to a sociological understanding of communication', in G. Liestøl, A. Moorison & T. Rasmussen (eds) *Digital Media Revisited. Theoretical and Conceptual Innovations in Digital Domains.* Cambridge, MA: The MIT Press.

Rheingold, H. (2003) *Smart Mobs: The Next Social Revolution.* Berkeley: Perseus Publishing.

Sandbothe, M. (2000) 'Interactivity, hypertextuality – transversality. A media-philosophical analysis of the Internet'. *Hermes, Journal of Linguistics* (24): 81–102.

Schuller, T., Baron, S. & Field, J. (2000) 'Social capital: A review and a critique', in S. Baron, J. Field & T. Schuller (eds) *Social Capital. Critical Perspectives.* Oxford: Oxford University Press.

Sennett, R. (2004) *Respect. The Formation of Character in an Age of Inequality.* London: Penguin Books.

Silverstone, R. & Haddon, L. (1996) 'Design and domestication of information and communication technologies: Technical change and everyday life', in Mansell & Silverstone (eds) *Communication by Design. The Politics of Information and Communication Technologies.* Oxford: Oxford University Press.

Ithiel de Sola, P. O. O. L. (1983) *Technologies of Freedom.* Harvard University Press.

Spigel, L. (1992) *Make Room for TV: Television and the Family Ideal in Postwar America.* Chicago: University of Chicago Press.

Sproull, L. & Kiesler, S. (1991) *Connections: New Ways of Working in the Networked Organization.* Cambridge, MA: MIT Press.

Tanis, M. & Postmes, T. (2003) 'Social cues and impression formation in CMC'. *Journal of Communication* 53(4): 676–693.

Toomi, I. (2002) *Networks of Innovation: Change and Meaning in the Age of the Internet.* Oxford: Oxford University Press.

Tribble, E. B. (1993) *Margins and Marginality: The Printed Page in Early Modern England.* University of Virginia Press.

DOI: 10.1057/9781137446466.0008

Turkle, S. (1997) *Life on the Screen: Identity in the Age of Internet.* New York: Touchstone.

Turkle, S. (1999) ' "Cybespace and identity" symposium'. *Contemporary Sociology Journal of Reviews* 28(6).

Turkle, S. (2011) *Alone Together. Why We Expect More from Technology and Less from Each Other.* New York: Basic Books.

Urry, J. & Elliott, J. (2010) *Mobile Lives.* London: Routledge.

Uslaner, E. M. (2004) 'Trust, civic engagement, and the internet'. *Political Communication* 21(2): 223–242.

van den Hooff, B. & De Ridder, J. A. (2004) 'Knowledge sharing in context: The influence of organizational commitment, communication climate and CMC use on knowledge sharing'. *Journal of Knowledge Management* 8(6): 117–130.

Watzlawick, P. et al. (1967) *Pragmatics of Human Communication: A Study of Interactional Patterns, Pathologies and Paradoxes.* New York: W.W. Norton.

Weber, M. (1958) 'From Max Weber. essays in sociology', in H. H. Gerth & C. W. Mills (eds). New York: Oxford University Press.

Webster, F. (ed.) (2001) *Culture and Politics in the Information Age. A New Politics?* London: Routledge.

Wellman, B. (1999) *Networks in the Global Village.* Boulder, CO: Westview Press.

Wellman, B. & Hampton, K. (1999) 'Living networked on and offline'. *Contemporary Sociology* 28(6): 648–654.

Wellman, B. & Haythorntwaite, C. (eds) (2002) *The Internet in Everyday Life.* Oxford: Blackwell.

Wellman, B. et al. (2001) 'Does the Internet increase, decrease or supplement social capital?: Social networks, participation and community commitment'. *American Behavioral Scientist* 45(3): 437–456.

Wenger, E. (1998) *Communities of Practice: Learning, Meaning, and Identity.* Cambridge: Cambridge University Press.

White, H. (1965/2008) 'White notes on the constituents of social structure'. *Sociologica* No. 1.

Willensky, J. (2006) *The Access Principle. The Case for Open Access to Research and Scholarship.* Cambridge, MA: The MIT Press.

Wittel, A. (2001) 'Toward a network sociality', *Theory, Culture & Society* 18(6): 51–76.

Wittgenstein, L. (1953) *Philosophical Investigations.* Oxford: Blackwell.

DOI: 10.1057/9781137446466.0008

Index

ambivalence, 11
appropriation, 27, 45, 53–55, 58, 124
archiving, 9–11, 83, 102
augmented reality, 97, 99, 100

Bateson, G., 100
Bauman, Z., 4, 13, 26
Baym, N., 86
Beck, U., 13, 26
Bolter, J., 24, 28, 93, 98, 99
Bourdieu, P., 3, 14, 24, 45
bricolage, 28
Burt, R., 14, 126

cascades, 117
category, 40, 82, 83
clusters, 116
Coleman, J., 14, 114, 122, 124, 126
communication, *passim*
communities of practice, 123
community, 64, 81, 82, 108, 110, 122, 123
complexity, 79, 107, 113
conversion, 54–55

de Certeau, M., 3, 27, 45, 56–59
domestication, 5, 9, 13, 53–54, 123

email, 19, 23, 28, 32, 44, 55, 68, 80, 92, 106, 111–112, 115, 121, 124

Facebook, 3, 23, 54, 56, 76, 78, 81, 106, 115, 117, 118–121, 125
Foucault, M., 13, 34–37, 60, 74, 109

Gadamer, H-G., 2
Giddens, A., 13, 24, 26, 118
Goffman, E., 2, 37–39, 62, 71, 73, 74
Google+, 115
Granovetter, P., 14, 108, 126

Habermas, J., 2, 13, 26, 36, 46–51, 58, 73, 74, 79
Husserl, E., 46, 47, 72–74
hypermediacy, 93, 95, 98, 99
hyperreality, 96

incorporation, 54, 55, 58
individualisation, 32–33, 40, 44, 60, 62, 65, 74, 101, 105, 112, 118
interaction, *passim*
Internet, 5, 19, 21, 32, 55, 80–82, 106, 109–111, 123
intersubjectivity, 50, 64, 72–74, 86
intimacy, 13, 20–21, 39, 40, 43, 44, 55, 62, 111

Langer, S., 93, 94, 95
Lazarsfeld, P., 70
lifeworld, *passim*
Ling, R., 2, 61

DOI: 10.1057/9781137446466.0009

LinkedIn, 10, 108, 115, 125
Luhmann, N., 13, 26, 62, 74–76, 79, 80, 81

mass media, 2, 4, 5, 6, 8–9, 17, 20, 37, 70, 71, 72, 80, 81
McLuhan, M., 14, 68, 88–92, 93, 95, 98
media theory, 69, 85–103,
message, 75, 76, 77, 79, 88
Meyrowitz, J., 14, 38, 92, 93, 94, 95
mobile, *passim*
modernity, 27, 34, 46, 47, 58, 60

objectification, 52, 53, 55
Ong, W., 27, 92
orality, 26, 27, 28, 37, 89
orientation, 9, 10

patterns, 62, 111, 118, 120
personal media, *passim*
personalisation, 5, 6, 13, 20, 31, 40–41, 45, 53, 54, 71, 123, 125
presentation, 10, 20, 24, 26, 36, 37–39, 45, 68, 101
publics, 70, 83, 106
Putnam, R., 14, 65, 122, 124, 126

Rasmussen, T., 11, 46, 48, 49, 54, 64, 86, 99, 116
remediation, 93, 99
Rheingold, H., 68
Rogers, E., 5, 70
Rorty, R., 72

Schütz, A., 2, 46, 47, 73
Simmel, G., 2, 43, 45, 56

simulacrum, 96, 100
skills, 52, 105, 107, 108, 114–15
Skype, 32, 44
SMS, 9, 10, 22, 23, 30, 55, 68, 101, 103, 111
social capital, 14, 33, 43, 61, 63, 105
social media, 10, 11, 53, 78, 80, 83, 105–109, 110, 111, 113–117, 122–126
social network, 3, 10, 12, 14, 22, 45, 61, 63–65, 81, 83, 102, 105–8, 110, 112, 113, 114, 115, 116, 117, 118, 121, 122, 123
sociology, 13, 17, 26, 33, 37, 45, 46, 47, 51, 52, 56, 61, 62, 64, 65–66, 72, 74, 108, 122
supernodes, 116–117
symbols, 48, 93, 94–95

trust, 15, 22, 26, 33, 39, 40, 43, 53, 65, 97, 107, 109, 110, 111, 112, 113, 114, 115, 116, 122–124, 126
Turkle, S., 12, 68
Twitter, 7, 10, 68, 81

Urry, J., 125

virtuality, 97

web 2.0, 80, 118, 119, 120, 121
Weber, M., 2, 4, 5, 11, 13, 46, 108
Wellman, B., 40, 64, 102, 124
Wikipedia, 120
Wittgenstein, L., 72

Youtube, 3, 68, 101,

DOI: 10.1057/9781137446466.0009